2003 Vol. 59, No. 1

Youth Perspectives on Violence and Injustice
Issue Editors: Colette Daiute and Michelle Fine

TRANSFORMATIONS FROM YOUTH THROUGH RELATIONSHIPS

2001 KURT LEWIN AWARD ADDRESS

George Levinger (1984–1987)
Joseph E. McGrath (1979–1983)
Jacqueline D. Goodchilds (1974–1978)
Bertram H. Raven (1970–1973)
Joshua A. Fishman (1966–1969)
Leonard Solomon (1963)
Robert Chin (1960–1965)
John Harding (1956–1959)
M. Brewster Smith (1951–1955)
Harold H. Kelley (1949)
Ronald Lippitt (1944–1950)

Journal of Social Issues, Vol. 59, No. 1, 2003, pp. 1–14

Youth Perspectives on Violence and Injustice

Colette Daiute and Michelle Fine*

The Graduate Center, City University of New York

This introduction presents the theoretical, methodological, and practical rationale for "Youth perspectives on violence and injustice," a special issue of the Journal of Social Issues. Our approach to youth violence research raises questions about what counts as normative youth behavior and broadens the nature of inquiry so that understandings and goals of young people, especially those from discriminated groups, contribute to re-defining the problem and its analysis. We also underscore how the articles in this issue illuminate youth perspectives via novel theoretical and methodological tools. After presenting the organizing themes of social justice and development: youth perspectives through history, culture, and community, youth confronting public institutions, and youth transformations through relationships, we preview themes in the integrative summary.

Questioning "Violence" and "Youth"

While much has been written *on* youth violence, it is still rare to read a scholarly text about violence written critically from the perspectives *of* youth (for exceptions see Boyd-Franklin & Franklin, 2000; Coles, 1991; Daiute, 2000; Fine, 1988; Flanagan, Bowes, Jonasson, Csapo, & Sheblanova, 1998; Garbarino, 1999; McIntyre, 2000; Noguera, 2001; Phillips, 2000; Pittman, 2002; Way, 1998). With this issue, we try to fill this space by presenting a series of articles written through "youth perspectives" on violence by drawing upon positive youth development theory as well as recognizing the vast and rich diversity among youth living under adverse conditions (Connell & Wellborn, 1991;

Correspondence concerning this article should be addressed to Colette Daiute, The Graduate Center, CUNY, 365 Fifth Avenue, NY, NY 10016 [e-mail: cdaiute@gc.cuny.edu]. The authors acknowledge the intellectually-supportive environment of The Graduate Center, City University of New York, especially their students as inspiration for research and collaboration. In addition Colette Daiute thanks the William T. Grant Foundation, Spencer Foundation, and Rockefeller Foundation for grants supporting the research reported here. Michelle Fine thanks the funders of her research, including Helenia Foundation, Spencer Foundation, Leslie Glass Foundation and Open Society Institute.

Flanagan & Tucker, 1999; Lerner, Fisher & Weinberg, 2000; Spina, 2000; Pittman, 2002).

The articles in this issue build on, but also challenge, traditional work within the field of youth violence (see Elliot, Hamburg, & Williams, 1998 for a beginning of this turn). Research in the field of youth violence often entails portraits and explanations that conceptualize youth deviance (Rhodes, 1999), but rarely reports from the standpoints of youths themselves, who may look at the world around them as problematic. Perhaps this is simply because adults project onto youth our growing concerns about violence. In the area of violence in the community, as has happened in examinations of sexual behavior (Fine, 1998), youth have become the site for our adult "moral panics" (Fine & Harris, 2002), panics that are especially virulent in relation to forthright expression by youth of color (Powell, 2001). Further, it is understandable that we, as adults—parents, educators, researchers, youth workers, and policy makers—find it difficult to accept youth violence as our *social* responsibility. It may be far easier to view violence as an individual problem of youth. There has, for some time, been a tendency for violence research to be conducted from a medical perspective whereby violence is examined as a stable trait or disorder (Loeber, 1982; Olweus, 1979) rather than as integral to ongoing histories, injustices, and social relations.

More recently, in the literature on youth violence, the assumption that violence is a disease has begun to give way to focus on the environmental circumstances influencing youth who become violent (Elliot et al., 1998), an approach most recently transformed by writing about youth in positive ways (Pittman, 2001). Some authors of large-scale research have, for example, become intrigued by the affective experiences of aggressive and violent youth, citing the need to step back from the exclusive focus on behavior (Aber, Jones, Brown, Chaudry, & Samples, 1998; Daiute & Buteau, 2002).

The researchers in this issue write to understand "youth perspectives" on violence, by which we mean young people's experiences with and explanations about the risks of violence to their physical and psychological well-being. Drawing on "standpoint theory" (Hartsock, 1983; Hill-Collins, 1991), the articles in this issue create a space for theorizing how youth diversity—cross race, ethnicity, class, gender, nationality, and sexuality—affects perceptions of, engagements with, and experiences of violence. When we listen intently to youth perspectives, a series of epistemological insights emerge. As normative institutions and practices become challenged, narrow definitions of "youth violence" broaden, and the range of methods required to research youth violence expands dramatically. We review these insights below.

First, youth perspectives challenge *normative perspectives* on social arrangements, as illustrated in papers by Daiute, Stern, and Lelutiu-Weinberger (this issue); Fallis & Opotow (this issue); Fine, Freudenberg, Payne, Perkins, Smith, and Wanzer (this issue); Phoenix, Frosh, and Pattman (this issue); and Tolman,

Spencer, Porche, and Rosen-Reynoso (this issue). Youth critique the very institutions and practices that adults take for granted and question those behaviors,
institutions, policies, and practices that seem most natural in mainstream adult
society, e.g., policing for public safety (Fine et al., this issue), heterosexual relations (Tolman et al., this issue), violence prevention programs in schools (Daiute
et al.; Mahiri & Conner, this issue) are re-cast, by youth, in a critical light. So too,
some behaviors viewed as troubling by adults, such as school cutting (Fallis &
Opotow, this issue), are reconceptualized by youth as understandable—if counter-
productive—responses to problematic educational institutions. By broadening the
focus of research from youth behavior to youth subjectivity and experience, these
papers expand the units of analysis from individual youth to youth in the contexts
of social institutions, dynamic relational processes, and symbolic media.

Second, once youth perspectives are engaged, a *broad range of topics* falls
within the territory of youth violence. By adopting a youth perspective, the researchers represented in this issue found it necessary to shift and expand the
terrain of youth violence to include research on violence enacted by youth (Hertz-
Lazarowitz; Solis; Spencer et al., this issue), violence witnessed by youth (Phoenix
et al., this issue), violence experienced by youth (Tolman et al., this issue), and
violence perpetrated institutionally and historically on youth (Cross, this issue;
Solis, this issue).

Commonly accepted distinctions between physical, cultural, historic and psychological violence blur, yielding significant insights about what makes young
people feel uncomfortable with their environments, adults and with themselves,
including being under unfair scrutiny, being isolated, and anticipating a range of
harms. Broadening notions of violence from the perspective of youth highlights
the ways in which accepted social arrangements "do violence" to some youth and,
accordingly, suggests an urgency about the need to generate developmental supports for youth identities, affiliations, activities that may be considered threatening
to the status quo.

Researchers seeking youth perspectives also question prevailing assumptions
about the nature and development of violence by providing social theory about
power relations (Daiute et al., this issue), a critical look at the need for scapegoats
(Mahiri & Conner, this issue), and challenges to those practices that maintain and
naturalize social stratification (Fine et al., this issue). Theory about mechanisms
of resilience in the face of such social oppressions has also extended youth violence research—where resilience occurs in social conflict as much as in individual
behavior.

This research, thus, invites an explicit reframing of violence studies and a
widening of the spaces in which we interrogate youth production of, resistance
against, and performance through violence, including physical domains of sexuality, music, group activities, and psychological orientations that interject new
meanings and resistances into cultural practices. In some ways, we expect young

people's perspectives to mirror mainstream adults' notions of violence done to them, such as rape, and by them such as shooting other people. Yet, just as we know that race, class, and gender matter, in this issue we learn that age, generation, status, and everyday social interactions also affect the many forms of violence that define us globally.

Third, the articles in this issue rely upon a *broad range of methods* including standard surveys, participant observations, discourse analysis, archival and historic research, ethnomethodology, content analysis, and statistical modeling. Research on youth violence typically seeks and documents *universal* explanations from large scale studies about the causes of violence. However, research methods that rely primarily on behavioral indicators and normative scales may miss some of the ways that youth from diverse socio-cultural backgrounds perceive and deal with social problems and, even more striking, may miss all the ways in which youth avoid and withdraw from violent circumstances.

We have included here research conducted with methods including broad-based surveys as well as context-specific qualitative analyses. All of the articles, however, offer textured understandings of how race, ethnicity, history, class, gender, sexuality, region, and social role affect exposure to, coping with, and resistance toward violence (see Daiute et al.; Spencer et al., this issue). These studies also probe broadly and creatively how young people understand and cope with violence, offering a much needed complement to both environmental and epidemiological explanations as the basis for education and policy.

As is evident in many of these papers, the integration of theory and method is important to clarifying youth perspectives. The papers combine quantitative and qualitative methods in different ways. In the Fine et al. paper, for example, quantitative methods are used to examine the range and prevalence of young people's experiences of surveillance while qualitative methods are applied to understand the depth of the impact of those experiences. Somewhat differently, the research by Spencer et al. employs quantitative methods to apply an innovative survey combining community, developmental, and phenomenological factors to two large samples of African American youth and qualitative "holistic interpretation of community violence." Daiute et al. offer a third approach to integrating quantitative and qualitative methods involving critical qualitative discourse analysis to identify and compare values across participants in a violence prevention program and quantitative analyses to examine the range of values across contexts and participants.

Archival analyses also provide an important mechanism for conceptualizing youth perspectives on violence in several of the papers. The papers by Cross, Solis, Hertz-Lazarowitz, and Mahiri and Conner conduct historical analyses of media, legal documents, and scholarly reports to examine prevailing assumptions about violence, yielding Mahiri and Conner's finding, for example, that the largest increase of violence is among White men approaching middle age rather than among young Black men, as commonly believed. The studies reported in this issue also use participant observation and interviewing to bring contemporary empirical interpretations to archival analyses.

In this way, the range of methods reflects the intellectual and methodological reach of researchers who seek to understand rigorously and deeply how young people view the circumstances in which they are situated; how they come to witness, engage in and avoid violence; how they reproduce the very violence imposed on them; and how they organize for change. Heinous cases of youth violence in recent years (Garbarino, 1999) and also evidence of the everyday micro-aggressions endured by youth (Boyd-Franklin & Franklin, 2000) increase the need for complex approaches. Researchers in this issue begin to integrate analyses of individual understanding, affect, and action with institutional analyses of families, schools, peer groups, (in)justice systems, and insidious forces of racism, sexism, and classism.

Expanding Definitions of "Youth"

"Youth" is conceptualized here as a socio-cultural concept. We consider "youth" only in part to be determined by chronological age. Unlike some references to teens or those in high school, the age groups we consider span from seven-year-olds through young adults attending college. We include this relatively broad range of young people because they all face social challenges with incredible intelligence and agency, even though they are young, legally, and materially dependent. It is clear from this collection of research studies that any continuous transition from vulnerability to agency posited by some developmental theory (Erikson, 1968) is a luxury that few experience. The papers in this issue explain how seven-year-olds make sense of serious social conflict, how college students struggle with identity in the context of ethnic wars, how pre-teens and teens reckon their own bodies with gender, sexual, and racial politics, and how young people identify with ambivalence the often duplicitous roles of "caring" institutions.

Violence and injustice challenge social relational maturity in children, require hopefulness among older teens, and provoke critical consciousness across all age groups. In seeking to elicit diverse perspectives on youth violence, we deliberately include a broad sample of young people's insights about school attendance, legal identity, police presence, sexuality, social values, and myths about violent acts. The young people cited support their own resiliency in the face of social forces that are sometimes supportive and sometimes oppressive. Activities like presenting one's self, learning, creating relationships, and hanging out require young people, especially those in urban settings, to address competing and, in some cases, hostile social forces from the time they move about independently. Since defining youth perspective also requires defining its context and abjectness, our conceptualization of "youth" encourages us to consider the networks of peers, parents, teachers, school administrators, law enforcers, and others who support and/or limit youth development.

Common Assumptions

This issue is organized around several conceptualizations of "youth perspective." In the most obvious sense, "youth perspective" involves gaining direct reflection from youth about how they perceive and analyze violence in their worlds. Such research invites youth to share their experiences through interviews, surveys, conversations with peers, and participation in projects over time, even as participants in the research process itself. Beyond gaining first person accounts from young people, however, these studies have deliberately crafted theoretical concepts and methodological tools to ask questions (research questions and interview questions), conduct data analyses, and interpret results from conceptualizations and categories that emerge in youth-centered research.

Adult-centered and -generated questions were considered a priori insufficient as the basis for many of these studies. Some of the studies involve youth researchers who help design survey questions (Fine et al.; Hertz-Lazarowitz, this issue), interpret conversations and data (Fallis & Opotow; Solis, this issue), express their views in peer groups (rather than with only adults; Daiute et al.; Mahiri & Conner; Phoenix et al., this issue). All of the studies foreground youth perspectives by broadening the unit of analysis beyond individuals—beyond what individual youth say about themselves and their environments to the expressions of groups with social, cultural, and political solidarity in the face of the powerful institutions that typically define youth development.

Once youth perspectives sit at the center of our analyses, the very complex impact of major social institutions on youth comes into evidence. Specifically, youths' contradictory relations with families, schools, communities, law enforcement, and popular culture become pronounced. While youth may disagree with their families, and families may violate the rights of their children, families emerge in these studies as the "breeding grounds" for shared knowledge, beliefs, and practices commonly known as "culture" (Cross; Solis, this issue). So, too, while romantic peer relations offer novel sites for intimacy and pleasure, (hetero)sexual relationships and the institution of "compulsory heterosexuality" come to be seen as potential sites for violent relations between young men and women (Phoenix et al.; Tolman et al., this issue). Just as public schools can expand the knowledge and agency of young people, these institutions are often distant from or oppressive to the ways of knowing and interacting of youth from racial and ethnic "minority" backgrounds (Daiute et al.; Fallis et al.; Mahiri et al.; Spencer et al.). Likewise, police and other "protectors" may "help" individuals and communities, but they also create problems that limit young people's development into responsible members of organized society (Fine et al., this issue). For these reasons, we offer scholarship on youth perspectives as they evolve across historical and cultural periods that create foundational motivations and boundaries, youth perspectives as they develop within and against public institutions that introduce specific moral imperatives and practices, and youth perspectives as they are shaped within close relationships defining intimacy and personal meaning.

Identifying Youth Perspectives Isn't Easy

Several problems make embarking on the task of gaining youth perspectives challenging. First, existent theories on violence and injustice provide little guidance for addressing interactions between institutional and personal factors—society and experience—and how these influences conspire to create lives. The papers discuss the ways in which gaining access to youth perspectives has required transforming theory and methods. These papers reveal how difficult and yet how significant it is to connect individual lives, personal narrations, and institutional effects. Second, those who are most interested in youth perspectives admit also that it is very difficult for adults to gain anything like "authentic" youth perspectives. In our call for papers, researchers were asked explicitly to address how their methods were designed to gather youth analyses. Humble as we are about the difficulty of gaining access to young people's standpoints, the authors of this issue explore creatively theory-based methods to access youth experiences of violence. Methodological decisions considered how the research interacted with the study contexts, how the purposes and goals of participants conformed to or challenged those around them, and how historic and institutional forces could be incorporated into the design. Studies in this issue represent a range of designs that aim to open inquiries into and with youth about their relationship to social violence. For example, eliciting youthful conversations about violence with peers, teachers, and researchers is a self-conscious design principle aimed at capturing the socially constructed and contextual nature of views about violence (Daiute et al., this issue). Teaching youth, themselves, to be researchers is another innovative approach discussed here (Fallis & Opotow; Fine et al.; Hertz-Lazarowitz, this issue) whereby youth, as researchers, come to view relations of violence as an object for study, asking different questions than if they were positioned as the object for study. Analyzing youth behavior and narratives in distinct contexts, that is, the same youth in school, community, with peers and at home, allows us to view the kaleidoscopic quality of youth perspectives (Mahari & Conner; Solis; Spencer et al., this issue).

We are cautious, however, of especially one peril of foregrounding youth perspectives. Since we seek theory and research that avoids the demonization of youth for society's ills, it may be argued that we, in response, idealize—that we err on the side of identifying, primarily, injustices that social structures have imposed on youth. With these reflections, we introduce this issue as a critical extension of—not a replacement for—the existent literature on youth violence.

Purpose and Plan

The goal of this issue of *JSI* is to theorize, explain, and illustrate youth as an analytic perspective rather than as the object of violence studies. Establishing the nature, circumstances, and consequences of youth perspectives will, we propose, increase clarity in youth violence studies, provide the basis for expanding research questions and methods, and offer new insights for subsequent research, practice, and policy. The papers are written by researchers who have re-focused the gaze of violence research to gain insights into how young people and their families perceive social problems. Contributors work from diverse disciplines, including social psychology, developmental psychology, clinical psychology, educational psychology, sociology, drawing on specific expertises in women's studies, Black identity theory, immigration studies, public health, and literacy. The research described occurred in urban and suburban classrooms, homes, community-based organizations, college campuses, and city streets on different continents—places where young people engage in some of their activities, thus embedding issues of practice and policy in the research designs—which some of the authors discuss as part of their results. The papers all explain how theory and method open up youth perspectives toward the creation of research for understanding and promoting issues of social justice and development. None of the contributing scholars conceptualizes youth violence as a disease, and all take seriously that violence against and by young people must be addressed as a social and political problem.

The issue is organized in three sections, focused on distinct contexts that foreground "youth perspectives" to forge conceptual breakthroughs about violence and youth's position in various kinds of violence. These organizing contexts offer youth perspectives through history, culture, and community; youth confrontations with public institutions, and transformation of understandings about violence through the examination of youth in relationships.

Section I: Youth Perspectives Through History, Culture, and Community

The papers in Section I present theoretical and methodological stances to highlight perspectives that are often only background themes in youth violence research. These papers assume the social world to be problematic for, if not assaultive to, youth and examine how youth negotiate social dangers and dilemmas. This shifting toward invisible, oppressed perspectives, moreover, offers insights about modes of violence like the imposition of "illegality" as an identity that challenges youth development and wisdoms known in "minority communities" about violence.

Each paper interrogates a realm of violence in terms of how youth in diverse oppressive or challenging settings must create identities and lives for themselves against the forces of history. In "Re-Thinking Illegality as a Violence Against, not by, Mexican Immigrant Children and Youth," Jocelyn Solis explains how, crossing the border, Mexican children walk into identities that make them criminals—hostile conceptualizations against which they must figure out how to live and be recognized in a society where they are not welcomed, in spite of the contributions they make to the society. In her research with Mexican American youth considering issues of border crossing in a social activist organization, Solis illustrates the entwined nature of physical and psychological violence around citizenship.

In "Vulnerability to Violence: A Contextually-Sensitive, Developmental Perspective on African American Adolescents," Margaret Beale Spencer, Davido Dupree, Michael Cunningham, Vinay Harpalani, and Michèle Muñoz-Miller present a measurement of subjectivity in community context to account for psychological effects of violence on African American adolescents. Describing Phenomenological Variant of Ecological Systems Theory, Beale Spencer and colleagues argue for a definition of "youth perspective" as a range of psychological profiles resulting from crime around Black youth and offering important links between community responsibility and youth experience in concrete ways, positioning young people at the center of specific social, cultural, and political realities.

In "Arab and Jewish Youth in Israel: Voicing National Injustice on Campus," Rachel Hertz-Lazarowitz explains how violence may become a performance of identities for Jewish and Arab youth attending the same university. Like Solis, Hertz-Lazarowitz uses historical analysis to explain the political inevitability of youth violence. Across their articles, these researchers offer provocative and compelling evidence that it is *in* the performance of violence, that many youth take the resilient step of attaching themselves to a particular version of identity in war. In an effort to carve a sense of racial and ethnic "self" in the midst of contested political and geographic borders, youth engage a violence of identities.

In "Tracing the Historical Origins of Youth Delinquency & Violence: Myths & Realities About Black Culture," William Cross uses a dialectic historical analysis to document how the mystique of Black criminality is at best a form of intellectual denial, which threatens future progress of the African American community in particular, and the larger project of a multi-racial democracy called America. The methods used to reveal the historical, cultural, and communal aspects of youth perspectives include archival studies, interviews, social action projects, and scale-based quantitative tools.

The papers in this section examine socio-political relations through historical and archival analysis—a methodology that is increasingly used to provide contexts for cultures and individuals. The papers argue that raising typically muted voices not only informs practice, policy, and research around issues of youth violence, but can also fundamentally change the subject under scrutiny.

Section II: Youth Confronting Public Institutions

The papers in Section II approach youth perspectives by shifting the critical gaze away from "what's wrong with youth" and toward those "caring" institutions that assume youth violence to include anti-social behavior and discourse, especially among historically oppressed racial, ethnic, and class-based groups. By explaining how public institutions contribute to—rather than contain—youth violence, these analyses raise new questions for research, practice, and policy.

The twentieth century was in many ways the century of the child in part because of the numerous institutions designed "for youth"—institutions designed to ensure rights, to protect, to support healthy development, to socialize, to educate, to inhibit, to serve as holding places, and to hold youth up as examples. The papers in this section focus on public schools and law enforcement as public institutions with roles that have evolved from serving society to increasingly posing limits on the needs and potentials of diverse groups of youth. Violence prevention is a social institution that unites school and law enforcement from different political, social, and developmental origins, often by "containing" youth and youth expressions of social, political, racial and religious conflict. These papers consider how the identification and prevention of violence by public institutions may conflict with meanings generated by youth.

Colette Daiute, Rebecca Stern, and Corina Lelutiu-Weinberger examine such contradictions directly in their paper "Negotiating Violence Prevention," which illustrates the different and conforming values of children, teachers, and curriculum developers around discrimination conflicts and social responses to such conflict. The paper explains how seven- through ten-year-old children sometimes resist the peace-at-all-costs curriculum as a means of expressing their own social realities, needs, and social responsibilities. In "Are Students Failing Schools or Are Schools Failing Students? Class Cutting in High School," Kirk Fallis and Susan Opotow examine students' use of class-cutting as a commentary on presumptions about trust and effectiveness of public high school education.

In "Black Youth Violence Has a Bad Rap," Jabari Mahiri and Erin Conner offer theory that popular culture positions urban youth as scapegoats, and although violence occurs in their lives, the longitudinal study of fifty young people of color shows that the nature and role of these youth in violence is very different from the portrayal in the media. The paper culminating this section shifts the gaze of violence toward law enforcement and other adults who engage the lives of young people on a daily basis. In "'Anything Can Happen with Police Around': Urban Youth Evaluate Strategies of Surveillance in Public Places," Michelle Fine, Nick Freudenberg, Yasser Payne, Tiffany Perkins, Kersha Smith, and Katya Wanzer offer information about the range of experiences of "micro-aggressions" in every day life of White youth, and even more so, in youth of color who emerge as those most likely to expect disrespect and powerlessness in the face of aggression from police officers, school personnel, and others.

In sum, the research reported in this section contributes data-based accounts of violations to youth trust and dignity by public authorities who tacitly and some-times overtly demonize youth whom they are supposed to support. These studies document how much can be learned by listening to the experiences of young people as they challenge public institutions about the nature and meaning of violence, the aggressions they face, and their own social responsibilities.

Section III: Transformations from Youth Through Relationships

Section III focuses on youth perspectives which emerge in intimate relationships that challenge development and well-being. While family and peer relationships are certainly influenced by broader social, political, and economic forces that operate in institutional/individual interactions, the emotional impact of connection/dominance is salient and intense for individuals and their relationships. It is in the interpersonal practices and meanings that personality forms, so violence in and around these relationships has an immediate impact. The papers in this section examine family and sexual relationships (separately).

In "Sowing the Seeds of Violence in Heterosexual Relationships: Early Adolescents Narrate Compulsory Heterosexuality," Deborah L. Tolman, Renee Spencer, Michelle V. Porche, and Myra Rosen-Reynoso examine young adolescents' experiences and perceptions of heterosexual relationships. Through interpretive analysis of interviews and focus groups, these researchers identify "cultural scripts of heterosexuality"—the expectations of male dominance and sexual aggression and presumption of female conformity to these expectations.

From a different vantage point on sexual politics, Ann Phoenix, Stephen Frosh, and Rob Pattman in "Producing Contradictory Masculine Subject Positions: Narratives of Threat, Homophobia, and Bullying in 11–14 Year Old Boys" explain and illustrate how the pressure of societal expectations that boys should be sexually and otherwise dominant, aggressive, and tough is at the root of tensions within boys' groups and in spite of understandings about the nature and injustice of such interactions.

The Integrative Summary

In the integrative summary, Linda Powell highlights themes that emerged in her reading of the articles in this issue, in particular as they relate to psychodynamic theory and several challenges of identifying and sustaining youth perspectives on violence and injustice. In addition to underscoring insights about the phenomenology of meaning making in theory and method across the studies and the need to address the biased nature of human environments when analyzing youth violence, Powell urges youth researchers to employ "clinical language about the unconscious" which provides "firepower to talk more authentically about the complexity of what happens within and between individuals and groups." Finally, she urges us to examine the implications of schooling, popular culture, and ourselves in the construction of youth violence and injustice.

The Benefits of Youth Perspectives

Three benefits of a youth perspective approach to research become apparent across the papers in this issue. First, by listening fully and deliberately to youth perspectives, we hear, broadly and painfully, about the ways in which the very taken-for-granted structures, institutions and relations of society may assault the dignity of youth. For some articles, this involves youth in general. For others, the impact is more particular to youth of color, undocumented youth, gay or lesbian youth. Across the volume, today's youth can be read as a generation growing up with a sense of adult betrayal and alienation.

Articles in this issue, for example, establish theory and methods that represent how public and private institutions sustain or mask normalized violence, e.g., school practices (Fallis & Opotow, this issue), legal definitions of "citizenship" (Solis, this issue), value-laden assumptions of a violence prevention program (Daiute, Stern, & Lelutiu-Weinberger, this issue), analyses that question gender-based violence (Phoenix et al.; Tolman et al., this issue). Such theory, methods, and results not only critique, but also offer alternatives to normalized strategies. Such material is crucial if we are to generate more responsive strategies for dealing with violence by and against and youth.

Second, we have learned the value of involving youth in design of research, policy, school reform, media, and university governance. The papers argue that institutions "for" youth, including media (Mahiri & Conner, this issue) and schools, must also be "of" youth and "by" youth. If not, the "for" may be thoroughly undermined by youths' sense of alienation from adult-centered policies and practices (Fallis & Opotow, this issue).

Many of the papers in this issue force us to revisit policies that advance problematic strategies for responding to youth violence, such as "zero tolerance" programs, which demonize and banish individual youth. By listening to and working with youth, the policy focus in this issue was developed at the intersection of social justice and development, seeking new understandings of youth violence and responses to violence *in context (not pushed out of significant contexts)*. Such scholarship is essential for reconceptualizing social research, practice and policy on youth violence (see Daiute et al.; Spencer et al., this issue).

Third, we have learned that providing young people with opportunities to challenge and critique the normalization of violence offers innovative research findings and strategies for organizing pedagogy and policy. This practice-based research offers strategies that involve youth critique to re-imagine curriculum (Daiute et al., this issue), schools (Fallis & Opotow, this issue), universities (Hertz-Lazarowitz, this issue), community based organizations (Solis, this issue), community policing (Fine et al., this issue), media portrayals of youth of color (Mahiri & Conner, this issue) and youth organizing for broader economic, racial, gender, sexuality and social change (Cross; Spencer et al., this issue). Via these efforts of shifting the gaze away from youth as perpetrators to youth as critics and engaged citizens, we learn about the power and strength of involving youth in short and long term strategies for social change. So many of these articles breath a sense of possibility, born of the creativity and imagination launched once youth are invited to contribute their critical understandings of social relations.

References

Aber, J. L., Jones, S., Brown, J. L., Chaudry, N., & Samples, F. (1998). Resolving conflict creatively: Evaluating the developmental effects of a school-based violence prevention program in neighborhood and classroom context. *Development and Psychopathology, 10*(2), 187–213.

Boyd-Franklin, N., & Franklin, A. J. (2000). *Boys into men: Raising our African American teenage sons*. New York: Dutton.

Coles, R. (1991). *The spiritual life of children*. Cambridge, MA: Harvard University Press.

Connell, J., & Wellborn, J. (1991). Competence, autonomy and relatedness: Motivational analysis of self system processes. In M. Gunnar & L. A. Sroufe (Eds.), *Minnesota Symposium on Child Psychology* (Vol. 23, pp. 43–77). Hillsdale, NJ: Erlbaum Publishers.

Daiute, C. (2000). Narrative sites for youths' construction of social consciousness. In M. Fine & L. Weis (Eds.). *Construction sites: Excavating class, race, gender, and sexuality among urban youth* (pp. 211–234). New York: Teachers College Press.

Daiute, C., & Buteau, E. (2002). Writing for their lives: Children's narrative supports for physical and psychological well-being. In S. J. Lepore & J. M. Smythe (Eds.), *The writing cure: How expressive writing promotes health and emotional well-being* (pp. 53–73). Washington, DC: American Psychological Association.

Elliot, D. S., Hamburg, B. A., & Williams, K. R. (Eds.). (1998). *Violence in American schools*. New York: Cambridge University Press.

Erikson, E. K. (1968). *Identity: Youth and crisis*. New York: Norton.

Fine, M. (1988). Missing discourse of desire. *Harvard Educational Review, 58*(1), 29–53.

Fine, M., & Harris, A. (Eds.). (2002). Theorizing counter stories. *International Journal of Critical Psychology, 4*.

Flanagan, C., Bowes, J., Jonsson, B., Csapo, B., & Sheblanova, E. (1998). Ties that bind: Correlates of adolescents' civic commitments in seven countries. *Journal of Social Issues, 54*(3), 457–475.

Flanagan, C., & Tucker, C. (1999). Adolescents' explanations for political issues: Concordance with their views of self and society. *Developmental Psychology, 35*(5), 1198–1209.

Garbarino, J. (1999). *Lost boys: Why our sons turn to violence and how we can save them*. New York: The Free Press.

Hartsock, N. (1983). The feminist standpoint: Developing the ground for a specifically feminist historical materialism. In S. Harding & M. B. Hintikka (Eds.), *Discovering reality* (pp. 283–310). Dordrecht: Reidel.

Hill-Collins, P. (1991). *Black feminist thought: Knowledge, consciousness and the politics of empowerment*. New York: Routledge.

Lerner, R., Fisher, C., & Weinberg, R. (2000). Applying developmental science in the 21st century: International scholarship for our times. *International Journal of Behavioral Development, 14*(1), 24–29.

Loeber R. (1982). The stability of antisocial and delinquent child behavior. *Child Development, 53*, 1431–1446.

McIntyre, A. (2000). *Inner city kids: Urban youth confront life and violence in an urban community*. New York: New York University Press.

Noguera, P. (2001). Finding safety where we least expect it. In R. Ayers (Ed.), *Zero tolerance*. New York: New Press.

Olweus, D. (1979). Stability of aggressive reaction patterns in males. *Psychological Bulletin, 86*, 852–857.

Phillips, L. (2000). *Flirting with danger*. New York: New York University Press.

Pittman, K. (2002). Balancing the equation: Communities supporting youth supporting communities. *Community Youth Development* (Special Anthology: Summer), 19–24.

Powell, L. (2001, August). *The hidden incompetence of elites*. Paper presented at the American Psychological Association meetings. San Francisco.

Rhodes, R. (1999). *Why they kill: The discoveries of a maverick criminologist*. New York: Knopf.

Spina, S. O. (Ed.). (2000). *Smoke and mirrors: The hidden context of violence in schools and society*. Lanham: Rowman & Littlefield Publishers, Inc.

Way, N. (1998). *Everyday courage: The lives and stories of urban teenagers*. NewYork: New York University Press.

COLETTE DAIUTE is Professor of Psychology at the Graduate Center of the City University of New York. She is a developmental psychologist focusing on social processes and symbolic systems in children's learning and social relations. Dr. Daiute is has been working for the past five years on a funded study on children's discourse and action around social conflicts in urban and suburban settings. Colette Daiute is author of *The development of literacy through social interaction* (Jossey-Bass Publishers) and *Computers and writing* (Addison-Wesley) as well as numerous articles.

MICHELLE FINE is a Professor of Social Psychology, Urban Education and Women's Studies at the Graduate School and University Center, City University of New York. Recent publications include (with Lois Weis) *The unknown city: Lives of poor and working class young adults*. Boston: Beacon Press, 1998; *Speedbumps: A Student Friendly Guide to Qualitative Research*. New York: Teachers College Press, 2000; and *Construction sites: Excavating race, class, gender & sexuality in spaces for and by youth*. New York: Teachers College Press, 2000.

Journal of Social Issues, Vol. 59, No. 1, 2003, pp. 15–31

Re-Thinking Illegality as a Violence *Against*, not *by* Mexican Immigrants, Children, and Youth

Jocelyn Solis*

Brooklyn College

Sociohistorical theory was used to examine illegality as a form of state violence that bears upon the formation of undocumented Mexican immigrants. This article proposes a theory of dialectical violence that integrates societal with personal enactments of violence through case illustrations of Mexican youth. In a grass-roots association defending immigrants' rights, youth develop within conflicting discourses about undocumented immigrants proposed by society, family, and community. Methods included ethnographic analysis of the association's documents, a workshop in which five participants authored a booklet with texts and illustrations about their lives in the city, and an interview with their mothers. Findings illustrate how Mexican youth enter a cycle of violence as a result of their undocumented status, socioeconomic class, language and ethnic-racial memberships.

The study of youth violence has persistently focused on members of minority groups from lower income backgrounds (Eron, Gentry, & Schlegel, 1994). This is an institutional injustice in research literature that produces a notion of minorities as worthy objects of inquiry only when they are emblematic of undesirable characteristics: being marginalized, poor, and likely to fail according to society's standards. Understandably, much research has addressed this institutional bias by portraying minorities in something other than in a deficit model, with a more positive light around a number of issues, such as language (Labov, 1968; Zentella, 1997), education (Gibson & Ogbu, 1991; Trueba, 1999; Valdes, 1997), or identity (Cross, 1995; Matute-Bianchi, 1991), and by re-conceptualizing

---

Correspondence concerning this article should be addressed to: Jocelyn Solis, School of Education, CUNY-Brooklyn College, 2900 Bedford Avenue, Brooklyn, NY 11210 [e-mail: jsolis@brooklyn.cuny.edu]. The author would like to acknowledge the thoughtful comments and suggestions for revisions by the editors and reviewers of this article, as well as the generous participation of those involved in the research. This article is part of a dissertation whose completion was funded by the Ford Foundation.

violence as resistance to social injustice (hooks, 1994; Walsh, 1987). Such previous research has attempted to portray its subjects from within their own complex set of cultural lenses. This article presents innovative theory and methods based on case illustrations of Mexican youth that address violence as a potential outcome of societal-individual dialectical relationships.

Illegality as a Societal-Institutional Violence

Research on violence in relation to the lives of minority youth needs to discuss critically the origins and development of violence within the particular situation of the population under investigation. In this article, I examine notions of illegality as an identity from the perspective of undocumented Mexican immigrants, particularly through the perspectives of children and youth. As I will describe, illegality is one kind of societal violence with which Mexican immigrants and their children are faced; I argue that illegality is produced on a societal level through social structures such as the mass media, immigration laws, and popular opinion where undocumented immigrants are "illegal" subjects worthy of disparagement in popular discourse, and of exploitation in popular practice (Espenshade & Belanger, 1998).

This article, however, posits that undocumented Mexican youth and the children of undocumented parents must confront conflicting perspectives that define who undocumented immigrants are. The arguments I present in this article are drawn from empirical research conducted in a grassroots organization defending the rights of Mexican immigrants. Within this special context, Mexican children and youth develop their identities through discourses of illegality proposed by society, family, and community. This article illustrates how a *dialectical* relationship of violence is formed as institutionally-assaulted Mexican youth become violent youth themselves.

Drawing from sociohistorical psychology (Scribner, 1985; Vygotsky, 1978), the original focus of the study involved examining the formation of identity in societal/institutional and individual contexts of illegality. Following from this premise, identity was conceptualized as a dialectal activity operationalized in the activities of a community-based organization and its individual members. This article intends to expand the theoretical and methodological literature on identity that only relatively recently began to take sociopolitical context and cultural variability into account (Harré & Gillett, 1994; Parker, 1997). Moreover, it expands the work of previous studies that stress the importance of race, ethnicity, and gender (Cross, 1995; Deaux, 2000; Hurtado, 1996) by adding a focus on immigration status as another institutional structure upon which identity may be based.

Vygotskian sociohistorical theory (1978) proposes that psychological forms emerge through cultural tools that mediate between material and psychological activity. In this sense, it is essential to locate the tools that are available for the formation of individuals' identities. I theorize that societal-institutional structures of immigration status, race, ethnicity, and language are available to Mexican immigrants and children in the context of U.S. relations of power; they are potential tools for meaningful, dialectical, psychological-material activity. This article presents initial steps toward considering whether personal acts of violence can be explained according to this theoretical premise, illustrated through case examples of Mexican youth.

Research Methods

This study traced youths' psychological development through societal and individual histories. Ethnographic fieldwork including participant observation of a grassroots organization in New York City took place during the years 1999–2000; during this time, I collected field notes, public documents such as brochures and press releases, as well as 16 issues of an information bulletin published monthly. As a participant of the organization, I continue to work with the staff on the writing of grant proposals, translations of important documents, and the planning of special projects. I also assist a number of cultural events, rallies, and manifestations.

The organization operates at the grassroots level for the purpose of defending the legal and human rights of Mexican immigrants in the city. All members are volunteers, primarily undocumented Mexican immigrants organized in community-based groups that convene in their neighborhood's parishes around the city's five boroughs. The organization estimates the population to currently stand at about 500,000 people, and it claims to reach over 10,000 Mexican immigrants through its 40 affiliate groups. At present, the organization is the largest Mexican institution in the city; in spite of its recent inception in 1997, it is a highly public organization that maintains close and frequent contact with the media.

In addition to such ethnographic methods, I designed an audio-taped writing workshop for children and youth in which 16 participants authored a booklet with written texts and illustrations about their lives in the city. (Titles of written documents [e.g., booklet, bulletins] produced by the organization, and proper names of participants have been avoided or changed in this article to protect confidentiality.) The purpose was to write this booklet for other Mexican children and youth whose families planned to migrate to New York. The mothers of five core participants were interviewed together after its completion.

The research questions raised in this article are:

(1) How do Mexican children and youth experience, understand, and discuss illegality?

(2) What kinds of violence are Mexican youth exposed to and how do they respond?

(3) What are the consequences of violence on youths' identities and general development?

My analysis rests primarily on triangulation methods (Denzin & Lincoln, 1994) that verified the general ideology and political position of the organization through both its general activities and local testimonies across participants. However, individual variability was also examined across adult and child participants, as well as within the group of children and youth with whom I worked closely to underscore the individuals' characterizations of illegality. In this chapter I focus on data classified under the general theme of violence, a grounded category among several (others included literacy, citizenship, and religion) that emerged in descriptions of Mexican youth, as well as the youths' descriptions of their own experiences of life in the city.

Insider Institutional Responses to Illegality

The community organization where the research was conducted was a critical site for youths' development as it provides an institutional re-framing of illegality as a societal violence *against* undocumented Mexican immigrants. The *Asociación Tepeyac* organizes Mexican immigrants so they can learn about and publicly defend their human and legal rights, maintain their cultural identity, and publicly expose the societal hypocrisy that underlies discourses about undocumented immigrants. Through its public rallies, protests, cultural events, and monthly information bulletin, it affords immigrants a common discourse with which to contest multiple acts of violence (such as human rights infractions, labor abuse, and racial discrimination) that result from both unfair practices and erroneous grounds upon which the identities particular to undocumented immigrants emerge on the societal level. The association attempts also to curtail personal acts of violence that are seen as consequences of these hardships by publishing texts that raise awareness about common problems and resources in the community. In this way, the association constructs both the cause and solution for Mexican migrants' violence externally. Its common discourse, emerging through the communication of shared experiences and practices during community meetings and published texts, portrays violence *toward* Mexican immigrants as a cause of acts of violence *by* Mexican immigrants, a cycle that begins with the actual immigration experience.

Although crossing over the Mexican–U.S. border is a potential solution to their severe economic hardships (Smith, 1996), crossing the border illegally is a traumatic experience for many immigrants. Hagan (1998) documents the physical dangers Mexican migrants face when they cross into the United States which include getting caught by the Border Patrol, swindled by smugglers, and robbed or killed by border bandits. Others become lost or lose their children who were accompanying them; some die of dehydration or hypothermia in desert areas (Hagan, 1998). Another harsh reality that I have observed the association address is the widespread violence against women who state they have been sexually abused in their attempt to cross the border. Their testimonies claim that their aggressors range from border bandits or "cholos" and smugglers, to Immigration and Naturalization Service (INS) officers.

This is a reality of abuse fostered by discriminatory immigration laws and economic relations that force Mexican migrants to enter an illegal underground culture of violence later reinforced by labor abuse and even racial or physical maltreatment, along with other problems more common to poor immigrants in general (see Suarez-Orozco, 1998 for a volume of research on Mexican immigration that discusses the range of hardships this population endures). I argue that the adaptation of Mexican immigrants in New York is a process grounded in special circumstances and experiences having to do with being poor, undocumented people of color. *Asociación Tepeyac* addresses such acts of violence against Mexican immigrants by raising awareness about border perils, pressuring civically both U.S. and Mexican governments to take actions to protect migrants' human rights, and defending migrants threatened with deportation by employers, landlords, or others as they live and work in substandard conditions. In addition, the association seeks services and alternative activities (that are both legal and non-violent) for those immigrants who become involved in gangs, who abuse substances and alcohol, or those affected by domestic violence. In the process, personal acts of violence against themselves and others are construed as consequences of their specially difficult life circumstances in the city.

The association's monthly information bulletins, for example, contain articles in which violence in the community is consistently explained as youths' reactions to violence and mistreatment directed toward them. For example, in one such article the Executive Director wrote that some immigrants take their anger out on others, even innocent victims, when they, themselves, have been exploited, mistreated, or paid unfairly. Such explanations point to a dialectical relationship: a cycle between the societal abuse *faced* by Mexican immigrants, and the personal acts of violence and abuse *enacted* by Mexican immigrants. The association seeks to involve youth in constructive activities that build a sense of community and empowerment, and that raise consciousness to motivate peaceful yet forceful action. In the next section I examine youths' narrations of violence, how they understand and respond to social violence, and how their personal experiences intersect with their own psychological formation and identities. I propose that illegality is one possible source of violent expression among Mexican youth when the societal violence imposed on them becomes a psychological tool with which they can re-define or relate to themselves and others.

Mexican Children and Youths' Experiences of Violence and Notions of Illegality

Mexican children's and youths' experiences of violence emerged indirectly as part of the audiotaped booklet project having to do with their general experiences of life in New York. They were primarily recruited through the "snowballing" method; although I met a total of 16 children and teenagers over the course of this project, five of them participated consistently. By examining their interpersonal relationships, youths' own experiences of violence inevitably emerged. Children and youth described their own confrontations with different kinds of violence, ranging from physical and verbal to racial and psychological. Therefore, my analysis of children's development examined the social positions of power (Harré & Gillett, 1994) they adopted with respect to themselves and their communities in order to understand how they identified themselves and others. Rather than limit my examination to their social role, I was interested in their specific position within a status and power hierarchy. Wherever possible, I also compared their power positions with information gathered from the audiotaped group interview with their mothers to further place their lives in a historical context; their opinions represented another kind of institution (the family) whose point of view children and youth are exposed to in a profound way. As the illustrations below will demonstrate, violence is afforded by society as a tool youth use to make sense of themselves, other people, and institutions. They use violence to make sense of their own and others' identities, and in their interpersonal relations and actions.

Since my intent is to portray the different kinds of violence youth experienced, even one mention of violence in their lives by one child or teenager was sufficient. In my analysis I subdivided findings according to institutional, inter-ethnic, intra-ethnic, reactive, and unexplained violence. Other researchers have similarly described aggression in terms of relational, proactive, or reactive terms (Crick & Dodge, 1996; Crick & Grotpeter, 1995), but in this study I place equal importance on the violent acts exerted by youth as to those directed toward them within the dialectical framework outlined above. In a Vygotskian sense (1978), a psychological tool develops from cultural artifacts and eventually mediates a dialectical relationship between individuals' cognitive and material functions. Therefore, I also examined whether violence carried psychological functions for Mexican children or youth.

The youths described their experiences of violence in relation to their race, ethnicity, language background, and immigration status. For example, some children mentioned having to defend their parents or themselves as English language learners when they first arrived in the United States. In addition, children and youth narrated stories of ethnic conflict, as they talked about fights they had with other Latinos or other Mexicans. A thirteen year-old girl narrated the following:

> *Se creen mucho los puertorriqueños* [Puerto Ricans think they're all that]. In my school, I had a fight with this Puerto Rican girl but all the girls, all of them, came up to me. I was like "What you want?" They were like "Oh why you talking shit." We had a fight. She called me a lesbian and stuff like that so I got mad, right? I started cursing at her, *todas me vieron* [all of them saw me], right? And they were like "Oh why you calling her this and that, you call her mother–." I was like no. My friends was like "Yo, what's wrong with you?" Then they wanted to suspend me. I was like "No, *deja eso* [drop that] ... I got sick of it ... I

usually like—all my friends are Puerto Rican. All of them. I'm like, I don't get it. I fight with Puerto Ricans, I have friends [who are] Puerto Rican."

Based on her description, it would seem that such conflicts, however irrational, stemmed from inter-ethnic rivalry. However, in the continuation of her narrative, we see that this is only one kind of ethnic rivalry, and that violence seems to be used as a means to address other, inexplicit and unresolved issues:

Actually, *con los que peleo más son con mi propia raza porque hay unos que, este, like, otras chamacas, mi misma edad, igual, tienen* [those I fight with the most are other Mexicans because there are some, like other girls my same age] 13, 14, whatever, right? *Traen pleito conmigo. Por nada. Son,* [They're carrying a fight with me. For nothing. They're,] um, *cholas.* I'm like, *ya van como dos veces que me paran diciendo que ando hablando de ellas* [already twice they've stopped me saying I'm talking about them], and I'm like *ni siquiera* [I didn't even] . . . *Yo una vez les dije, sí, o sea, ustedes dicen que yo hablo de ustedes y todo. O mejor si se quieren pelear conmigo ya díganme* . . . [Once I told them, ok, you say I'm talking about you and all. Better yet, if you're looking for a fight with me, tell me . . .] I'm like "shit!" *Eso me aburre ya* [I'm tired of it already]. I was like, *ya mejor se quedaron quietas* [then they finally stopped still].

This teenager resorted to violence, in light of having to defend herself and in her frustration at failing to understand why she was the object of others' hostility. From her narrative it seemed that she has had a great deal of contact with other Mexican youth, and had mentioned earlier that she was involved in organizing a folkloric dance group for the Mexican youth in gangs in her neighborhood. Wondering whether her contact with Mexicans and experiences of violence were taking place outside of the association's activities, I asked her if there were other Mexicans in her school to which she responded:

En la mía sí. En la mía creo que hay más mexicanos pero la verdad son como muy callejeros. Pero, se creen, ves [In mine there are. In mine I think there are mostly Mexicans, but the truth is they're really street kids. But they're snobs, see]. No, I don't get it. It's like, *mira,* in my school, *o sea ¿no?* [right?] In my school, *en todas partes, cuando hay bailes* [everywhere, when there are dances] and stuff, *todos vamos y cuando acaba el baile, a la mitad, en medio* [we all go and when the dance ends], in middle of the dance, there's fighting. Mexicans *con* [with] Mexicans. Mexicans, they try to kill each other. I'm like—they try to take knives out *y que pistolas y que* [and guns and], but I'm like "what the–?" That's why my mother doesn't take me to dances anymore.

Throughout her narrative, this teenager contrasted herself with other Latino and Mexican youth who start fights for no reason. She continually positioned herself as a (potential) victim of violence who resorted to violence as a personal defense against the harm toward which she was drawn under racial/ethnic segmentations and sub-divisions.

Aside from narrating such personal experiences of violence that children and youth faced and reacted to, others also discussed their exposure to risky conditions in their neighborhoods. After being questioned on one occasion about how one might meet other Mexicans in the city, an eleven year-old boy suggested youth in gangs in Mexican neighborhoods.

The particular experiences of violence that children narrated positioned them against other racial/ethnic groups as well as against members of their own ethnicity or nationality. Each of these youths' narrations of violence pointed to a circular or dialectal developmental pathway between societal and personal violence, that is, a society where racial and ethnic differences exist affords youth with racist means to address their conflicts. Without direct means and critical thinking skills to understand and address their conflicts, racial/ethnic violence is perpetuated.

However, my participants' confrontations with violence did not emerge from only racial/ethnic, or intra-ethnic conflicts, but were discussed also in relation to illegality. Therefore, I examined also how the children's individual experiences of violence intersected with their understanding of illegality according to institutional definitions of "illegal" immigrants. One must consider the impact that illegality as a societal violence can have on undocumented Mexican immigrants who, without organization, are silenced and easily exploited, as well as how this bears upon their children's development.

The children and teenagers who had lived in Mexico long enough to remember what it was like living there were well aware of the dangers of border-crossing and consequent injustices that Mexican immigrants faced in the United States. For instance, a fourteen year-old girl who participated only once in the booklet project narrated this knowledge. I had asked her if she had been born there and what she remembered about Mexico. She stated:

> I remember some stuff. It was hard to live there. There was no money and . . . the food was a lot of money. You buy like four things and it was already two hundred something [pesos]. You can't survive there. [JOCELYN: That's why a lot of people come here.] But everyone's dying when they come over here, you know, they have to close that part [of the border]— the desert. When they come, you know, they have to pass by the desert 'cause they don't have papers so in the desert they say there's a lot of snow and everything and, you know, they don't survive in there.'

Using her personal experience of economic hardship and cultural knowledge of the dangers of border-crossing, this teenager juxtaposed Mexican migrants with an unidentified "they," an authority who had the power to close the border. She repeated the use of "survival," first to describe Mexicans' difficult economic situation, and later to describe the risk they took by crossing the border under hazardous conditions. Poverty and protected borders both lie outside of Mexican migrants' individual control, and work against them as societal barriers to their survival. She had commented earlier that she sometimes dislikes Americans who say they hate immigrants, but make them work hard for little pay. Thus, she was aware of the economic hardships and immigration-related violence that Mexican migrants faced, and used this knowledge to expose her understanding of social injustice and power imbalances.

Based on my reading of their collective experiences, Mexican children and youth must make sense of the illegitimate U.S. membership they, their families, and/or communities are afforded as a result of their undocumented status, *and* racial, class, and language backgrounds. This is a violence that they must confront using whatever means they have available to them. "Violenced" children and youth, without appropriate tools to defend themselves, are set up to become violent youth themselves. In addition to becoming frustrated and angry as described in their narrations above, such violence may have consequences on their identities ranging from children's affiliation with marginalized communities, to a complete rejection of Mexican identity and assimilation to mainstream beliefs.

A Case Study: The Emergence of David's Critical Consciousness and Limitations

To illustrate one particular case of how multiple kinds of violence intersect with an individual's identity formation, I will discuss the case of David, one of the booklet project's main participating youths. In our conversations, David, at 14, was the eldest participant who most frequently narrated experiences of violence, largely in relation to racial tensions and illegality. Interpersonal conflicts between David and his peers and teachers, who were not necessarily aware of his immigration status, were attributed to racial tensions taking place in school. Therefore, I begin by describing David's narrations of violence in general and end specifically with his own experience and beliefs about illegality.

David was a freshman in a small all-boys Catholic high school whose population consisted primarily of African American and Latino youth with virtually no Mexicans. The school was located in a different borough from the one in which David lived. His home's neighborhood was primarily Puerto Rican. According to his mother's narration of her family's history in the United States, David remembered when he crossed the border illegally with her and his two year-old sister, Karina, when he was four years old. He disliked talking about this experience openly because of the psychological turmoil that ensued; upon arriving in New York, his fears about his migration experience manifested themselves in nightmares re-enacting his own persecution by helicopters. Unaware of the circumstances under which they would cross the border, David knew only that he would soon be re-united with his father.

During our first meeting as a group when I introduced the booklet project, David was completely silent. However, over the course of the ten weeks we met he became the most talkative of the group, narrating many stories of experiences he had lived in the United States although he hesitated to write them down. He described himself as a student who did not often receive good grades and who was sure to end up in summer school because he was failing 9th grade math. He often spoke of being misunderstood by his teachers who would punish him for conflicts and physical fights he did not start, but that he engaged in frequently because of other students' disrespect and outright racist remarks. In fact, David recalled one occasion in which he felt ignored by a teacher who would not call on him in class. When David muttered something about his teacher being racist, he claimed the teacher conceded, "Yeah, I am."

In the interview with my participants' mothers, all of them agreed that racism was prevalent in their children's schools, even though they admitted having had a hard time believing it at first. The mothers agreed that when they saw school authorities mistreating some students over others, or when they witnessed their own children's racial confrontations with their teachers, they finally believed that their children's accounts about racism in school were true.

Aside from racism on the part of school authorities that David narrated and that his mother confirmed, David also frequently narrated stories about racial conflicts with his peers to which he would react in a violent manner. Similarly to the teenage girl I quoted earlier, David's uses of violence reported in our conversations also displayed a defensive function. He described his engagement in violent acts as a reaction to other people's assaults or discrimination. However, he did not always describe himself as being provoked into violent confrontations. In addition to such acts of violence with unclear provocation, David reported other experiences of violence that seemed gratuitous. Although hard to judge their truthfulness, such seemingly irrational acts of violence were even more alarming in this dialogue:

> DAVID: On the way back from school we was burning things. Yeah we—, I brought a lighter and then they was givin' out flyers about clubs … I burned like three of them [laughs]. Threw them in the sewer. It was right next to the gas station too, that was hilarious.
> JOCELYN: You could start a fire.
> DAVID: It wasn't gonna be my fault.
> JOCELYN: I don't know.
> DAVID: I woulda thrown the lighter in the sewer or somethin'. Where do you see my fingerprints? Nobody saw nothin'.

Undoubtedly, David had been both a victim and a perpetrator of numerous kinds of violence. His case indicates that violent behavior is one means he has available to act upon the world. Violence toward others was aimed at societal institutions and its representatives as well. For example, David's irreverence toward the severity of his own acts was displayed at other moments as irreverence toward certain authorities. Other than his teachers whom he often qualified as dumb because they could be outsmarted by his continual mischief, David also invoked the Immigration and Naturalization Service by drawing a maze from Mexico to New York with two dead ends labeled *la Migra* (the INS). In this situation and in others, David positioned himself in contempt of structures of control which were conversely positioned by David as repressive social means. This is illustrated further in the following narration:

> I wanna go on my bike and all that joint … I go to this place … They have like a ramp …
> going down. It's mad fast. It's like a real steep hill. It's like next to a police precinct. They

[the police] be kicking them out all the time. Last time they went after me. But I was on my bike and they was on foot, so who has the advantage?

David also questioned the practices of reporters, as he witnessed an occasion when journalists from a local television cable channel visited the offices of the association to interview one of the staff people. He witnessed how the reporters fabricated the piece of news they wanted to portray: "It was like a fake report cause they showed . . . M– . . . walking into a room talking. He wasn't even talking! They just . . . wanted like a shot of them. I don't know."

Although he later conceded that this was probably done to leave the public with a realistic activity of the association, one could argue that the media is one kind of authority whose word the public is supposed to trust, yet creates stories that often do not do justice, but injustice, to the people whose lives they are reporting. David's range of experiences lent themselves to his mistrust and irreverence toward authorities and structures of power. This is consistent with Fine, Freudenberg, Payne, Perkins, Smith, and Wanzer's finding (this issue) that Latino youth mistrust police, social workers, and other public servants. Much of David's experiences seemed to be disrespectful of authority figures, and in our meetings, he enacted this in playful ways. For instance, he consistently sought ways to outsmart me and the other participants by engaging us in power plays and playful teasing. He also inserted playful threats, usually directed at his sister, during our conversations: e.g., "I'm gonna go over there and slap her!" or "Smack her over the head, Jorge." At other moments, he used racism as discrimination to taunt his sister: "Oh this is my sister['s drawing] . . . with her skinny-ass people . . . See, that's all she draws. Skinny people. She's racist against fat people" [laughter].

In the next example, Karina shamed her brother by tattling on his own racial epithets used as a means to bully her:

KARINA: for real, he bullies me! He['s] like [pretends to be pushed], "What, nigger? What, nigger? What you gonna do?" . . . He hits me. He goes, "Ow! [pretends to get pushed] What, nigger? Ow! What? What you gonna do?"

As one can see from these examples, even David's sense of humor was laden with violent undertones. While David could not react with violence directly toward the structures of power that impose illegality and other oppressive identifying markers on him, he could use violence to address other people in contexts where he occupied a dominant position of power, such as a brother toward his younger sister or a physically larger boy toward his smaller peer. This would not have been detected if David's multiple positionality and history had not been taken into account. During another session in which I suggested that the group co-author a story to accompany a drawing Margarita, a 6 year-old participant, had made of two children walking in front of tall buildings, David's suggestions also exemplified his dark sense of humor:

"They get mugged on the way home."
"They meet the pimp who lives downstairs."
"They start a fire in the elevator."

Most of David's suggestions were intended to tease Margarita who insisted that she wanted the story to be a "happy" one. On the other hand, David's own illustrations sometimes conveyed the generalized negativity with which he associated the city. In one illustration, he drew the Hudson River as a waste dump including a car wreck, a dead body, a bomb, and dead fish.

In terms of illegality, David also consistently demonstrated a great amount of cultural knowledge about being "illegal" in his comments about new immigrants implicitly assumed to be poor and undocumented. He described them as being afraid of the police, easily exploited by employers, and hard-working, rather than abusive of government services. David positioned himself repeatedly as an advocate of immigrants, questioning both the ethics and authority of government control along the border. On one occasion, David criticized stereotypes about Mexicans depicted as natives slumped by a cactus sleeping with their heads bowed under a large sombrero. In response to a drawing, he asked me afterwards why "we" could not act similarly and close the border to keep Americans out of Mexico. After I explained that each country has its own immigration laws, and that Mexico's weaker economy has something to gain by allowing Americans to enter and spend their money there, David simply shook his head in annoyance. He was aware that Mexican immigrants face injustices in the United States, and that being undocumented places constant barriers on him, his family, and his community. In our interview, his mother discussed how she had to confront her son about his undocumented status when he insisted that he wanted to work. Adamant about getting his working papers, his mother told David that he could not work legally in the country because of his undocumented status. In the process, she pointed to expectations both about herself and her children. While it is alright for her to work illegally in the United States as a means to support her family, she expected her children to surpass her own lifestyle in spite of their shared illegal immigration status. David is not allowed to work illegally, and must negotiate parental expectations to achieve academically along with the negative experiences that turn him against school, as well as the structural barriers he must face as an undocumented youth.

All of the mothers that I interviewed saw being undocumented as a necessity for economic survival and social mobility that was unattainable for them in Mexico. Although they had achieved some financial stability and saw the possibility for further mobility, living as undocumented immigrants was somehow functional to their goals. For this reason, they did not present themselves as being hostile toward Americans or to the country in spite of the injustices and hardships that they, themselves, faced. As David's mother put it, her initial motivation to migrate had to do with her daughter's health. Karina was becoming epileptic in Mexico where her family could not afford treatment. In New York, she found free medical care for her daughter in spite of their undocumented status, and Karina eventually recovered completely. Only after this medical problem was resolved did Rosa begin planning her family's financial security. She also contrasted her position of gratitude with other Mexicans' hostility toward the United States.

For David, however, being undocumented was not functional; it was a barrier to the fulfillment of his goals and a source of violence against him. This, coupled with the racism he confronted in school and parental expectations to achieve academically, is a source of psychological conflict for him as seen in his ambivalence about going to college: " . . . Cause I don't wanna go to college but I do. But if I do go to college, I wanna go really far away. I swear. Really far away." In his answer to a peer-conducted interview in which we asked what he liked least about New York, he stated racism. Thus he associated school and New York City with a series of race and immigration-related assaults committed against him, and expressed this in his narratives, illustrations, power plays, and even in his sense of humor.

David's range of cultural knowledge and personal experiences provided a basis for him to understand himself and his community in relation to certain authorities. His participation in the *Asociación Tepeyac* had also served as an enabling means for him to develop a critical eye and a mistrust for authorities and structures of power. In addition, he counted on the cultural knowledge and expectations passed on to him by his parents, as well as exposure to both of his parents' involvement as community leaders in their own neighborhood. He, himself, has attended protests and demonstrations in defense of immigrants' rights.

David's experiences of violence and access to cultural knowledge, which mainstream U.S. society ignores, has placed him in a special position to think critically; he can detect conflicting perspectives and question public information or social practices that identify him, his family, and his community in disrespectful ways. He was aware that social *mis*-representations lead to violent outcomes such as death on the border, abuse in the workplace, or class and race discrimination. Social theories of identity should take into account not only how social representations mediate between individuals and societal beliefs (Augoustinos & Walker, 1995), but also how individual identities are constructed through activities working within multiple and conflicting social representations. Although David's consciousness has liberatory potential (Freire, 1996) it will remain limited as long as violence continues to be lived privately and ignored publicly, *and* as long as the means to respond to violence other than with violence remain unfamiliar to him.

Understanding the Dialectics of Violence

Where does the blame for violence lie? Rather than blaming the victim or blaming society as opposing sources of violence, I posit that violence needs to be understood as a dialectical process that is constantly unfolding between social structures and individuals. This article attempts to understand violence in relation to identity formation through its social origins and psychological development. At first glance, David's case may seem typical of a working-class minority youth who demonstrates resistance to authorities and institutions representative of his group's oppression (Walsh, 1987). However, when his personal situation is examined in more detail, one can locate the particular experiences and multiple memberships in institutions that have fostered his own personal consciousness, knowledge, and actions. His defensive and destructive attitude, alienation by society, and contempt toward higher authorities are consequences of a social system of violence. While undocumented Mexican immigrants are positioned by society as unbelonging outsiders (Mirandé, 1985), the association's critical perspective re-positions them as victims of social injustice for the purpose of mobilization. On the other hand, the means that individuals like David can find to re-position themselves within these power struggles is exactly what the association tries to prevent: violence itself.

My analysis, based on triangulation of the youths' statements, the association's texts, and three years of my own participation in it indicates that society affords youth with violence as a tool to understand, reject, and defend their own and others' identities. In order to understand this development, one must look to the structural and institutional conditions that afford individuals both limitations and possibilities for further action. David's violent actions originate as a response to violence on a societal level and as a defense against personal, psychological harm, yet will continue and may be deployed upon those in weaker positions of power unless changes are made dialectically between him and the society in which he lives. That is, violence must be understood in its social origins, personal understanding and adoption, and consequent effects on both the individual and society (Mead, 1934; Wertsch, 1985). Without access to tools that allow David (and others like him) to address directly and effectively the violence with which they are confronted, children and youth will be positioned to become violent youth themselves. This is an alarming realization that begs for both personal and institutional levels of intervention.

Is Society Prepared for Mexican Children and Youth, Their Families, and Communities?

The theoretical grounding laid forth in this article was drawn from ethnographic work and case examples of Mexican youths' direct experiences of violence. Empirical research needs to test this argument further by delving more deeply into the personal histories of youth, while simultaneously considering the potential responsibility of the state in making certain structures of power available to exert violence as a means of positioning oneself and relating to others. Therefore, we must first accept that violence has social origins rather than a natural, or inherently individual basis. Second, we must agree that societal violence may be internalized, and that personal acts of violence are caused by multiple external factors. This implies that individually-exerted violence can be curbed by simultaneous interventions on both personal and societal-institutional levels that present alternative structures upon which self-understanding is formed. As long as borders remain closed to some, societal representatives (such as the immigration policymakers or media that provide a popular conception of undocumented immigrants) must first acknowledge publicly the presence of undocumented immigrants as a steady, continuous population that exists, in part, for the sake of U.S. economic interests (Mirandé, 1985). Institutions of power must take responsibility for misrepresentations of the undocumented by ensuring that measures are taken to deter violence against undocumented immigrants, which, in turn, may serve to prevent the formation of violent youths. Otherwise, the repercussions will be long-term as Mexican families continue to settle permanently in the United States in spite of their undocumented status (Hondagneu-Sotelo, 1994).

Community-based organizations such as *Asociación Tepeyac* can structure collaborative projects between families and schools to inform each other about common problems their children face, to educate each other about their respective institutions' cultures, and to design together violence prevention programs that are culturally meaningful. The association has consistently sought ways to develop cultural and recreational programs through such activities as folkloric dance, soccer training, and other activities with the intention of providing a positive sense of community in safe spaces. Indirectly, this is a measure against violence through which youth develop social skills and community values in a supportive environment. However, mental health professionals could also aid the association in developing interventions or conflict resolution training that address explicitly violence-related problems and non-violent means to resolve them. Mexican youth need to be provided with cultural-psychological tools relevant to their own knowledge, experiences, and goals so they can identify personal and historical causes of emotional tensions and conflicts through critical reflection.

Also, teacher education programs should include curricula that prepare educators to recognize the special needs of students from immigrant populations. Educators need to be capable of understanding and recognizing potential sources of psychological conflict that affect students' identities, academic participation, and relationships with peers and teachers. Institutionally, schools should be prepared to reach out to their students as well as other institutions potentially involved and interested in their educational success. Finally, researchers must examine also how their work can facilitate such collaboration between institutions, and reflect on how their research is used to reproduce or transform the social standing of marginalized populations. By using multiple levels of historical analysis (in this case, of society, community organization, and individuals) through multiple design methodologies (ethnography, interviews, and case studies) to understand the psychosocial developmental trajectories of children and youth, we can achieve a rich understanding of the complexity and variability of human development, its broad implications and possibilities.

References

Augoustinos, M., & Walker, I. (1995). *Social cognition: An integrated introduction*. Thousand Oaks, CA: Sage.

Crick, N. R., & Dodge, K. A. (1996). Social information-processing mechanisms in reactive and proactive aggression. *Child Development, 67*(3), 993–1002.

Crick, N. R., & Grotpeter, J. K. (1995). Relational aggression, gender, and social-psychological adjustment. *Child Development, 66*(3), 710–722.

Cross, W. E. (1995). Oppositional identity and African American youth: Issues and prospects. In W. Hawley & A. Jackson (Eds.), *Toward a common destiny: Improving race and ethnic relations in America* (pp. 185–204). San Francisco: Jossey-Bass.

Deaux, K. (2000). Surveying the landscape of immigration: Social psychological perspectives. *Journal of Community and Applied Social Psychology, 10*(5), 421–431.

Denzin, N. K., & Lincoln, Y. S. (Eds.). (1994). *Handbook of qualitative research*. Thousand Oaks, CA: Sage.

Eron, L. D., Gentry, J. H., & Schlegel, P. (Eds.). (1994). *Reason to hope: A psychosocial perspective on violence and youth*. Washington, DC: American Psychological Association.

Espenshade, T. J., & Belanger, M. (1998). Immigration and public opinion. In M. M. Suárez-Orozco (Ed.), *Crossings: Mexican immigration in interdisciplinary perspective* (pp. 363–403). Cambridge, MA: Harvard University Press.

Freire, P. (1996). *Pedagogy of the oppressed*. New York: Continuum.

Gibson, M. A., & Ogbu, J. U. (Eds.). (1991). *Minority status and schooling: A comparative study of immigrant and involuntary minorities*. New York: Garland Publishing, Inc.

Hagan, J. (1998). Commentary. In M. M. Suárez-Orozco (Ed.), *Crossings: Mexican immigration in interdisciplinary perspective* (pp. 357–361). Cambridge, MA: Harvard University Press.

Harré, R., & Gillett, G. (1994). *The discursive mind*. Thousand Oaks, CA: Sage.

Hondagneu-Sotelo, P. (1994). *Gendered transitions: Mexican experiences of immigration*. Berkeley, CA: University of California Press.

hooks, b. (1994). *Teaching to transgress. Education as the practice of freedom*. New York: Routledge.

Hurtado, A. (1996). *The color of privilege: Three blasphemies on race and feminism*. Ann Arbor, MI: University of Michigan Press.

Labov, W. (1968). *A study of non-standard English of Negro and Puerto Rican speakers in New York City*. New York: Columbia University Press.

Matute-Bianchi, M. E. (1991). Situational ethnicity and patterns of school performance among immigrant and nonimmigrant Mexican-descent students. In M. A. Gibson & J. U. Ogbu (Eds.), *Minority status and schooling: A comparative study of immigrant and involuntary minorities* (pp. 205–247). New York: Garland Publishing, Inc.

Mead, G. H. (1934). *Mind, self, and society from the standpoint of a social behaviorist*. Chicago: University of Chicago Press.

Mirandé, A. (1985). *The Chicano experience: An alternative perspective*. Notre Dame, IN: University of Notre Dame Press.

Parker, I. (1997). Discursive psychology. In D. Fox & I. Frillektensky (Eds.), *Critical psychology: An introduction*. London: Sage.

Scribner, S. (1985). Vygotsky's uses of history. In J. Wertsch (Ed.), *Culture, communication and cognition* (pp. 119–145). New York: Cambridge University Press.

Smith, R. C. (1996). Mexicans in New York: Membership and incorporation in a new immigrant community. In S. Baver & G. Haslip-Viera (Eds.), *Latinos in New York: Communities in transition* (pp. 57–103). Notre Dame, IN: University of Notre Dame Press.

Suarez-Orozco, M. M. (1998). (Ed.). *Crossings: Mexican immigration in interdisciplinary perspective*. Cambridge, MA: Harvard University Press.

Trueba, H. T. (1999). *Latinos unidos: From cultural diversity to the politics of solidarity*. New York: Rowman and Littlefield.

Valdes, G. (1997). *Con Respeto: Bridging the distances between culturally diverse families and schools: An ethnographic portrait*. New York: Teachers' College Press.

Vygotsky, L. S. (1978). *Mind in society: The development of higher mental processes*. Cambridge, MA: Harvard University Press.

Walsh, C. (1987). Schooling and the civic exclusion of Latinos: Toward a discourse of dissonance. *Journal of Education, 169*(2), 115–131.

Wertsch, J. V. (1985). *Vygotsky and the social formation of mind*. Cambridge, MA: Harvard University Press.

Zentella, A. C. (1997). *Growing up bilingual: Puerto Rican children in New York*. London: Basil Blackwell.

JOCELYN SOLIS recently earned her doctorate in Developmental Psychology at the CUNY Graduate Center. The title of her dissertation was *The (trans)formation of illegality as an identity: A study of the organization of undocumented Mexican immigrants and their children*. Currently, she is an Assistant Professor in the Graduate Literacy Program of the School of Education at Brooklyn College. Her research interests are in cultural psychology and the development of identity, language, literacy, and bilingualism.

Journal of Social Issues, Vol. 59, No. 1, 2003, pp. 33–49

Vulnerability to Violence: A Contextually-Sensitive, Developmental Perspective on African American Adolescents

Margaret Beale Spencer*
University of Pennsylvania

Davido Dupree
University of Pennsylvania

Michael Cunningham
Tulane University

Vinay Harpalani
University of Pennsylvania

Michèle Muñoz-Miller
University of Pennsylvania

Spencer's Phenomenological Variant of Ecological Systems Theory (PVEST) is presented as a theoretical framework to analyze potential effects of being a victim or co-victim of a violent crime. Data are presented from a sample of African American adolescents residing in a Southeastern metropolitan area. Victims (n = 20) and non-victims (n = 332) are compared on their self-reporting of clinical symptoms normally associated with violent or traumatic experience during middle childhood and early adolescence. Results suggest that observed symptomatology

*Correspondence concerning this article should be addressed to Margaret Beale Spencer, W. E. B. Du Bois Collective Research Institute, University of Pennsylvania, 3440 Market St., Suite 500, Philadelphia, PA 19104 [e-mail: marges@gse.upenn.edu]. The research described was supported by funding to the first author from the W. T. Grant Foundation, Commonwealth Fund, and The Spencer Foundation. Support for the writing of this manuscript was made possible by grants to the first author from the NIMH, Kellogg, NSF, and Ford Foundations.

33

may not be solely attributable to actual victimization. Discussion includes possible mechanisms by which factors such as cognitive developmental status, physical and social context, and previous victimization of the adolescent or a family member of the adolescent can influence symptomatology.

Violence among youth in America is a major public health concern with multifaceted effects. Victimization itself can lead to injury or death, and co-victimization, the direct observation of perpetration of violence against another individual, can lead to severe psychological and emotional distress. The recent rampage of school shootings has brought increased attention to violence among adolescent youth. Among males aged 15–24 in the United States, the rates are currently approximately four to five times higher than those in most other industrialized nations (Fingerhut & Kleinman, 1990; Snyder & Sickmund, 1995). Metzenbaum (1994) offers the shocking statistic that handguns alone have killed more American children within the past fifteen years than the total number of American soldiers who lost their lives in the Vietnam War. Moreover, the problem is particularly serious among African American youth; homicide has been the leading cause of death for Black youth aged 15–24 (Hamburg, 1998), and according to some estimates (Cohen & Swift, 1993), homicide rates among Black males in this age range are over ten times those of their White counterparts. Thus, researchers concerned with violence must pay particular attention to the challenges facing African American youth.

In order to understand the impact of violence on youth (and particularly African American youth), it is helpful to utilize a sound conceptual framework that takes into account the experiences of youth in context. Several issues must be considered to properly understand the complexity involved. Social context is central to understanding violence; for example, Cubbin, Pickle, and Fingerhut (2000) note the links between urbanization, socioeconomic conditions, and homicide. Issues of normative development must be considered, and these are particularly salient during adolescence, when physical, social, and psychological maturation occurs, often in rapid and noticeable fashion. For African American youth, issues of race and gender identity are especially important, as these may interact to create unique experiences of stress and dissonance (Spencer, 1995, 1999).

Spencer's (1995) Phenomenological Variant of Ecological Systems Theory (PVEST)

Spencer's (1995) Phenomenological Variant of Ecological Systems Theory (PVEST) provides a comprehensive theoretical framework to integrate salient issues of context and development. In doing so, application of PVEST can help illuminate the relation between various factors and outcomes associated with direct and indirect effects of violence. PVEST integrates a phenomenological perspective with Bronfenbrenner's Ecological Systems Theory (1989), linking

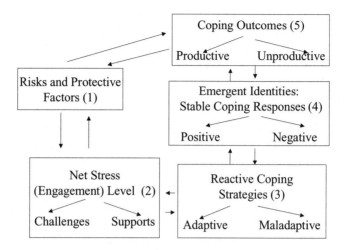

Fig. 1. Phenomenological Variant of Ecological Systems Theory (PVEST)

context with perception. In doing so, it captures the meaning-making processes underlying foundational identity development and outcomes (Spencer, 1995; Spencer, Dupree, & Hartmann 1997; Spencer, 1999). PVEST differs from ecological systems theory in that it is a process-oriented, development-emphasizing framework designed to describe individual life course development; in contrast, Bronfenbrenner's model, while certainly developmentally-sensitive and relevant, explicitly describes context rather than development.

A systems theory, PVEST consists of five components linked by bi-directional processes (Figure 1); it is a cyclic, recursive model that describes identity development throughout the life course.

The first component, *risk contributors*, consists of factors that may predispose individuals for adverse outcomes such as violence or associated psychosocial stressors. For urban minority youth, risks include socioeconomic conditions such as poverty, socio-cultural expectations such as race and sex role stereotypes, and socio-historical processes including racial subordination and discrimination—all of which can be associated with violence and pose threats to healthy development. The risks, of course, may be offset by *protective factors* (e.g., cultural capital). Self-appraisal is a key factor in identity, and how minority youth view themselves depends on their perceptions of these conditions, expectations, and processes.

Net stress engagement, the second component of PVEST, refers to the actual net experience of situations that challenge one's psychosocial identity and well-being, and the supports that are present to help cope with these challenges. These are essentially risk contributors that are actually encountered and manifested in everyday life and may be offset or balanced by available supports. For example, experiences of discrimination, violence, and negative feedback are salient stressors for minority youth, and positive adult supports can help mitigate experiences of stress. In response to stress, *reactive coping methods* are employed to resolve dissonance-producing situations. Reactive coping responses include strategies to solve problems that can lead to either adaptive or maladaptive solutions.

As coping strategies are employed, self-appraisal continues, and those strategies yielding desirable results for the ego are preserved. Accordingly, they become stable coping responses, and, coupled together, yield *emergent identities*, the fourth component of PVEST. Emergent identities define how individuals view themselves within and between their various contextual experiences. The combination of cultural/ethnic identity, sex role understanding, and self- and peer appraisal all contribute to and define one's identity. Particularly during adulthood, one's work and parental roles also contribute to identity processes in significant ways. Identity lays the foundation for future perception and behavior, yielding adverse or productive *life-stage, specific coping outcomes,* the final component of PVEST. Productive outcomes include good health, positive relationships, and high self-esteem, while adverse outcomes include poor health, incarceration, and self-destructive behavior.

The PVEST framework recycles and recourses through the lifespan as individuals balance new risks against protective factors, engage new stress levels, are given challenges potentially offset by supporters, try different coping strategies, and redefine how they and others view themselves. With regard to violence, the use of PVEST can, for example, (a) help elucidate mechanisms that may link exposure to violence at one life stage and aggressive behavior in another, and (b) facilitate identification of relevant interventions that may prevent intermittent maladaptive coping and mitigate negative outcomes.

Vulnerability to Violence: Impact on Psychological Well-Being

From a PVEST perspective, race and socioeconomic status are risk factors for exposure to violence. Both direct and indirect experiences with violence constitute stress engagement. Research findings suggest that in some communities, children and adolescents may be exposed to some form of violence on a regular basis (e.g., Bell & Jenkins, 1991; Gladstein, Rusonis, & Heald, 1992). For example, Shakoor and Chalmers (1991) found that close to 75 percent of African American youth surveyed in Chicago schools had been "co-victimized," directly witnessing the perpetration of serious violence (e.g., shooting, stabbing) on another person. According to a study done by Fitzpatrick and Boldizar (1993), nearly 85 percent of their non-clinical sample of African American youth (7–18 years of age) had witnessed at least one act of violence, and for more than 43 percent the witnessed violent act was murder.

Case studies of youth who have experienced problems linked to a violent experience indicate that a single violent experience may not have lasting effects.

However, chronic violence or cumulative experiences with violence may have far reaching effects on the psychological and cognitive development of adolescents (Gladstein et al., 1992). Garbarino, Dubrow, Kostelny, and Padro (1992) suggest that continuous exposure to violence does not desensitize children to its effects. Rather, it seems to "increase their susceptibility to developmental harm and post-traumatic stress" (Garbarino et al., 1992, p. 49). Co-victimization can lead to post-traumatic stress disorder (PTSD), and exposure to violence has been linked to perpetration of violence (DuRant, Cadenhead, Pendergrast, Slavens, & Linder, 1994). Specifically, Martinez and Richters (1993) found that witnesses of violence often reported symptoms such as anxiety, intrusive thoughts, depression, and sleep problems. Fitzpatrick and Boldizar (1993) also reported that, on average, their participants presented five PTSD symptoms, with only a very small number of participants being entirely symptom-free. More generally, co-victimization has been linked to both internalizing and externalizing symptomatology in children, with the former being the more prevalent response cluster (Kliewer, Johnson & Oskin, 1997). Garbarino et al. (1992) likens these symptoms displayed by co-victims to those seen in survivors of war.

Vulnerability to Violence: Impact on Cognitive Development

If experience with violence has developmental implications, age-specific developmental tasks would be affected. In general terms, one example of such a task is the development of abstract thought and hypothetical reasoning. More specifically, relationships among responses to violence, abstract thought, and hypothetical reasoning may be best understood with respect to attention. Attention plays a central role in memory and learning, and adolescents who have been exposed to violence may be affected in ways that influence their ability to pay attention or to focus their attention on task-relevant information (Wine, 1982).

For example, as a result of experience with violence, adolescents may become more sensitive to the threat of violence. Frieze, Hymer and Greenberg (1987) suggest that the reason for this perceived loss of security is that it becomes easier to envision oneself in a vulnerable position after having been victimized. Unfortunately, reports of the effects of experience with violence on adolescents have been more clinical in conceptualization (e.g., Gardner, 1971; Pynoos & Nader, 1990). Thus, most of the available literature reports the observable relations between reported violent experiences and observed symptoms. While often insightful, they offer little description of the cognitive mechanisms that must underlie the cognitive functioning they seek to explain. Clinical observations have revealed such themes in response to exposures to violence as fear of aggression directed at one's self (Bell & Jenkins, 1991; Dyson, 1989; Gardner, 1971; Pynoos & Nader, 1988) and a fear of not being able to control one's impulse to counter-aggress (Gardner, 1971). When considered in terms of attention and distraction, such responses can serve as distracters to the learning process. After exposure to violence, an adolescent may concentrate too much on his or her willingness, ability, and need to respond aggressively to perceived threats. Such adolescents may consequently become pre-occupied by feelings of self-consciousness, fear, anger, or guilt, and consequently have trouble paying attention to school-relevant information (Overstreet & Braun, 1999).

May (1986) further suggests that adolescents may develop a perceptual bias based upon past violent experiences. She conducted a study with secondary school males concerned with perception of violence among more and less violent males. May presented them with six pairs of experimental slides. One pair was a neutral scene, while the other was a violent one. The pairs were shown tachistoscopically for 0.5 seconds, which was short enough to keep the subjects from actually focusing on either one of the slides, but long enough for them to see both of the slides separately. May found that boys with a history of violent or aggressive behavior reported more violence in the tachistoscopic presentation. May argues that these results represent a perceptual bias as opposed to a response bias. The boys did not perceive violence in neutral slides; they were simply more sensitive to the violent slides. She further offers that since past research reveals that perceptual biases can be learned, "chronic exposure to violent acts or interpersonal violence educates selective attention to violent cues" (May, 1986, p. 25). A possible explanation is that as victimized youth become more selectively attentive to violent cues, they will become less attentive to other cues (e.g., school-relevant material and discussion, social cues during interpersonal interactions) or cope in ways that decrease maximum fit with school values (Spencer, 1999). Indeed, studies have shown (Osofsky, Wewers, Hann, & Fick, 1993; Shakoor & Chalmers, 1991) that survivors of community violence often suffer cognitive and academic delays. This may be due to attentional difficulties.

Additionally, adolescent victims may display certain symptoms that are repre-sentative of PTSD (Overstreet, 2000). However, relatively few display the complete constellation of symptoms associated with PTSD that would identify them as re-quiring clinical attention. When symptoms representative of PTSD are recognized in children and youth, attention is drawn to endemic problems in a community. However, what is potentially misleading about a diagnosis such as PTSD is that most accounts of the phenomena are based on children and youth who have obvi-ously been affected strongly enough by an identifiable experience that they need clinical attention. When an identifiable experience is assumed to be the origin of the symptomatology, there is less emphasis placed on individual vulnerability. A more appropriate focus might be an examination of issues related to individ-ual vulnerability as opposed to the incidents that expose this vulnerability (i.e., experience with violence).

To give an example, *Diagnostic and Statistical Manual of Mental Disor-ders*, Third Edition (American Psychiatric Association, 1980) criterion states that

PTSD can be characterized by the re-experiencing of previous trauma. It offers also that a predisposing factor for PTSD is pre-existing psychopathology. Both assertions are acknowledgments of pre-existing vulnerability, but they also both assume pathology. Conversely, vulnerability may be understood also by comparing PTSD symptomatology with cognitive changes that are normatively associated with adolescence, as understood in the context of social and cultural factors. For example, adolescent thought may be marked by an increased sensitivity to the implicit relationships among the activities that occur within one's community, one's immediate experience, and the actual physical make-up of the community (including oneself and other people). The ability to think more abstractly and hypothetically also affords adolescents the opportunity to become more vulnerable to their own unchecked anxiety, imagination (e.g., personal fable, imaginary audience), reasoning, and increased introspection (Irwin & Millstein, 1986). This can lead to inordinate self-focused attention, drawing away from other tasks (e.g., school). Thus, increased sensitivity to violence may detract from these important activities.

Vulnerability to Violence: Examining Normative Adolescent Development in Context

While an understanding of adolescent cognitive development alone may give insight into those adolescent-specific manifestations of distress (e.g., Schonert-Reichl & Beaudoin, 1998) that are a response to an identifiable experience with violence, it does not help one to understand the influence of the contexts which adolescents develop in and try to make meaning of. Violence does not occur in a vacuum. There are correlates of violence including conditions that offer the opportunity for violence or threat of physical harm (i.e., inappropriate sexual activity, run-down housing, overcrowding, illegal drug activity, poverty), "communal" coping mechanisms (e.g., peers or family members carry weapons, hang around kids who get in trouble a lot), as well as individual coping strategies (e.g., carrying a weapon). These correlates of violence may lead to the same distress symptoms that have been attributed to violence.

Correlates of violence that contribute to adolescents' social and physical context may actually inhibit aspects of development. For example, the physical characteristics of a community—possible correlates of violence—can have an effect on intellectual development. In a study of the characteristics of effective schools, Edmonds (1986) found four sets of correlates, one of which deals directly with the context. Effective schools were operationally defined as those schools in which the proportion of low-income students demonstrating academic mastery is close to being identical to the proportion of middle class students showing academic mastery.

Edmonds found that effective schools are relatively cleaner, relatively safer, relatively more orderly, and relatively quieter. Disorderliness, noise, and concerns about safety are correlates of violence that can serve as stressful distracters that can divide learners' attention to the point that learning is inhibited. Consequently, intellectual development is inhibited.

Edmonds's (1986) findings suggest that an important factor influencing learning is the degree of adaptation one has to make in a context where conditions are so stressful that they are distracting. More importantly, researchers become better analysts when recognizing that although isolated and cumulative experiences of violence may provide easily identifiable points of reference, acts of violence may be the catalyst and not the origin of the observed symptomatology in children and adolescents that develop in violent contexts.

Behavioral expressions that are associated with violence (sometimes mistakenly) should also be considered in context. Stevenson (1997) describes how African American youth are "missed" and "dissed" by mainstream American society, and how this treatment in conjunction with neighborhood factors relates to African American youth becoming "pissed" while trying to manage their anger. Black youth are "missed" as stereotypical media-based images distort the meanings of their social and affective displays—usually in negative terms. Hence, these unique cultural displays are devalued and viewed with insolence—"dissed." In conjunction with these misrepresentations, many Black youth reside in high-risk contexts where anger display may be an appropriate coping mechanism (Cunningham, 1999). Anger may indeed become a form of competence for social and emotional viability in certain high risk contexts. Hence, misrepresentation, disrespect, and hazardous contextual factors interact in creating the anger of Black youth (i.e., "pissed").

In conducting this study, Stevenson (1997) used Spencer's PVEST model to identify and investigate the risks and stressors that contribute to different coping methods involved in anger expression or suppression. Stevenson's (1997) findings indicated that fear of adverse outcomes may diminish expressions of anger, although not feelings of anger. However, his data also indicated that this relation might not hold in high-risk contexts, where situations may necessitate mitigation of fear and display of anger. Both the expression and suppression of anger have many health risks that may be related to violence.

Current Study

With the aforementioned concerns in mind, this study was designed to identify preexisting risk factors or patterns of vulnerability in addressing the effects of experience with violence. The research questions are as follows:

(1) Is there a statistically significant difference in the self-reports of symptoms associated with PTSD by adolescents who report having been a victim of assault or some other violent crime compared to adolescents who have not

reported being victimized? If so, are the differences in self-report predicted by self-report of those symptoms prior to being victimized?

(2) Is there consistency in the symptomlogy of adolescents who report having been a victim or assault or some other violent crime?

Methods

Participants. The students in this study were drawn from a sample of 562 African American male ($N = 394$) and female ($N = 168$) adolescents from a Southeastern metropolitan area. The students were participants in the first author's six-year longitudinal study, Promotion of Academic Competence (PAC) Project. The data reported were collected during the 1989–1990 and 1990–1991 academic years. Students were in the sixth, seventh, and eighth grades in the initial year of data collection. However, due to high retention rates for African Americans in the school districts from which the students were drawn, the participants' ages ranged from eleven to fifteen. The students were originally enrolled in four middle schools in the same Southeastern metropolitan area. Three of the four schools have populations that are over ninety percent African American, with over sixty percent in the fourth school. From parent-reported family income information, it was determined that fifty-eight percent of the subjects' families met federal poverty guidelines (for a family size of four, the criterion for poverty was an annual family income of $13,950 or less).

A subset of students was drawn from this sample. Students were selected to be in one of two comparison groups, victims or non-victims, based on two criteria. The victim group consisted of students (17 males and 3 females) who reported having been personally victimized in the second year of data collection, but who did not report victimization of self or a family member during the first year of data collection ($n = 20$). The non-victim group (214 males and 118 females) consisted of students who did not report having been victimized in the second year; nor did they report victimization of self or a family member in the first year of data collection ($n = 332$).

Procedures. As part of the PAC sample, each student was seen in small groups at their respective schools. They completed survey instruments over the course of three sessions. During the small group sessions, the majority of the testers were the same race as the participants. All testers were well-trained graduate students, undergraduates, or other adults who were hired specifically as adolescent interviewers. The adolescents were also engaged in one-on-one interviews that were conducted by interviewers of the same race and gender.

Instruments. The Stressful Life Events Report (Newcomb, Huba, & Bentler, 1981) is a list of thirty-nine positive and negative events that the student may have experienced in the past year. The respondent indicates whether he or she has experienced any of these events. If so, the respondent also rates the perceived impact of the event from very bad (-3) to very good ($+3$). Sixteen additional items were added to the survey to reflect incidences considered possible sources of stress for PAC project participants. The items were indications of occurrences in urban environments such as witnessing violent acts in the neighborhood or having personal knowledge of someone who was a victim of a violent act (Spencer, 1989). Two items from this instrument were selected for use in this study: "I was assaulted or the victim of some other violent crime" and "A family member was assaulted or the victim of some other violent crime." Data were collected using the Stressful Life Events Report in years 01 and 02.

Youth Self-Report (Achenbach, 1991) is a measure designed to obtain self-reports of clinical symptoms as well as competencies. The measure contains one hundred and nineteen behaviors to which the child indicates whether or not they are characteristic of his or her self. Thirteen items were selected for use in this study: "I can't keep my mind off certain thoughts," "I daydream a lot," "I am afraid of going to school," "I am afraid I might do something bad," "I act without stopping to think," "I like to be alone," "I have nightmares," "I feel too guilty," "I am self-conscious or easily embarrassed," "I am suspicious," "I have trouble sleeping," "I am unhappy, sad, or depressed," and "I keep from getting involved with others." This subset of thirteen symptoms represents clinical symptoms associated with experience with violence (i.e., PTSD symptoms). The possible responses are $0 =$ Not at all true, $1 =$ Somewhat true, and $2 =$ Very true. Data were collected using the Youth Self-Report in years 01 and 02.

Data analysis. Analyses of covariance (ANCOVAs) were used to compare differences in symptoms among victims and non-victims in year 02. Symptoms reported in year 01 were used as covariates to control for any prior differences in self-report of the symptoms of interest. A primary assumption underlying the use of ANCOVA is that the variable used as a covariate (e.g., self-report for "I like to be alone" in year 01) is significantly correlated with the dependent variable in the analysis (e.g., self-report for "I like to be alone" in year 02). Accordingly, if the covariate variable and dependent variable are not significantly correlated, then the ANCOVA is not appropriate. Correlations were computed for each pair of the thirteen selected symptoms for years 01 and 02 for the entire sample (i.e., victims and non-victims). If appropriate, two by two (2×2) ANCOVAs were conducted to compare victims and non-victims by gender on their reporting of each of the selected symptoms from the Youth Self-Report during the second year of study. Their self-reports for each symptom in the first year were used as a covariate. The analysis of covariance requires that the slope of the covariate by independent variable be the same for all levels of the independent variable. In order to test that assumption, ANCOVAs were first run including an interaction term, victim status by self-report of the symptom in year 01. If the self-reporting of the symptom in year 02 was significantly different for the levels of the interaction term, then there was no further analysis for that symptom.

Results

The results indicated statistically significant correlations ($p < .05$) for each pair of self-reports for each symptom except for "I like to be alone" and "I keep from getting involved with others."

The preliminary ANCOVAs, including the interaction term and the victim status by self-report of symptom in year 01, indicated that self-reports in year 02 were significantly different based on the interaction term for "I have nightmares" and "I have trouble sleeping." Accordingly, no additional analyses were conducted for those symptoms.

The final ANCOVAs indicated that when self-reporting of the symptom in year 01 is used as a covariate, there are significant differences between victims and non-victims for the following symptoms: "I can't keep my mind off certain thoughts" ($F(3, 328) = 4.67, p < .05$), "I am afraid of going to school" ($F(3, 339) = 4.92, p < .05$), "I act without stopping to think" ($F(3, 337) = 4.87, p < .05$), "I am self-conscious or easily embarrassed" ($F(3, 335) = 6.65, p < .05$), and "I am suspicious" ($F(3, 328) = 4.63, p < .01$). Differences in degrees of freedom reflect missing data for specific items. The numbers of subjects in each analysis are as follows (NV = non-victims, V = victims): "I can't get my mind off certain thoughts" ($n_{NV} = 322, n_V = 19$), "I am afraid of going to school" ($n_{NV} = 326, n_V = 20$), "I act without stopping to think" ($n_{NV} = 325, n_V = 20$), "I am self-conscious or easily embarrassed" ($n_{NV} = 324, n_V = 19$), and "I am suspicious" ($n_{NV} = 321, n_V = 18$).

Students who reported having been victimized in year 02 were more likely to report these symptoms than non-victims. Students' self-reports for "I am afraid I might do something bad," "I feel guilty" and "I am unhappy, sad or depressed" in year 02 were predicted by students' self-reports for the same symptom in year 01. However, there were no differences based on victimization. Students' self-reports for "I daydream a lot" were predicted by their self-report in year 01 and gender. Females reported daydreaming more often than males. Again, there was no difference based on victimization.

The symptom profiles in Table 1 were created based on students' self-reports. The profiles show the different manifestations of symptoms for the twenty students who reported having been victimized in year 02. The number of symptoms—reported by these students—ranges from 0 to 11. There is no one symptom that appears in each profile. However, there are four symptoms that over 50 percent of the victims report experiencing including: "I can't get my mind off certain thoughts" (55 percent), "I daydream a lot" (65 percent), "I act without stopping to think" (60 percent), and "I like to be alone" (65 percent).

Table 1. Symptom Profiles (Based on Self-Report) of Students Who Reported Being Victimized in Year 01

	Females
Subject 1	daydream a lot; afraid might do something bad; act without stopping to think; like to be alone; self-conscious or easily embarrassed
Subject 2	daydream a lot; afraid might do something bad; like to be alone; have nightmares
Subject 3	can't get mind off certain thoughts; daydream a lot; afraid of going to school; afraid might do something bad; like to be alone; have nightmares; self-conscious or easily embarrassed; have trouble sleeping; unhappy, sad, or depressed; keep from getting involved with others

	Males
Subject 4	no symptoms
Subject 5	can't get mind off certain thoughts; afraid might do something bad; act without stopping to think; like to be alone; self-conscious or easily embarrassed
Subject 6	can't get mind off certain thoughts; like to be alone; self-conscious or easily embarrassed; suspicious; unhappy, sad or depressed; keep from getting involved with others
Subject 7	can't get mind off certain thoughts; daydream a lot; afraid might do something bad; act without stopping to think; like to be alone; have nightmares; self-conscious or easily embarrassed; suspicious
Subject 8	daydream a lot; like to be alone; feel too guilty; self-conscious or easily embarrassed; suspicious
Subject 9	can't get mind off certain thoughts; daydream a lot; act without stopping to think; have nightmares; keep from getting involved with others
Subject 10	can't get mind off certain thoughts
Subject 11	can't get mind off certain thoughts; daydream a lot; afraid of going to school; afraid might do something bad; act without stopping to think; like to be alone; have nightmares; feel too guilty; self-conscious or easily embarrassed; suspicious; have trouble sleeping; unhappy, sad, or depressed; keep from getting involved with others
Subject 12	can't get mind off certain thoughts; daydream a lot; afraid of going to school; afraid might do something bad; act without stopping to think; like to be alone; have nightmares; feel too guilty; self-conscious or easily embarrassed; suspicious; have trouble sleeping; unhappy, sad, or depressed; keep from getting involved with others
Subject 13	daydream a lot; afraid might do something bad; act without stopping to think; like to be alone; have nightmares; unhappy, sad, or depressed; keep from getting involved with others
Subject 14	can't get mind off certain thoughts; daydream a lot; afraid of going to school; afraid might do something bad; act without stopping to think; like to be alone; have nightmares; feel too guilty; self-conscious or easily embarrassed; suspicious; unhappy, sad, or depressed; keep from getting involved with others
Subject 15	act without stopping to think; have nightmares; self-conscious or easily embarrassed; have trouble sleeping; keep from getting involved with others
Subject 16	can't get mind off certain thoughts; act without stopping to think; like to be alone; suspicious
Subject 17	daydream a lot; afraid of going to school; act without stopping to think; like to be alone; feel too guilty; self-conscious or easily embarrassed; suspicious; have trouble sleeping; unhappy, sad or depressed; keep from getting involved with others
Subject 18	can't get mind off certain thoughts; daydream a lot; afraid might do something bad; have nightmares; self-conscious or easily embarrassed; unhappy, sad or depressed; keep from getting involved with others
Subject 19	afraid might do something bad; act without stopping to think; have nightmares; suspicious
Subject 20	daydream a lot; afraid of going to school; afraid might do something bad; have nightmares

Discussion

This study used Spencer's (1995) PVEST model to determine whether the self-reports of adolescents who have been victimized indicate preexisting risk or vulnerability related to symptoms associated with post-traumatic stress disorder. Results suggested that "I like to be alone" was the only symptom that was predicted solely by having been victimized. Self-report in year 01 was not a significant predictor. Thus, withdrawal or social isolation is probably experienced as a result of the reported victimization.

Results also suggested that, when self-reports of the same symptoms in year 01 were taken into account, adolescent victims were still more likely to report five out of thirteen selected symptoms ("I can't keep my mind off certain thoughts," "I am afraid of going to school," "I act without stopping to think," "I am self-conscious or easily embarrassed," and "I am suspicious"). Within the PVEST framework, impulsivity (acting without stopping to think), distractibility (can't get mind off certain thoughts, self-conscious, or easily embarrassed), anxiety (afraid of going to school), and inability to trust (suspicious) can be seen as preexisting risk factors. Experiencing these symptoms prior to their reported victimization in year 02 may indicate a greater vulnerability to those particular distress responses. Thus, victimization may not have led to the reported symptoms but rather aggravated them. Reporting such symptoms prior to victimization does not necessarily indicate innate vulnerability or biological differences in the temperament of the students. Rather, it suggests that they might have had other experiences that have not been identified yet which still have had an impact on their psychological well-being.

Students' self-reports for "I am afraid I might do something bad," "I feel guilty," and "I am unhappy, sad, or depressed" in year 02 were predicted solely by students' self-reports for the same symptom in year 01. Students' self-report of "I daydream a lot" was predicted by their self-report in year 01 and by gender. These findings suggest that, even if the adolescent victims had reported those symptoms, victimization did not lead to those symptoms.

These findings suggest that it may be more appropriate to consider the responses to experiences with violence in a broader context. That is, responses to experiences with violence may be influenced by prior behavior and experiences. Furthermore, it may be inappropriate to attribute reported cognitive and behavioral problems to a single experience—adolescents may be experiencing multiple stressors over time. Thus, one may observe diverse responses to experience with violence. As our victim profiles indicate, two different adolescents may display four symptoms after reporting an experience with violence but they may each report a different constellation of symptoms and, thus, actually manifest a different perception and response to the experience with violence. Each response to being victimized may have its basis in different preexisting risk factors (i.e., likes to be alone, self-conscious or easily embarrassed). Responses to being victimized may be related also to the developmental status of the student. For example, analyses revealed that adolescents who had experienced violence were more likely to report adult-like responses to trauma such as detachment (i.e., likes to be alone) as well as the adolescent-specific response of self-consciousness (i.e., self-consciousness or easily embarrassed).

From a policy perspective, this study has two major implications. First, and most importantly, public funding should allow mental health support and services to be available to students without requiring a diagnosis for a particular disorder. There should be non-stigmatizing opportunities for students to talk about and receive support to respond in constructive ways to their experiences with violence and other life stressors. This is especially salient because the majority of the students did not report being victimized and were not identified from a population of students receiving counseling or other mental health services for experience with violence. Rather, they were drawn from a more general population of adolescents from four middle schools in an urban Southeastern city. The self-reported victims, in particular, may have experienced PTSD-like responses to violence or other stressors yet may not have received any support because the problem behavior was not identified as such for any number of reasons (e.g., the behavior was not believed to be associated with experience with violence, the behavior was observed or experienced before the experience with violence, particular symptoms associated with experience with violence may also be experienced by a peer who has not been victimized).

Second, in terms of broader implications of the PVEST perspective on vulnerability to violence, future prevention and intervention programs for adolescents should incorporate issues that are more salient during adolescence. As adolescents experiment with potential adult roles, coping strategies and identity constructs can influence outcomes such as school engagement and achievement (Cunningham, 2001). For example, each of the symptoms that were predicted by experience with violence was related to focus of attention. Attention is a necessary function of learning. Feelings of fear, distraction or self-consciousness in response to experiences with violence can interfere with normative learning processes. In a society where African American males, in particular, are perceived as violent, and exposure to violence is prevalent for these youth, it is important to promote adaptive coping skills and positive identity formation. This can only be accomplished by devising developmentally and contextually sensitive interventions.

References

Achenbach, T. M. (1991). *Manual for the Youth Self-Report and 1991 profile*. Burlington, VT: University of Vermont Department of Psychiatry.
American Psychiatric Association. (1980). *Diagnostic and statistical manual of mental disorders* (3rd ed.). Washington, DC: Author.
Bell, C. C., & Jenkins, E. J. (1991). Traumatic stress and children. *Journal of Health Care for the Poor and Underserved, 2*, 175–185.

Bronfenbrenner, U. (1989). Ecological systems theory. In R. Vasta (Ed.), *Annals of child development* (pp. 187–248). Greenwich, CT: JAI Press.

Cohen, L., & Swift, S. (1993). A public health approach to the violence epidemic in the United States. *Environment and Urbanization, 5*, 50–66.

Cubbin, C., Pickle, L. W., & Fingerhut, L. (2000). Social context and geographic patterns of homicide among U.S. Black and White males. *American Journal of Public Health, 90*, 579–587.

Cunningham, M. (1999). African American adolescent males' perceptions of their community resources and constraints: A longitudinal analysis. *Journal of Community Psychology, 27*, 569–588.

Cunningham, M. (2001, April). *School and community-based influences on resilience in adolescent males.* Presented at the biennial meeting of the Society for Research in Child Development. Minneapolis, MN.

DuRant, R. H., Cadenhead, C., Pendergrast, R. A., Slavens, G., & Linder, C. W. (1994). Factors associated with the use of violence among urban Black adolescents. *American Journal of Public Health, 84*, 612–617.

Dyson, J. L. (1989). The effect of family violence on children's academic performance and behavior. *Journal of the National Medical Association, 82*, 17–22.

Edmonds, R. (1986). Characteristics of effective schools. In U. Neisser (Ed.), *The school achievement of minority children: New perspectives* (pp. 93–104). Hillsdale, NJ: Lawrence Erlbaum Associates.

Fingerhut, L. A., & Kleinman, J. C. (1990). International and interstate comparisons of homicide among young males. *Journal of the American Medical Association, 263*, 3292–3295.

Fitzpatrick, K., & Boldizar, J. (1993). The prevalence and consequences of exposure to violence among African-American youth. *Journal of the American Academy of Child and Adolescent Psychiatry, 32*, 424–430.

Frieze, I. H., Hymer, S., & Greenberg, M. S. (1987). Describing the crime victim: Psychological reactions to victimization. *Professional Psychology: Research and Practice, 18*(4), 299–315.

Garbarino, J., Dubrow, N., Kostelny, K., & Pardo, C. (1992). *Children in danger: Coping with the consequences of community violence.* San Francisco: Jossey-Bass Publishers.

Gardner, G. E. (1971). Aggression and violence: The enemies of precision learning in children. *American Journal of Psychiatry, 128*, 445–450.

Gladstein, J., Rusonis, E. S., & Heald F. P. (1992). A comparison of inner-city and upper-middle class youths' exposure to violence. *Journal of Adolescent Health, 13*, 275–280.

Hamburg, M. A. (1998). Youth violence is a public health concern. In D. S. Elliott, B. Hamburg, & K. R. Williams (Eds.), *Violence in American schools: A new perspective* (pp. 31–54). New York: Cambridge University Press.

Irwin, C. E., & Millstein, S. G. (1986). Biopsychosocial correlates of risk-taking behaviors during adolescence: Can the physician intervene? *Journal of Adolescent Health Care, 7*, 82S–96S.

Kliewer, W., Johnson, P. D., & Oskin, D. (1997, March). *Violence exposure and psychological symptoms in urban minority youth.* Poster presented at the biennial meeting of the Society for Research in Child Development, Washington, DC.

Martinez, P., & Richters, I. E. (1993). The NIMH Community Violence Project: II. Children's distress symptoms associated with violence exposure. *Psychiatry: Interpersonal & Biological Processes, 56*, 22–35.

May, J. M. (1986). Cognitive processes and violent behavior in young people. *Journal of Adolescence, 9*, 17–27.

Metzenbaum, H. M. (1994, March 1). Statements on introduced bills and joint resolutions. *Congressional Record* (Daily ed.; pp. S2169–S2183).

Newcomb, M. D., Huba, G. I., & Bentler, P. M. (1981). A multidimensional assessment of stressful life events among adolescents: Deviations and correlates. *Journal of Health and Social Behavior, 22*, 400–415.

Osofsky, J. D., Wewers, S., Hann, D. M., & Fick, A. C. (1993). Chronic community violence: What is happening to our children? *Psychiatry, 56*, 36–45.

Overstreet, S. (2000). Exposure to community violence: Defining the problem and understanding the consequences. *Journal of Child and Family Studies, 9*, 7–25.

Overstreet, S., & Braun, S. (1999). A preliminary examination of the relationship between exposure to community violence and academic functioning. *School Psychology Quarterly, 14*, 380–396.

Pynoos, R. S., & Nader, K. (1988). Psychological first aid treatment approach to children exposed to community violence: Research implications. *Journal of Traumatic Stress, 1*, 445–472.

Pynoos, R. S., & Nader, K. (1990). Children's exposure to violence and traumatic death. *Psychiatric Annals, 20*, 334–344.

Schonert-Reichl, K. A., & Beaudoin, K. (1998). Social cognitive development and psychopathology during adolescence. In R. E. Muuss & H. D. Porton (Eds.), *Adolescent behavior and society: A book of readings* (5th ed., pp. 368–372). New York: McGraw-Hill.

Shakoor, B. H., & Chalmers, D. (1991). Co-victimization of African-American children who witness violence: Effects on cognitive, emotional, and behavioral development. *Journal of the National Medical Association, 83*, 233–239.

Snyder, H. N., & Sickmund, M. (1995). *Juvenile offenders and victims: A national report*. Washington, DC: Office of Juvenile Justice and Delinquency Prevention.

Spencer, M. B. (1989). *Patterns of developmental transitions for economically disadvantaged Black male adolescents*. Proposal submitted to and funded by the Spencer Foundation, Chicago.

Spencer, M. B. (1995). Old issues and new theorizing about African American youth: A phenomenological variant of ecological systems theory. In R. L. Taylor (Ed.), *Black youth: Perspectives on their status in the United States* (pp. 37–70). Westport, CT: Praeger.

Spencer, M. B. (1999). Social and cultural influences on school adjustment: The application of an identity-focused cultural ecological perspective. *Educational Psychologist, 34*, 43–57.

Spencer, M. B., Dupree, D., & Hartmann, T. (1997). A phenomenological variant of ecological systems theory (PVEST): A self-organization perspective in context. *Development and Psychopathology, 9*, 817–833.

Stevenson, H. C. (1997). "Missed, dissed, and pissed": Making meaning of neighborhood risk, fear and anger management in urban Black youth. *Cultural Diversity and Mental Health, 3*, 37–52.

Wine, J. D. (1982). Evaluation anxiety: A cognitive-attentional construct. *Series in Clinical & Community Psychology: Achievement, Stress, & Anxiety*, 207–219.

MARGARET BEALE SPENCER, PhD, is the Board of Overseers Professor of Education at the Graduate School of Education and Professor of Psychology in the School of Arts and Sciences at the University of Pennsylvania. She is the Director of the W. E. B. Du Bois Collective Research Institute and the Center for Health Achievement Neighborhood Growth and Ethnic Studies (CHANGES) where she conducts her theory-driven research on resiliency correlates among low-resource multi-ethnic pre-pubertal and adolescent urban youth.

DAVIDO DUPREE, PhD, is a Research Associate at the Center for Health Achievement, Neighborhood Growth and Ethnic Studies (CHANGES) at the University of Pennsylvania. His work focuses on research and program design to support and promote the development of at-risk children and youth including using evaluation and assessment to support activities to build the capacities of the families and communities of children and youth.

MICHAEL CUNNINGHAM, PhD, is an Associate Professor with a joint appointment in the Department of Psychology and the Department of African & African Diaspora Studies at Tulane University, New Orleans, LA. His work examines how perceptions and experiences of social context impact the identity formation and coping patterns of African American adolescents. Prior to his current position, Dr. Cunningham was a post-doctoral fellow of CHANGES at the University of Pennsylvania.

VINAY HARPALANI is a PhD candidate at the University of Pennsylvania, in Interdisciplinary Studies in Human Development in the Graduate School of Education, and a Master of Bioethics candidate in the School of Medicine. He is also a Spencer Foundation Fellow and senior research assistant at CHANGES and the W. E. B. Du Bois Collective Research Institute, and a graduate associate at the W. E. B. Du Bois College House.

MICHÈLE MUÑOZ-MILLER is a PhD candidate at the University of Pennsylvania, in the Interdisciplinary Studies in Human Development program in the Graduate School of Education. She is also a Spencer Foundation Fellow and research assistant at CHANGES.

Journal of Social Issues, Vol. 59, No. 1, 2003, pp. 51–66

Arab and Jewish Youth in Israel: Voicing National Injustice on Campus

Rachel Hertz-Lazarowitz[*]

Haifa University, Israel

Haifa University (HU) is the stage for a prolonged social drama between Arabs (20%) and Jews. 86 students (38 Arabs and 48 Jews) were interviewed on their experiences of injustice. Three major differences emerged. For the Arabs, 92% of injustice took place on campus compared to 40% for the Jews. Arabs attributed injustice to discrimination (60%), Jews to the actors' personal characteristics (58%); the Arabs transformed injustice events into a political struggle for national recognition, identity, and narratives. The analysis intimates that Arabs' "social being" is developing through the staging of negative expressive acts, namely, respect/contempt and power/weakness. Thus actors at HU can stage social processes, and change sites of surveillance and injustice into places of reconciliation and coexistence.

Youth can encounter injustice individually or as a group (Daiute & Fine, this issue). On April 4, 2000, a highly violent conflict took place on the Haifa University (HU) campus, involving Arab (minority) and Jewish (majority) students, the police, and HU authorities. It was one more act in a persistent pattern of conflictual rituals that disturb the seemingly serene routine of academic and social coexistence on campus, and launch the Arab and Jewish students into annual "campus wars" (Arthur & Shapiro, 1995). Often those conflicts are the outcome of deep feelings of injustice and surveillance experienced by different groups of students.

Campuses in general are significant and symbolic spaces for youth empowerment around the world, for example, the United States, South Africa, and Israel

Correspondence concerning this article should be addressed to Rachel Hertz-Lazarowitz, Faculty of Education, The University of Haifa, Haifa, Israel 31905 [e-mail: Rachelhl@construct.haifa.ac.il]. Thanks to my students in the 2001 seminar at HU, and particularly to Shoshi Avidan and Manar Mahmoud. This seminar was highly inspired in its initial stages by the work of Michelle Fine, and was facilitated through the help of Yasser Kairo, both of the Psychology Dept., The Graduate Center, City University of New York.

(Hare, 1985). University campuses have become a stage for political activism, with violent and sometimes non-violent conflicts. By confronting authorities of power, students are the "actors" who are "playing" various types of "social being" in order to test and redefine power, status, identity, and majority-minority relations, including the legitimacy of opposing collective narratives.

Harre, in his theoretical construction of the Social Being (1979), suggests a model of a Social Drama, applying concepts from the theater to social psychology. During the past 25 years HU campus has indeed become a major stage in Israel for intergroup social drama. In keeping with this model, feelings of injustice and surveillance on the campus are studied and conceptualized here first on the *academic personal level* and then as they shift to the *ethnic and national group level*. This transformation takes place when the actors, Arab and Jewish students and their leaders, realize the significance of their acts.

Based on Arthur and Shapiro (1995), *Injustice* is defined as personal experiences of unjust actions by one person or group against another without consent and causing harm and feeling of anger and alienation. *Surveillance* exists when these actions are transposed from the personal level to the collective level and are interpreted as acts against the collective. *Violence* is reactive or proactive actions to disturb the routine of teaching and research on campus.

This study continues my inquiry into social developmental processes within HU's unique *Umwelt*, this term being defined by Lewin (1935) as the physical environment crossing its social meaning. An earlier study (Hertz-Lazarowitz, 1988) of the perennial conflicts between Arabs and Jews followed the Harre model and focused on the physical environment of this *Umwelt*, including the architecture of the setting, the sequence of events, and the presentation of the conflict in the public sphere (printed documents). The present study focused on the "social meaning" of the *Umwelt* by means of interviews seeking data on experiences of injustice and surveillance as perceived by Jewish and Arab students and their leaders. It is argued that lessons learned from the HU *Umwelt* and conflict on campus can suggest directions to restructure Arab-Jewish relations on the HU campus and in Israel.

The study probed two issues: first, the relationship between personal experiences of injustice and justice and the culture of perceived surveillance on campus, and the way it shaped students' social being, and second, how students' leaders transformed their own and other students' personal experiences into collective messages. Our basic assumption on both issues was that the university is a space for advantaged and disadvantaged groups of students to achieve academic excellence in a just and moral way. The qualitative data based on personal interviews served to conceptualize and discuss the messages/themes voiced by the students. This may further social scientists' understanding of the causes of conflict or coexistence to the campus and lead to the experience of and experimentation with new visions of a more peaceful social drama on campus.

The Dramaturgical Model

Harre's (1979) dramaturgical model guides the theoretical current analysis of injustice and surveillance on campus. Harre's focus was on interpersonal relationships, but in an earlier study (Hertz-Lazarowitz, 1988) we found the model highly applicable to the Israeli intergroup conflict situation. In the present study we rely on Harre's three pairs of concepts, as were modified to actions of injustice and acts of surveillance of ethnic and national relationships on HU campus. The three original pairs of concepts are presented with examples from HU *Umwelt* and a fourth pair developed in our 1988 study is added. The first pair is *Practical/Expressive* aspects of social activity, in which activities viewed by one group as practical, are interpreted by the other as expressive, and vice-versa. For example, at HU, the speaking of Arabic by Arabs openly on campus or their socializing in large groups in central areas of Eshkol Tower (the main building on campus, with 30 stories) are viewed by the Arabs as natural and *practical social activities*. But the Jews consider them *expressive* of threat to the Jewish identity of the HU, and metaphorically to the future of the Jewish homeland.

The second pair, *Action/Acts*, differentiates a sequence of behavior, namely, the Actions, from their interpretation and meaning, namely, the Acts. Each ritual can be analyzed as a sequence of action types. For instance, kissing, handshaking, and nodding are interpretable as the Greeting Act. In the sequential structure of conflict, Actions such as shouting, catcalling, and fighting during a demonstration constitute either an Act violating freedom of speech on campus or an Act of war between the minority and majority groups. Every facet of the social drama on campus requires interpretations of behaviors as Actions, and of Actions as Acts: "the very stuff of social life" (Harre, 1979). The dynamic of the contradictory interpretation of Actions and Acts is the reflection of expressive activities of people striving to present acceptable and recognized selves.

The third pair, the *Respect/Contempt duality*, refers to publicly expressed opinions (e.g., policies, newspapers, and other documentation) and to private feelings (e.g., personal interactions, interviews, and self-reports). Based on our earlier study we concluded those relations between Arabs and Jews on campus are highly motivated by the ritual of Respect and Contempt. For some participants in the drama these forces may operate unconsciously, and for others it is highly conscious.

The fourth pair, the *Power/Weakness* duality, was developed following the Hertz-Lazarowitz study (1988). Jews referred to this duality more then the Respect/Contempt duality. Power is expressed in terms of control and moral legitimacy while threat and fear of losing the homeland express weakness. This cultural difference was supported by social scientists, claiming that Respect/Contempt has a significant meaning, as an expressive Act, within the Arab culture (Dwairy, 1998) while Power/Weakness has a significant meaning as an expressive Act in the Jewish culture (Bar-Tal, 2000). In relating to those pairs the reader should be ever aware of the significance of the shift across the duality in each pair of activities, in relating to personal and group events of injustice and surveillance.

Using this theoretical model, we sought to document young people in conflict and confrontation using events of injustice and surveillance to develop critical and political thinking. Thus they could create space for negotiation about their social being as expressed in themes of recognition, identity, and narratives. In doing so they could alter inter-group relations on campus (and off campus), and offer social scientists a new understanding of the interplay between personal and collective factors (Hertz-Lazarowitz, 1988; Hofman, 1988; Stephan, 1999).

Haifa University, Israel—A Site for Conflict and Coexistence

Despite its small size and population (about six million), Israel, like most societies in the Western world, is becoming ever more diverse in the economic, social, and cultural spheres. Social scientists in Israel name four major cleavages in Israeli society. These are the national cleavage between Jews (80%) and Arabs (20%); the religious cleavage between orthodox (14%) and secular Jews; the ethnic cleavage between Jews of Middle Eastern origin (Sephardim, about 50%) and Jews of European and American origin (Ashkenazim); and most recently the cleavage between immigrants, mostly from former Soviet Union (17%), and non-immigrants (Horowitz, 2000; Smooha, 1997).

Notwithstanding some changes in the intensity of the cleavages among the different groups, the Jewish–Arab cleavage has persisted since 1948, the year of the birth of the State of Israel. It centers on issues of narratives, identity, civic equality, loyalty, domination, and oppression. Within the Arab minority in Israel today, constituting 20% of the population, the majority is Muslims (85%), the rest are Christians (10%), Druze (5%), and other small groups of non-Jewish citizens. Most Jews and Arabs live in segregated cities or villages, and enroll in a fully segregated educational system (Al-Haj, 1998; Mar'i, 1978). The University is the sole place for meetings and interaction, hence the unique experience of HU for both groups.

HU with its 13,000 students, is located in one of the five mixed cities in Israel, and for the last 25 years HU had the largest Arab student body in Israel, which equals Arabs proportion in the population (20%). The contribution of HU to meet the academic aspirations of the Israeli Arabs is well documented (Al-Haj, 1998; Hofman, 1988; Hofman, Beit Hallahmi & Hertz-Lazarowitz, 1982; Mar'i, 1978).

On the HU campus, "The structure of a setting may be an icon of the social theory . . . . The physical settings are not neutral, they contribute to the action" (Harre, 1979, p. 192). In HU the Arabs' presence gives them an expressive sense of power and respect, which they had not experienced before, in a mixed *Umwelt*. Conversely it makes many Jews feel threatened by the loss of power and the weakening of the Jewish identity of their *Umwelt* (Stephan, 1999). Consciously or unconsciously the HU campus proclaims messages of power, territory, distance, and a struggle over recognition and control. Arabic, which is heard predominantly in the halls, has caused folk culture to label HU as "Palestine University" and "Fatahland." Thus, the architecture of Haifa University creates a social topography of distance and power (Lewin, 1935) between the actors in the social drama. Over the years, with the annual social drama taking its course, the two groups have become aware of the remarkably expressive meaning of the architecture and its messages (for a detailed analysis see Hertz-Lazarowitz, 1988).

Method

Participants

Participants were 86 students, 38 Arabs and 48 Jews. They were interviewed on campus or around it. Of them 26 were males (14 Jews and 12 Arabs) and 60 were females (26 Arabs and 34 Jews) from different department, and in age they ranged from 19 to 31 (average age of Arabs 23 and of Jews 25). In addition in-depth interviews (lasting each 3–4 hours) were conducted with a group of Arab ($N = 10$) leaders in the *Vaad*—the nonrecognized union of the Arabs—and Jewish ($N = 5$) leaders in the *Aguda*—the recognized student union (Avidan, Mahmoud, & Shochat, 2001).

Procedure

All participants were approached individually in the main space of the campus or elsewhere. They were asked: "Are you willing to participate in the study and tell about an event in which you felt that someone of authority controlled or acted toward you in an unjust way." Almost all students agreed; a time and a quiet place were assigned for the interview. The leaders' interviews began with the same 15 questions as described above and then moved on to their history, goals, and visions.

Interviewers

The interviewers were students enrolled in a research seminar (11 Arabs and 11 Jews). They worked in mixed cooperative teams (Miller & Harrington, 1992; Hertz-Lazarowitz, 1993; Deutsch, 1994) to obtain qualitative (interviews) and quantitative (questionnaires, not reported here) data. They were trained in interview procedures and analysis within the seminar meetings (about 12 hours).

Each team conducted a structured interview with five university students and the same number of high school students from the same national group. (The high school interviews are not reported here.) Interviews were in Hebrew (Jewish interviewers with Jewish interviewees) and Arabic or Hebrew (Arab interviewers with Arab interviewees).

Interview Measures

The interview included 15 open-ended questions and lasted 30–45 minutes. All interviews were tape-recorded, and transcribed to 3–4 typed pages. The transcription was analyzed by categories derived from Fine et al. (this issue) and Hertz-Lazarowitz (2001). The categories, derived directly from the 15 open questions, were: (a) context; (b) location; (c) participants; (d) feelings of the person under surveillance (A); (e) self-description; (f) interpretation (A's); (g) focus of the harm done; (h) whom A told about it; (i) coping; (j) generalizations; (k) internalization; (l) negotiations between A and B; (m) perception: can A see B's point of view? (n) voice in key quotes; (o) unique elements.

Based on the 15 categories a text-table summary form was developed for each interview; this served for later summaries across nationality. Agreement (reliability) of three Jewish and Arab readers, judging each transcript as to its categories, reached 90%.

Table 1 presents an example of the analysis by categories regarding a security check event on campus as reported by Jewish and Arab male students.

Results

Cases of Injustice as Perceived by Arab and Jewish Students

In the university context the two groups reported on perceived injustice related to *personal and academic matters*, such as unjust grades, not being listened to, and not being treated fairly. About half of these events occurred in private between the students and the teacher, the other half in public such as in a lecture. The Arabs reported more severe cases of perceived injustice in public, such as discrimination in security check (see Table 2).

The most notable difference between the Arabs and the Jews lay in the contexts (university and other contexts) and sites/locations (private vs. public). Of the Arabs, 92% reported on injustice at HU, while only 40% of the Jewish students did so ($\chi^2 = 22.84$, $p < .001$).

Yet we found similarities also between Arabs and Jews regarding perceived unjust events. Both groups stated that the injustices caused personal harm (80%), and they told friends and family members about them (85%). They shared similar feelings of anger, rage, and loss of self-worth (90%), and they developed negotiation and coping skills. The major difference was in the way the two groups interpreted, internalized, and generalized the cases of injustice. The Arabs consistently attributed every specific unjust event to a general context of discrimination against them (23 students; 60%). A race related attribution was mentioned by only three Jews (6%). Nasarin, a young Arab student who scored 84 on a paper when 85 would have won her exemption from the final test, applied for this point and

Table 1. Categories for Analysis of the Interview on Perceived Injustice: The Security Check Event

Category	Jewish Student	Arab Student
Context	The student had in his car some heavy apparatus that he had to deliver to the faculty building. He asked the guard to let him drive into the reserved campus car park for few minutes, but his request was refused.	The student noticed that the Russian security guard made a thorough search only of Arab students and not of Russian students. He refused to be searched. A conflict developed and the security officer was called in.
Location	Entrance gate to the campus area (for cars).	Entrance doors to the campus building (for people).
Participants	Security officer and student–driver.	Security guard, security officer, student, other students.
Feelings	Upset, angry, tense.	Angry, humiliated.
Self-description	They don't care about the students.	He is racist because I am not a Russian.
Interpretation	They are rigid and make life unpleasant, it could easily be changed if they were a little more flexible.	Feeling fierce discrimination and deciding to rebel.
Harm done	Helplessness at being unable to solve the problem; how can one lug the apparatus to the faculty building so far away?	To his honor and dignity.
Told it to	Other students in his faculty.	Other students.
Coping	Either find someone who has an entrance permit or tell a lie that is believed.	Getting in an argument about the way the guard treats Jews and non-Jewish students.
Generalization	Devaluing his faculty, concerned about telling lies.	This is what is going on at the university every day.
Internalization	Not giving up, telling the authorities that they are unjust.	One more evidence to the discrimination.
Negotiation	Every time he tried to explain the problem and they made impractical suggestions.	Open conflict with the guard. He insists on calling the security officer.
Perception of the other	They represent the university; they have their work to do; they could be more flexible.	Perhaps he wanted to appear considerate and nice to his own people.
Voice	They don't trust you; they don't believe you; they devalue the faculty.	Everyday we are put into such situations, we are used to it.
Unique elements	Telling a lie in order to drive into the campus.	Insisting on the involvement of the security officer who reproached the guard.

was refused. She said in the interview: "I think the grading was discriminative on purpose. It cannot be that all Jews got grades that exempted them from the test and no Arab or immigrant got this grade . . . . Why should I feel I always need to beg for a good grade? Especially on one point." The Jews attributed events to personal

Table 2. Context and Location of Unjust Events: Arab and Jewish Students

Context		Jews (N = 48)		Arabs (N = 38)	
		N	%	N	%
University					
Public sites	Classes	5	11	7	18
	Tests	3	6	4	11
	Library	2	4	1	3
	Entrance	1	2	4	11
	Halls on floors 6 & 7 of the Main Building	—	—	2	5
	Coffee shop	1	2	—	—
	Total	12	25	18	47
Private sites	Lecturers' offices	6	13	14	37
	Committees (discipline)	1	2	3	8
	Total	7	15	17	45
Workplace		10	20	1	3
Army		12	25	—	—
Other		7	15	2	5

characteristics of the people (40%). Haggit said: "I was late in submitting my research seminar paper, I was penalized by losing 10 points from my grade. I felt very
distressed. The teacher hardly talked to us. I realized he does not see me as a person,
just a number . . . . I never thought the university could be such a cold place."

For the Arabs, talk of discrimination, backed by feelings of rage and being
regarded as worthless, had become a collective and generalized voice, as expressed
in over 60% of their interpretation statements of the events. They charged the university with maintaining a culture of control and surveillance. The Arab students
concluded, "many of our teachers will always favor the Jewish students." They
developed strategies of finding out who were the more tolerant professors, taking their courses, and avoiding the others as much as possible. They could tell
many stories of injustice and surveillance, and they believed firmly in their own
interpretation on the reality.

Gender differences were found in the sites of injustice; Arab females experienced similar injustice in private academic spaces (offices) as did Arab males
(overall 18%). Unexpectedly Arab females experienced more injustice in lectures
(16%), and in tests (11%; overall 27%), than did Arab males (6%) or male Jews
(16%). Females in general did not experience, as males did, discrimination in security checks. Females shared their injustice experiences with more participants
than did males, and Jewish females shared the most.

Cases of Injustice as Perceived by Arab and Jewish Leaders

All of the ten Arab leaders reported on political and national injustice. The Jewish leaders reported on personal-students' life issues. Both groups were engaged

in political intergroup issues: the Arabs on identity, recognition, and political calendar, and the Jews in keeping HU as a Jewish-Israeli University. As a result clashes between Jews and Arabs, initiated mostly by Arab leaders, took place, often expressing the national and political power/weakness duality. The Arab leaders transformed Actions (for example; events of academic disagreements with professors) to Acts (such as planned discrimination). Most of their own and others' personal experiences with actions on campus, were perceived as acts of injustice, non-recognition and contempt on a national level. The Arabs did not question their own perception or the legitimacy of a given action. They voiced strong views that HU policies and regulations were acts of surveillance, beyond injustice: "They are afraid of our becoming educated." In this way academic events/actions became an issue of identity legitimization and civic rights. This transformation from personal to political awareness was voiced in most of the leaders' interviews.

Kullud said:

> I felt discrimination right from my first semester on campus. I compared what I got from the university after I left the classroom with what the new immigrant got. How they got all the help and how we did not. How I felt I was placed in the margins and they in the center. Therefore I decided to center on these issues and help new students on campus so they would have it better.

Her development as a strong (and controversial), locally and nationally political leader is a typical example of the transformation of the Arab leaders on campus. Overall three themes emerged from all the interviews with the Arab leaders: recognition, identity, and the war of opposing narratives. Those are presented and discussed on the basis of Harre's (1979) concepts with students' voices.

The Politics of Recognition

The dilemma of recognition was voiced by the Arab leaders first and foremost based on their shared experience that they were *not recognized* as a unique group of students on campus, a feeling that was intensified when they observed the recognition and privileges of Jewish groups of students. The Arabs rejected the explanation of HU authorities that practical matters explained the different allocations of money (that from the Jewish agency being only for immigrants). They perceive this as an *expressive* act of a policy of discrimination. The significant meaning of higher education for Arabs, and the hardships they encounter on campus to succeed and graduate, colored every experience with a feeling of being held in *contempt* in relation to their identity, language, culture, religion, and history. They did not see the positive aspects of HU and its doing for them, a position that frustrated many Jews on campus.

For the Arabs, recognition as a national group on campus was perceived as crucial to attain their academic goals. The leaders conducted a prolonged struggle for an Arab Union (the *Vaad*), in addition to the recognized *Aguda* (Students'

Union, which includes all students on campus). For many years the *Vaad*, not formally recognized, has been the most influential Arabs' representation and agency of communication with HU authorities (Hertz-Lazarowitz, 1988).

The leaders' most declared goal is to receive recognition, respect, and political power as a collective on the institutional and national level. They are very active politically on campus and are in coordination with national political parties. Many of the Jews, students, and faculty interpret this as an Act of political uprising against Jews and rejecting the Jewish identity of the State/University. Those contradictory perceptions of the Actions and Acts are rarely discussed openly between and within the groups at the university, so the same troubled plot of the social drama continues on campus.

The dilemma of recognition is also rooted in HU vision and perspectives. No doubt HU is the most tolerant institution of higher education in Israel. Political activities at HU are encouraged, under a set of regulations, in contrast to other universities where political actions on campus are restricted. HU perceives its role as significant to empowerment of Arab students, and the Dean of the Students develops new and examines old regulations to increase justice. However, all political actions of Jews and Arabs include the need for permission and security approval for public functions; obeying Israeli laws; and observing HU regulations. The sanction arm of the university is its disciplinary committee.

Most of the interviewed Arab leaders were in the *Vaad* and the Jewish leaders were in the *Aguda*. They took leading roles in protest and demonstrations that sporadically result in conflicts and violence on campus. The Arabs struggle for more rights, while the Jews guard the existence of a Jewish university. All leaders understand that the social drama is rooted in the dilemma of the politics of recognition. Taylor (1995) expresses this notion by writing:

> [It] is given urgency by the links between recognition and identity where this latter term designates something like a person's understandings of which they are, of their fundamental defining characteristics as a human being. The thesis is that our identity is partly shaped by recognition or its absence, often by the misrecognition of others. (p. 249)

Mirroring this feeling, Manar, an Arab women student, described an event where a conflict with an old Jew in a bus about whether to keep open a window inflicted contempt on the personal level and transformed from personal misrecognition to the core of her national identity. In this conflict she heard the following: "You Arabs should leave the country, this country does not belong to you, go and live in Arab countries." Manar said,

> This made me feel very bad. I felt he was thinking of us as inferior, uneducated, not part of the society, with no respect and no feelings for us. I felt that this incident reflects the views of many Jews who feel they can look down on Arabs as second-rate people. But at the same time it sharpened my feeling that I should stick to my identity and demand my rights, and make Jews accept us as equals and not test us all the time under a magnifying glass.

The Message of Identity

All of the leaders, Arabs and Jews, discussed identity as a major issue on campus. Following the unrest on campus in 2000, HU became more sensitive to the issue of academic equality and gave more resources and help to the Arab students. But the leaders (and many of the Arab students) see now the root of injustice in the politics of legitimization of identity and their narratives. Identity is a central theme for Jews and Arabs. It is a dynamic field of research (Hofman, 1988; Rouhana, 1997; Smooha, 1997), where dramatic changes took place in the way the Israeli Arabs and the Israeli Jews (the definitions commonly in use since the 1960s) redefine their identity. However, the common assumption held in Israel, namely, that national and civic definitions (Israeli-Jew and Israeli-Arab) will coincide, cannot be taken for granted with respect to young Palestinian citizens of Israel within its 1948 boarders. Dramatic political events in Israel and/or in the West Bank and Gaza and/or in the neighboring Arab countries are milestones that have changed the ways Arabs and Jews define their own and others' identities. Within this framework, students at HU are significant agents, functioning as seismographs to predict changes in identity definitions.

In 1988–1989 in the shadow of the first Intifada 12th grade high school students already documented a dramatic change in their self and mutual identity definitions (Hertz-Lazarowitz, Kupermintz, & Lang, 1999). That study investigated the impact of coexistence programs on a variety of social measures, including data on identity definitions and political orientations. High school students ($N = 929$) were asked to rate the appropriateness of eight identity definitions.

A principal component analysis of the ratings revealed two main factors in the Arab identity definitions. The first was *Palestinian–Arab Identity*; the second factor was *Israeli–Palestinian*. The results showed that in 1989, 52% of the Arab youngsters chose a definition that integrated two national definitions, namely, Palestinian and Arab, and 31% chose the definitions of either "Palestinian in Israel" or "Palestinian Arab in Israel." Thus the great majority used a double national categorization identity with no civic (Israeli) identity. This is in contrast to how Jewish youth defined the Arab identity: 74% of them integrated the national (Arab or Palestinian) and the civic (Israeli) identity, while only 26% used the definition Palestinian Arab. The growing detachment of the Arabs from the Israeli civic identity shown then was re-documented a decade later by Suleiman's (in press) findings among HU students:

Our results also show that the Palestinian respondents view their national identity as more central to their self-identification and alienated from their civic identity ... [t]his minority perceives its national and civic identity as diametrically opposed and rejects the latter as part of its collective identity ... The fact that Israeli Jews use the term Israeli Arabs to define the minority is not new. This term was coined by Jewish "Arabists" and not by indigenous minority members.

At this stage we find an incisive dissociation of the Arab students from the civic (Israeli) identity, which may be explained by two processes. The first is rage turned upon civic discrimination, which is not perceived as a personal action but as a collective Act. Even if the Arab students misjudge those events, it becomes political. Second, the identity of the minority is interfaced with the political orientations of the majority. The fear of the Jews from Arabs' identity formation is rooted in its impact on future peaceful coexistence. The fear of the Arabs is rooted in maintaining privileges to Jews. Thus both groups are threatened by the double definitions. Specially when national events and local events become critical, further research on identity using qualitative methodologies is important in order to understand the powers that re-define identities and also those who serve as levers to dialogues.

The Political Calendar of Opposing Narratives

Identities strive to voice their personal stories and collective narratives expressed utmost in an emerging political/national calendar. Recently Arab students on HU have resisted the dominant Israeli-Jewish narrative and moved from the periphery to the center. The rise of the opposing narrative is part of the debates in Israeli society, where the "new historians" rewrite some of the dominant and oppressed narrative of Jews and Arabs (Pappe, 1995). Most Israeli Jews expect, from the Arabs, greater civic respect for and identification with Israel's national symbols, the flag and the anthem, and greater loyalty to the Jewish state as part of Arab-Israeli citizenship. The major themes dominating the conflictual relations between the two groups have transformed. In the 1980s it centered on the right to "freedom of speech" (Hertz-Lazarowitz, 1988). In the early 1990s it became the battle of identity, and now it is a war of narratives and calendars, as a symbol for one side's legitimacy and a challenge of the other side's. This has changed the course of what is just and unjust on campus, and became the source for several stormy and violent demonstrations.

In the interviews all leaders referred to four such calendar dates: March 30 commemorates a bloody demonstration within Israel (1976). May 15 marks the birth of the state of Israel (1948). June 5 commemorates the outbreak of the Six-Day War (1967), and December 9 is the anniversary of the outbreak of the Intifada (1987). The Arab leaders perceived these days as symbolic markers, expressing their identity by seeking legitimizing for their opposing narratives. They plan ceremonies on campus, which often develop into open conflicts. Two events are described below.

March 30, Land Day (Yawm al-ard)

On this day (in 1976) a large-scale demonstration was held in an Arab village in Galilee, protesting the Israeli government's policy of land confiscation. The police intervened, and several Arab citizens were shot and killed. Since then Arabs in Israel commemorate this day by demonstrations. In recent years Arab students began to ask permission to mark the day on campus.

On April 4, 2000, the students at HU engaged in an unauthorized demonstration on the campus, which turned into a major violent conflict. A large police force entered the campus and the riots continued for several hours. Khulud said in her interview about the April 4 demonstration:

> We asked permission to protest because of Land Day and because of the murder of the old woman. [This is the interviewee's terms. The autopsy indicated that the 74-year-old woman had died of a heart attack; but the Arabs have never accepted this medical finding.] The authorities authorized it for the next day but we wanted to do it the same day, so we decided to make our protest at Cafe Deshe [an outdoors eating area adjacent to Eshkol Tower]. The next day the police came and wanted to arrest Raja [a student leader] because of a complaint that he had hurt a Jewish student [this proved to be a provocation by a right-wing student who called the police and impersonated the head of the security on campus]. Raja refused to get into the police car. He studies law and knows that the police may not enter and detain students on the campus grounds. The police pushed him into the police car by force. I went and called the students who were on floors six and seven to come. In 15 minutes there were over 500 students. We blocked the roads around the university and the police could not take Raja. We argued with the police, and a big crowed gathered. The Jewish right-wing students came in large numbers and confronted us. They sang the Jewish anthem Hatikva, and we started to sing Biladi, Biladi ("My land, my land"). We had posters stating I am a Proud Palestinian.

This confrontation lasted over four hours, and was at last settled through negotiations between an Arab Knesset (Parliament) member who was called to the scene and the president of the university. Raja was taken to the campus security office, which handled the matter thereafter, and the Arab students lifted the siege of the university. The demonstration won nationwide coverage in the press and on TV. Some headlines in the Jewish Hebrew press read: "Land Day Riots Move to Haifa University" (*Yediot Aharonot*, 2000), "A Nationalist Battlefield on Haifa Campus: Back to the Sights of the Eighties" (*Yediot Aharonot*, 2000), "Coexistence Is a Daily Reality but It Has Been Crushed" (*Kolbo*, 2000). As a result of these serious demonstrations the HU president suspended the right to hold political activities on campus and called for a short time-out (Shochat, 2002).

It was evident from the interviews that the Arab leaders were driven by the motive of ". . . We have to change the situation, because we are not only leaders of the students but also national leaders of the Arabs."

May 15, Nakba Day (Yawm al-nakba)

Nakba Day commemorates the events of 1948. It is the opposite narrative to the Jewish Independence Day. For the Jews it is the celebration of the birth of Israel, for the Arabs it is the day of the disaster (catastrophe, holocaust) when they mourn their national destruction. In recent years Nakba Day has acquired a central place in the rewriting of the Arab–Palestinian narrative in Israel. The Arab students request permission of the HU authorities to mark Nakba Day on campus, where it is invariably a source of tension as the Arab students are watched closely by the security personnel. Because of differences between the Jewish and the Gregorian calendars, Independence Day and Nakba Day coincide only once in 19 years.

In May 2001 the Arab students wanted to mount a photographic exhibition of the destruction of the Arab villages in 1948. They appealed to the Dean of Students for permission, which was granted on a very small scale. The Arab students organizers perceived this as an extreme sign of surveillance and injustice (Mahmoud, 2001). On HU campus the Nakba Day (May 15) is a source of concern in each academic year, and the Arab *Vaad* (Union) is planning ahead ceremonies that are perceived by the Jews as opposing the core existence of Israel.

Conclusions

From Surveillance to Reconciliation

Jewish and Arabs students alike are intent on being recognized and respected, as individual and group members. Their academic goals have to be guarded in a caring and just context. In the university *Umwelt*, the political and the personal cannot be separated. Personal injustice, as well as territory, power, identity, language, calendar, and narratives, are metaphysical representatives of having a homeland or being homeless (Gur-Ze'ev, 2000).

Each of the messages presented suggests transformation from injustice and violence to recognition and reconciliation and a potential for negotiation and dialogue. The remaking of the social drama is more on the majority group but the minority group has also a significant role. Following the violent Land Day events, a new treaty of "Justice and Fairness on Campus" was negotiated. The University took measures to give more rights to the students as individuals and collectives. Constantly open lines of communication with Arab and Jewish students' leaders were established, relating to the main messages described in the paper. And indeed the academic year of 2001 was more peaceful then 2000. Notwithstanding coexistence is always fragile. Following the social drama model, extreme people or extreme political events inside or outside the campus might cause it to revert to a violent confrontation.

University education has to be viewed as a political matter related to the power structure of the society (McLaren & Giroux, 1994). HU as an institution can do far more to transform Arab-Jewish relations. Based on its diverse student body it can build a field of academic knowledge and reduce ignorance about Arabs and Jews (Stephan & Stephan, 1996). HU has students who desire to gain and develop knowledge based on their experiential learning and become change agents in the field. From other work with mixed communities in Israel, it was shown that a spirit of synergy, democracy, coexistence, and academic excellence can inspire a system-wide change (Hertz-Lazarowitz, 1999). Haifa University, more than other Israeli universities, developed the vision, and the leadership to pursue it. The mission of continuing the dialogue, within a conflictual reality, is a never-ending challenge.

References

Al-Haj, M. (1998). *Education, empowerment and control: The case of the Arabs in Israel.* Albany, NY: SUNY Press.

Arthur, J., & Shapiro, E. (Eds.). (1995). *Campus wars.* Boulder, CO: Westview Press.

Avidan, S., Mahmoud, M., & Shochat, I. (2001). *Surveillance and violence on campus: Background and interviews.* Unpublished manuscript, University of Haifa.

Bar-Tal, D. (2000). *Shared beliefs in a society.* Thousand Oaks, CA: Sage.

Deutsch, M. (1994). Constructive conflict resolution: Principles, training and research. *Journal of Social Issues, 50,* 13–32.

Dwairy, M. (1998). *Cross-cultural counseling: The Arab Palestinian case.* New York: Haworth Press.

Gur-Ze'ev, I. (2000). Introduction. In Ilan Gur-Ze'eV (Ed.), *Conflicting philosophies of education in Israel/Palestine* (pp. 1–6). Dordrecht, The Netherlands: Kluwer.

Hare, A.P. (1985). *Social interactions as drama: Application from conflict resolution.* Beverly Hills, CA: Sage.

Harre, R. (1979). *Social being.* London: Blackwell Publishers.

Hertz-Lazarowitz, R. (1988). Conflict on campus: A social drama perspective. In J. E. Hofman (Ed.), *Arab-Jewish relationships in Israel* (pp. 271–299). Bristol, IN: Wyndham Hall Press.

Hertz-Lazarowitz, R. (1993). Using group-investigation to promote Arab-Jewish relationships at Haifa University. *Cooperative Learning, 13*(3), 26–28.

Hertz-Lazarowitz, R. (2001). *Manual for the analysis of the interview on violence and injustice on HU campus.* Unpublished manuscript, Haifa, Israel. (Hebrew).

Hertz-Lazarowitz, R., Kupermintz, H., & Lang, J. (1999). Arab-Jewish students' encounters. In E. Weiner (Ed.), *Handbook of interethnic coexistence* (pp. 565–585). New York: Continuum.

Hofman, J. E. (Ed.). (1988). *Arab-Jewish relationships in Israel.* Bristol, IN: Wyndham Hall Press.

Hofman, J. E., Beit Hallahmi, B., & Hertz-Lazarowitz, R. (1982). Self-concept of Jewish and Arab adolescents in Israel. *Journal of Personality and Social Psychology, 43,* 786–792.

Horowitz, T. (2000). *Violence as a social phenomenon.* Jerusalem: The Szold Institute. (Hebrew).

Lewin, K. (1935). *Principles of topological psychology.* Trans. F. Heider and G. E. Heider. New York: McGraw Hill.

Mahmoud, M. (2001). *Perceptions of Arab students' leaders on surveillance at Haifa campus.* Paper submitted as part of the requirements in a research seminar, Faculty of Education, Haifa University.

Mar'i, M. (1978). *Education in Israel.* Syracuse, NY: Syracuse University Press.

McLaren, P., & Giroux, H. A. (1994). *Between borders: Pedagogy and the politics of cultural studies.* New York: Routledge.

Miller, N., & Harrington, H. J. (1992). Social categorization and intergroup acceptance: Principles for the design and development of cooperative learning teams. In R. Hertz-Lazarowitz & N. Miller (Eds.), *Interaction in cooperative groups* (pp. 203–227). New York: Cambridge University Press.

Pappe, I. (1995). Critique and agenda: The post-Zionist scholars in Israel. *History and Memory, 71*(Spring–Summer), 66–90.

Rouhana, N. (1997). *Palestinian citizens in an ethnic Jewish state: Identities and conflict.* New Haven, CT: Yale University Press.

Shochat, I. (2002). *Students' political achievement as a result of the Arab-Jewish conflict (April–May 2000) on Haifa campus.* Unpublished manuscript, Haifa University.

Smooha, S. (1997). Ethnic democracy: Israel as an archetype. *Israel Studies, 2*(2), 198–241.

Stephan, W. (1999). *Reducing prejudice and stereotyping in schools.* New York: Teachers College Press.

Stephan, W. G., & Stephan, C. W. (1996). *Intergroup relations.* Boulder, CO: Westview.

Suleiman, R. (in press). Perception of the minority's collective identities and voting behavior: The case of the Palestinians in Israel. *The Journal of Social Psychology.*

Taylor, C. (1995). The politics of recognition. In J. Arthur & E. Shapiro (Eds.), *Campus wars* (pp. 243–269). Boulder, CO: Westview.

Turner, J. C. (1978). Social categorization and social discrimination in a minimal group paradigm. In H. Tajfel (Ed.), *Differentiation between social groups.* London: Academic Press.

RACHEL HERTZ-LAZAROWITZ, PhD, is a social-educational psychologist in the Faculty of Education at the University of Haifa. Her areas of research include the study of existence and co-existence of different ethnic and national groups in Israel. She works and conducts research within educational systems such as schools, universities, and Arab and Jewish co-existence organizations, and with leadership groups in mixed communities. The social psychological principles of cooperation inspire her work. In the last ten years Prof. Hertz-Lazarowitz has worked in Acre, a mixed Jewish-Arab city, where she studied change in large systems. She has published widely in English and Hebrew. Her edited book (with Norman Miller) *Interaction in cooperative groups: The theoretical anatomy of group learning* was published in 1992 by Cambridge University Press.

Journal of Social Issues, Vol. 59, No. 1, 2003, pp. 67–82

Tracing the Historical Origins of Youth Delinquency & Violence: Myths & Realities About Black Culture

William E. Cross, Jr.*

City University of New York

The negative effects of slavery have been theoretically linked to contemporary problems faced by African Americans, such as family instability, low achievement motivation, and high rates of juvenile delinquency and youth violence. Combining historical, sociological, and psychological materials, the current analysis argues that Blacks exited slavery with the necessary social capital, inclusive of proactive family attitudes and patterns as well as high achievement motivation, for rapid acculturation into mainstream America. Shifting to the present, it is shown that the co-existence of high Black crime rates and Black cultural integrity are not contradictory, especially when systemic forces neutralize or undermine the ameliorative potential of Black culture.

In analyses of the dynamics, structure, as well as historical origins of Black social problems, such as youth violence and delinquency, part of the variance is attributed to systemic issues such as protracted poverty (Wilson, 1978, 1997), and another component to racism—sometimes referenced as modern racism—to distinguish it from the more virulent forms of the past (Dovidio & Gaertner, 1986; Swim & Stangor, 1998). To keep things honest, balanced, and objective, an unknown but critical part of the remaining variance is attributed to problems and pathologies emanating from within the Black community (Frazier, 1939; Ogbu, 1991; Patterson, 1998). Explanations that place too much weight on forces external to the Black community are critiqued as evasive of personal responsibility (Steele, 1990) or, in the case of arguments that seem to defend Black culture, as blatantly romantic (Patterson, 1998). This has led observers to essentialize problems when

---

*Correspondence concerning this article should be addressed to William E. Cross, Jr., Professor and Head, Doctoral Program in Social Personality Psychology, Graduate Center – CUNY, Psychology, 6th floor, 365 Fifth Avenue, NY, NY 10016 [e-mail: wcross@gc.cuny.edu].

Blacks are involved, and to be more systemic when Whites and other social groups are highlighted (Coontz, 1992).

The essentialist versus systemic perspective is highlighted in events that took place about ten years ago. In the winter of 1992, a factory closed in Perry, Florida and *USA TODAY* ran a front-page story (Stone, 1992) on the economic ripple effects of the closure. Small photos of eleven laid-off workers, ten of whom were White, formed the border of a full-page pictorial schematic of the community. The photos, schematic, and accompanying article explicated how lost wages cut into the economic health of the surrounding community, with fewer dollars being spent in 31 local commercial establishments (jewelry store, cable television company, bank, ice-cream shop, hairdresser, volume of advertisements for local newspaper, etc.). The connection between employment, individual agency, taxpayer partici-pation, safe and affordable housing, and community vitality could not escape the average reader. There were no suggestions that the laid-off workers would become lazy, unmotivated, and addicted to welfare. Around the same time period, the *New York Times* (July 5–10, 1992) ran a series of front-page articles (Roner, 1992) on the need for welfare reform. The focus tended to be on Black people and other people of color residing in urban centers. Only nominal reference was made to the links between employment and community vitality, and the tone of the series was that Blacks had somehow positioned themselves to be on welfare, independent of economic forces. Juxtaposing the two stories one notes that when the focus is on Whites, the social policy implication is how to create economic activity and new jobs, but in the case of Blacks, the need is to get people off welfare. In one case, systemic forces explain worker redundancy, while in the other, the emphasis shifts to an implied history that has resulted in a mindset or psychology that is peculiar to Black people.

The current *issue of JSI* focuses on delinquency and youth violence and when Black youth are highlighted, the issues of implied history and peculiar mindset become immediately evident. According to the literature reviews by Taylor (1995) and Payne (2001), empirical research depicts Black youth in general, and Black males in particular, as originating from broken or unstable families, and exhibiting certain negative psychological traits: low achievement motivation, an estrangement from schooling and formal learning activities, negative self-concept and negative self-esteem, and a propensity toward delinquency and crime. Key scholars of the Black experience such as Wilson (1987), Patterson (1998), and Ogbu (1991) have tried to show that *contemporary problems in the Black community can be traced in a linear fashion to the legacy of slavery and past discrimination*. They depict Blacks as having been crippled by slavery, and claim that the era of Jim Crow, which lasted from the turn of the century to the late 1960s, never afforded Blacks a chance to right themselves psychologically or culturally speaking. The overall recession in 1973, which hit the Black community more like a depression, laid bare such Black vulnerabilities, leading to an explosive growth in single parent Black families and an epidemic of crime and Black-on-Black violence. Such notions of "the Black-underclass" and "Black oppositional identity" are premised on a certain understanding or theorizing about Black history. That is to say, Black kids do such-and-such negative and self-destructive things today because historically these negative propensities have existed all along, just below the surface of Black culture, waiting for an economic downturn to trigger latent tendencies into full-blown self-destructive patterns (Scott, 1997).

In this paper I construct a counterstory to show that whether the focus is on Black family structure, Black achievement motivation, or Black delinquency patterns, the historical linkage to slavery is problematic and dubious, and that contemporary systemic causal factors are repeatedly underestimated. In addition to not coming to terms with the real causes of contemporary Black youth violence, myths about Black history are another form of violence, only in this instance the violence is directed toward Black culture and Black people as a whole.

Black Family Instability as a Historical Antecedent to Black Youth Violence

After trivializing the works of Gutman (1976) and other revisionists who find themes of resilience, coping, and normal family functioning in Black history, Patterson (1998) argues that one of the greatest intellectual stumbling blocks to the development of realistic social policy about Black social problems, such as youth crime and violence, is the failure of Black as well as White scholars to fully appreciate the extent to which slavery dehumanized Black individuals and distorted Black cultural and family dynamics. He thinks the Black family and the basic relationship between Black men and women has never been adequate and positive, and that children raised in such chaotic family circumstances are at risk for turning to crime. As proof of his contention that the Black family has been unstable since the end of slavery, Patterson concentrates on the percent of single-parent Black households found in census reports, recorded between 1880 and 1910, which show 25% or more were headed by women.

Patterson points out that Frazier (1939) reported similar figures in 1939 and it was Frazier who first affirmed that the primitive and thus fragile rural Black family was headed toward disintegration in the aftermath of Black migration to urban centers. However, Frazier's fragility-deterioration thesis was not confirmed by subsequent census reports from either 1940 or 1950 (Gutman, 1976). In both instances, 70% or more of Black families are recorded as intact (both parents present) as opposed to broken (one-parent family structure). About thirty years after Frazier's work, Moynihan (1965) underscored an intact Black family rate of close to 70% but for the extremely poor the rate seemed to be getting smaller and it is on this basis that Moynihan predicted a decline in Black intact families. In effect, starting with early census reports from 1880, and continuing through the publication of Frazier's figures in 1939, and the appearance of the Moynihan report in 1965, intact Black families accounted for 70% and higher of all Black families. Given all the ecological, political, and sociological challenges Blacks faced between 1880 and the early 1960s, one could argue that a constant intact rate of 70% or higher is hardly a sign of instability (Hill, 2001).

Patterson is suspect of this 70% rate and argues that poor Black women often get pregnant and have a child out-of-wedlock with one man, and soon thereafter marry someone else, and record this second person as the actual father. This means, in the context of collecting census data, out-of-wedlock births could be underestimated, and the stability of the Black family could be overestimated. However, Patterson completely overlooks the fact that a similar pattern is readily isolated in the history of White women and out-of-wedlock birthing. Solinger's important book-length study, *Wake Up Little Suzie: Single Pregnancy and Race Before Roe v. Wade* (Solinger, 1992), shows that from the late 1930s onward, White women who became pregnant outside of marriage often "disappeared" before they began to show and were secretly cared for in special facilities, such as the Cradle in Evanston, Illinois. For the duration of the pregnancy, the officials, social workers, religious figures, and psychiatrists linked to the facility coerced the woman into placing her baby up for adoption, at the point of birth. In exchange, the woman was allowed to return home, as if nothing had happened, and the adoption agency had a new, highly sought after White infant. As importantly, Solinger points out that the reverse was true for Black girls and Black women positioned in the same circumstances. The adoption agencies, which welcomed the White girls, turned their backs and were unavailable to Black girls and Black women, and the public social agencies to which Blacks were forced to turn for help pressured them to keep their infants. Solinger determined that Black women were viewed by social welfare agencies as primitive and irresponsible in their sexual habits and undeserving of a "second-chance." So effective was society in hiding the out-of-wedlock patterns of White females that by the time society got around (circa the 1980s and 1990s) to doing something about welfare as we know it, out-of-wedlock birthing was depicted as a problem unique to Blacks (see Solinger, 1992, especially pages 187–204; Coontz, 1992; Patterson, 1998; Scott, 1997).

The so-called crash of the Black family—that is, the point at which out-of-wedlock birthing becomes extreme—is not evident until the mid-1960s. However, before one can turn to the bad culture or legacy of slavery arguments, it must be recalled that from the late 1950s onward, American cities lost hundreds of thousands of good paying, heavy industry jobs and Blacks, more so than Whites, were disproportionately affected by such turn of events (Goozner, 1990). Patterson (1998) and others seem to want Black families to "stay-together" even when there is no material basis for sustaining marriage. If, as Newman (1988) shows in her book, *Falling from Grace,* once stable middle and high income White families, in the face of protracted unemployment due to job layoffs and restructuring, can become the focus of father abandonment, divorce, and lower academic aspirations in children—all within one generation—then what stops us from comprehending that Black families, far removed from slavery, may encounter in the here and now socio-economic circumstances that negate whatever cultural strengths they may bring to the table? Coontz (1992) points out that *the employment rate for Black men was as high as 80% in 1930 but dropped to as low as 56% in 1983; and, as significantly, the average real income of Black men fell by almost 50% between 1973 and 1986.* Coontz underscores that the biggest losers were unskilled or undereducated Black men, who, between 1930 and the late 1960s, could, by the mere dint of hard work and strenuous effort, make an adequate income to support marriage and a family (Coontz, 1992, p. 245).

It is ironic that not too long after the appearance of Moynihan's report in 1965, the out-of-wedlock birthing for *poor White* girls and young women skyrocketed, and as they were never slaves, the weight of the legacy of slavery or inherent instability of Black family arguments were made all the more problematic. When, in the late 1970s and 1980s, Whites, in increasing numbers, joined the ranks of Blacks in the loss of good-paying, high-benefit jobs (Newman, 1988), a strange thing happened and White families started to look and behave like Black families (Ehrenreich, 2001). Moynihan eventually tried to explain how he "missed" the out-of-wedlock trend among White families, and to his credit, his revised analysis places more explicit weight on economic forces, although his perspective on the Black family has not changed (Moynihan, 1996).

In short, a discussion of the Black family in and of itself provides few clues as to why Black family instability and a parallel rise in Black delinquency took on monstrous proportions from the late 1970s onward. If anything, the recording of a 70% stability rate for Black families shortly after the end of slavery, before and after waves of migration to urban centers around the turn of the 20th century, during and after the Great Depression of the 1930s, and across the periods of racial oppression of the 1940s and 1950s, would seem to eliminate the viability of the *legacy of slavery thesis* for serious consideration as a primary cause of contemporary Black problems such as Black youth violence.

The Legacy of Slavery on Black Achievement Motivation & Crime Rates

Focusing less on family dynamics than does Patterson, and more on issues of schooling, identity, and a drift into the underground economy and crime, Ogbu (1978; see also Gibson & Ogbu, 1991) claims that slavery blocked the development of positive Black achievement motivation, turned the Black self-concept into a site of racial self-loathing as well as hatred of anything White ("oppositional identity"), and that such factors cause Black youth to drift away from mainstream models of success and toward involvement in delinquency and crime. While his theory of oppositional identity is not simplistic, Ogbu nevertheless implies that one can draw a fairly straight line between contemporary Black problems and the effects of slavery, especially with regard to (low) Black achievement motivation and a Black attraction to crime and the underground economy. There is a great deal of research on each of these factors, and what follows is an exploration of the evidence that contests Ogbu's legacy of slavery thesis.

Black Achievement Motivation

There is very little historical evidence that Blacks, en masse, resisted formal educational opportunities in the immediate aftermath of slavery. To the contrary, the scope of the educational demands that the masses of ex-slaves placed on themselves and on the larger society can be comprehended only as a *social movement for education*. In fact, as Spencer, Cross, Harpalani, & Goss (in press) noted, one is hard pressed to think of any White ethnic group entering the United States at the turn of the 20th century who exhibited the level of high and positive achievement motivation as did Blacks when they exited slavery. Had the larger society moved to cultivate, reinforce, and authenticate the ex-slaves' organic drive toward achievement and acculturation, Blacks today might well be disproportionately distributed among the highly educated. As it turned out, southern society, with the cooperation of the North, made extraordinary efforts to blunt, mangle, and where possible, destroy Black achievement motivation (Bullock, 1967; Du Bois, 1935; Harlan, 1958; Kluger, 1977; Steinberg, 1989, pp. 173–200). Even so, historians have documented that the positive value ex-slaves held toward education was passed on from one generation to the next, and did not appear to dissipate until the Great Depression of the 1930s (Anderson, 1988) and perhaps not even then (Spencer, Cross, Harpalani, & Goss, in press). Let us review the evidence.

It has long been recognized that there was much educational activity, involving the ex-slave population, immediately following the Civil War. Initially, historians linked such activity to forces and influences outside of the Black community such as enlightened members of the Union Army, White teachers and educational officials from the North, and the predominantly White Federal Freedman's Bureau, which was the federal agency responsible for the ex-slaves' transition to freedom (Bullock, 1967). However, revisionist historians such as Butchart (1980) and especially Anderson (1988) have shown that well before any of these external agents made their presence felt, the ex-slaves, themselves, organized and began to carry out educational ventures designed to spread literacy and enlightened citizenship among Black adults and their children. Given their mistrust of White southerners, the first impulse of the ex-slaves was to control their own education. Thus, except for collaborations with Black teachers from nearby free Black communities, the earliest forms of Black education were organic (Anderson, 1988). When White northern educators and federal officials first became involved in the education of the ex-slaves, they wrote in their diaries and field reports that they were often given the cold shoulder by Blacks who were already educating themselves

(Butchart, 1980; Anderson, 1988). White officials and White teachers were sometimes dumbfounded that a group just beyond the shadow of slavery was expressing not a resistance to or a lack of awareness about the value of education, but a level of positive achievement motivation that in some ways exceeded that which they associated with the achievement aspirations of free White families and children of the North (Butchart, 1980; Anderson, 1988).

The attitudes and behavior of the ex-slaves stretch our understanding of the concept of achievement motivation, which is generally defined at the level of the individual. Anderson (1988), Butchart (1980), and Du Bois (1935) depict the ex-slaves' educational demands and aspirations as reflecting a yearning for (a) schools for themselves and their children and (b) standards of personal excellence that would transform them from illiterate adults and children into valued and productive people capable of negotiating the political, economic, cultural, religious, and educational choices which, in their eyes, defined meaningful freedom. Progress within and across each of these domains necessitated literacy. As Butchart (1980) stressed, they wanted a future defined by social justice and achievement, both at the level of the individual and for the community as a whole. Their *individual-communal achievement motivation* redefined history:

> The eagerness to learn among American Negroes was exceptional in the case of a poor and recently emancipated folk. Usually, with a protective psychology, such degraded masses regard ignorance as natural and necessary, or even exalt their own traditional wisdom and discipline over "book learning"; or they assume that knowledge is for higher beings, and not the likes of us. The American Negroes never acted thus. (Du Bois, 1935, pp. 637–638)

As their resistance gave way to acceptance, the ex-slaves took advantage of the material and funding support provided by the Federal Freedman's Bureau and joined hands with educational agents from northern benevolent societies, hundreds of mostly female White teachers transplanted from the North, and Black teachers from free Black communities, to create what can be comprehended only as a social movement for education (Spencer, Cross, Harpalani, & Goss, in press; Du Bois, 1935). The historical record clearly shows that more times than not, those who stepped forward to help the ex-slaves in one educational venture or another were often startled and overwhelmed by the educational demands the ex-slaves made of themselves, their children, and their new-found White educational friends from the North. When a good mix of Blacks' demands, external leadership, and resources were provided, the result was an unheard of level of progress within a short span of time. For example, Du Bois (1935) pointed out that under the leadership of the Union Army General Nathaniel P. Banks, New Orleans and the State of Louisiana established Black schools throughout the state, including rural districts, all within a few years following the abolition of slavery. When this new system came under threat, ex-slaves organized and signed petitions in favor of its continuance, inclusive of one 30-foot long petition that showed the marks of 10,000 ex-slaves (Du Bois, 1935, p. 644).

The White teachers from the North, the White educational officials from the northern benevolent societies, and officials from the Federal Freedman's Bureau did not have to spend time instilling a sense of achievement motivation in the ex-slaves and their children. Rather, these external friends of the ex-slaves were often beside themselves in trying to keep up with the ex-slaves' educational demands. One sign of the scope of this pressure is how quickly officials moved to establish Black colleges, even before the dust from slavery and the Civil War had settled, in order to produce enough teachers to serve the emergent Black students and schools (Du Bois, 1935). Eventually, the spirit and influence of the drive for Black education overlapped with the general politics of the region, and as Du Bois (1935) first proclaimed and Bullock (1967), Butchart (1980), and Anderson (1988) have supported, the codification of the need for and right to public education was written into the southern state constitutions as a "gift" from the Black community.

That the ex-slaves would make education a priority the instant they achieved freedom means that the value of education and the groups' collective achievement motivation was in evidence *before* they were free. That is, they somehow developed a value for and appreciation of education not afterwards, but during, slavery even though it was officially against the law to educate slaves. There was no absence of Black educational activity during slavery, as Woodson (1919) discovered, when, in 1919, he set out to write a pamphlet on Black education during slavery. His modestly conceived project eventually grew into a 454-page book, because it took that much scholarship to summarize the scope of educational activities that were directed at the slaves and free Blacks throughout the history of slavery. Woodson's research helps to explain how, during slavery, literacy was characteristic of free-Black communities, and this community of free-Blacks produced many teachers, who were some of the first persons to engage the ex-slaves as they exited bondage (Butchart, 2002). However, it is from more recent scholarship that we have come to understand how the masses of illiterate slaves fashioned a world view and value system that reflected a level of achievement motivation generally associated only with certain White ethnic groups who entered the United States some 40 to 50 years after slavery (Spencer, Cross, Harpalani, & Goss, in press).

Certainly the slaves were influenced by the presence of free Black communities the majority of whose members were literate. Free Blacks found ways to communicate through the slave grapevine about the importance of knowing how to read and write (Webber, 1978; Woodson, 1919). Slaves sometimes witnessed the power of education in the hands of a fellow Black, as in 1755, when White southern Presbyterians from North Carolina decided—as an experiment—to see if Blacks could succeed at the college level, and sent the slave John Chavis to Princeton University (Bullock, 1967). Upon returning to the South, Chavis opened a school that was attended only by the White children of the slave owners. The irony of an educated slave teaching the master's children could not help but influence the slave community's attitudes about the importance of education. Free Black communities wrote and performed plays, held festivals that required written communications, and built and established Black churches, the activities for which were driven by the membership's ability to read the Bible. And, on occasion, some free Blacks wrote and secretly distributed, among the slaves, pamphlets arguing for the destruction of slavery.

But had there been no free Black communities, the slaves would still have seen the power of literacy as a result of the stratification of the White community. Blacks could readily see that the lowly overseers and poor Whites, who were on the margins of the plantation system, could not read and often were landless and without the right to vote. It must be recalled that poor Whites were seldom viewed by slaves to be role models of Whiteness, as they were frequently accorded a status beneath that of slaves—certainly beneath those slaves who were skilled craftpersons (Gutman, 1976; Webber, 1978). By comparison, the slave-plantation owners were often highly literate and were surrounded by evidence of the power derived from formal educational experiences. The slave grapevine knew about laws, the Constitution, newspapers, contracts, books, letters or written correspondence, etc. Almost every slave enclave had a few members whose missing fingers, ears, or whip-scarred backs revealed the price slaves were willing to pay to learn how to read or write (Webber, 1978). Bondage effectively prevented the spread of literacy among the captive Africans, and the masses of ex-slaves could be accurately described as illiterate. But, attitudinally, the slaves understood the value of education and they exited slavery with a hunger for education that, when assisted by others friendly to their cause, exploded into a social movement for education. That is the legacy of slavery, not some sort of "oppositional identity."

The foremost expert on the history of Black education in the South, James Anderson (1988), has traced this legacy of positive Black achievement motivation well into the 20th century, and Spencer, Cross, Harpalani, & Goss (in press) suggest that the educational problems of the so-called Black underclass are much more contemporary than is typically understood. It is not being romantic to suggest that, at the end of slavery and thereafter, had the larger White society taken advantage of the positive attitudes the slaves held about education and acculturation, then the proportion of Black people who are poor today would be dramatically diminished, and Blacks would likely be more proportionately represented across the social classes. Given that the ex-slaves had educational attitudes that put them ahead of poor Whites, it is not inconceivable that today Blacks might be a major force within the educational establishment in most southern states.

But this was not the White response. No sooner had General Banks and Blacks from Louisiana established a statewide system for educating Black children in 1864 (recall this was mentioned a few pages back), then other Whites turned around to destroy it (Du Bois, 1935). In 1880, when Blacks seemed to be educating their children too aggressively and threatened to produce Black high school students whose knowledge base and competencies might place them ahead of their White peers, the White community responded by shutting down the Black high school. It would be nearly 40 years before Black children in that area of Georgia would again have access to a high school (Anderson, 1988, pp. 188–193).

We typically think of the American Civil War in a singular sense, but there were two wars, the one between the North and South and the other "silent" civil war within the South itself, during which the White South defeated and subjugated its Black citizens. Black civil rights were eliminated, their place and future in the social order was truncated and fixed at a lowly status, and a segregated school system was created that was anything but separate and equal (Harlan, 1958). Tax dollars, which should have been distributed equally, were proportioned such that White children received far more and Black children far less than would have been the case under an equal distribution system (it was not uncommon that for every dollar spent on a Black child, 12 or more were spent on a White child; Harlan, 1958; Anderson, 1988; Bullock, 1967). This resulted in the exaggerated funding and accelerated development of White children as compared to the severe *under-funding and consequent underdevelopment* of Black children. In the early 1900s southern Black migrants practically matched the educational profiles of White immigrants pouring into the country—essentially both groups were undereducated (Lieberson, 1980). However, by the 1940s and 1950s, when the 2nd major wave of Blacks migrated from the South to the North, states such as Mississippi, Louisiana, Georgia, and South Carolina could speak with confidence that they had, over a 40–50 year period, carried out government-sanctioned social policies that effectively underdeveloped the social capital of hundreds of thousands of Black people and their children (Jaynes & Williams, 1989). Once in the North, life would not necessarily get better, for as Homel (1984) and Clark (1965) have noted, the underfunding of urban Black school districts, in conjunction with housing segregation and employment discrimination, would be commonplace from the late 1930s to the present. Such containment policies had the power to neutralize any level of achievement motivation Blacks might continue to hold. In point of fact, historians and educators have not pinpointed when low Black achievement motivation would become such a problem as to cause Ogbu (1991) and Wilson (1987, 1997) to theorize about the underclass and oppositional identity. One thing is for certain: low achievement motivation and undervaluing the role of education are not cultural themes carried over from slavery.

The Origins of Black Crime—Black Culture or Systemic Forces?

The current tendency to see Black juvenile delinquency as having a "life of its own" can be traced back to Frazier's (1939) text on the Black family (Frazier, 1948). In chapter seventeen, titled "Rebellious Youth," Frazier argues that the

Black delinquency rate steadily increased between 1930 and 1940, with greater crime involvement in the more run-down sections of the Black community, where broken Black families resided. He thought this trend became attenuated, as one moved outward to those sectors of the ghetto where more accomplished, intact Black families lived. According to Frazier:

> [A] decline in delinquency coincided with the decline in dependency, family desertion, and illegitimacy in the . . . zones indicating the expansion of the Negro population. The rates were high in those areas characterized by physical decay and the lack of organized community life. In these areas the customary forms of social control, as represented by the family and simple folk culture of the migrants from southern communities, tended to break down or disappear altogether. (Frazier, 1948, p. 279)

Frazier presented cases that underscored the failure of broken or dysfunctional Black families to monitor their children, flooding the streets with a steady stream of Black youth. He weaves issues of poverty and oppression into the discussion, but the emphasis is clearly on problems internal to the Black family and the Black community. More recently, Ogbu (1978, 1991) emphasized the same kind of thinking as did Frazier in viewing high rates of Black crime as emanating from within Black culture. However, new research suggests that the crime rise Frazier observed and to which Ogbu makes reference may have been the result of key structural and institutional problems over which Blacks had little control.

In 1984, Homel published an important book on the education of Blacks in the public schools of Chicago for the period covering 1920 to 1941 (Homel, 1984). Like Frazier, Homel, in a section dealing with family life, community, and the schools, makes note of the high delinquency rate which often characterized portions of the Black community. However, unlike Frazier, who emphasized the role of community and family dynamics, Homel discovered a more systemic and oppressive origin to Black delinquency: *the schools.* For the same time period stressed by Frazier (1930 to 1940), Homel found that the White ethnic population stabilized and began to decline in terms of percentage of ethnic White children attending public schools. Consequently, by 1940, overcrowding was not much of a factor in the administration of schools attended by the children of White, ethnic parents. The reverse was true for Blacks, as their numbers and the percentage of children in Chicago schools increased rather steadily between 1930 and 1940. In a report dated 1941, which recorded the enrollment capacity of a large number of Black elementary as well as Black high schools, the schools were said to have an official capacity of 18,800 students but the actual enrollment for all the schools was 28,673 or 35% more students than the actual legal capacity. A few of the elementary schools were running 30–40% over capacity, but most alarming was the overcrowding at Black high schools. Du Sable High had an official capacity of 2,400 students but was serving as many as 4,000 students. Phillips High, with a capacity of only 1,500 students, was being asked to accommodate the incredible figure of 3,600 students or an overcapacity of nearly 240%! These figures reflect also the density of racial segregation in Chicago; for the time period in question, Black areas of the South Side of Chicago had 90,000 people per square mile, while for nearby White neighborhoods the density was 20,000 residents per square mile. As Homel underscores, the impact of residential overcrowding was evident in ghetto classrooms.

Part of the problem was that officials were hesitant to invest in new schools for Blacks, and even with the White school population on the decline, new facilities were more likely to be built in White than Black districts. With limited investments in Black school construction, the school board resorted to other remedies to relieve overcrowding at Black schools, namely, the use of temporary structures and something called double shifts (Homel, 1984, pp. 79–80). To maintain school segregation, officials provided dismal, damp, and unhealthy temporary structures called portables, *but more important to our discussion of Black juvenile delinquency rates was the double shift remedy.* School schedules were altered and one school might serve two or *more* shifts of students every school day! Although rare in White neighborhoods, the number of multiple-shift schools in the ghetto climbed from four in 1931, to seven in 1936, and to thirteen in 1940. Compared to White students, Black students were spending 20% to 40% fewer hours in school. At Black high schools where overcrowding was most acute, the situation was nearly impossible. *For the age cohort most vulnerable to delinquency trends, Black adolescents were literally being turned out into the streets by the very institution designed, in part, to prevent delinquency through educational engagement.* The consequences of this predicament were predictable:

> School overcrowding . . . hurt both youth and the community as a whole by offering double-shift students too many chances to get into trouble. Observers pointed out that the shift system made it easy for pupils to become truants. A white women's club officer testified, "Any child on the street at any hour can explain his presence by saying, 'I went to school this morning,' . . . or 'I go to school in the afternoon.'" Even youngsters who were dutiful about attending classes had, in the words of the civic leader Irene McCoy Gaines, "a half day in school and a half day on the street." Children from households that had no adult home during the day spent their afternoon or morning without supervision. Half-day sessions, grumbled one South Sider, allowed boys and girls "time to learn all kinds of devilment." Children barred from school by seat shortages passed their time on the street corners, in adult entertainment establishments, and in unchaperoned apartments. "We have seen dozens of boys traveling in gangs for want of anything to do," a black newspaper columnist reported . . . Journalists, Urban League personnel, and PTA leaders blamed shortened school hours for the ghetto's high incidence of youth crime. As Alterman Earl B. Dickerson asked rhetorically in 1941, "Is it any wonder that our juvenile delinquency rate is one of the highest in the country?" (Homel, 1984, pp. 82–83)

In effect, Frazier's assertion that crime and juvenile delinquency go hand and hand with a pathogenic Black culture was more about myth making than fact. Frazier earned his doctorate from the University of Chicago and his work on the Black family and Black adolescence was published by the University of Chicago in 1939. A great deal of the information that went into the making of his text on the Black family reflected the observations he made of Black families living in Chicago. How he came to miss the role of school overcrowding and double-shift schools is not clear. It is interesting to note that his chapter on rebellious youth, which was described a few paragraphs back, contains not a single reference or commentary about schools or the school system.

Today, in a similar fashion, we do violence to Black people in general, and Black males in particular, by accepting as fact that Blacks are genetically pre-disposed (Duster, 1992) or "culturally" primed (Payne, 2001) for involvement in crime, drug usage, and drug trafficking (Lusane & Desmond, 1991). We are so accepting of the Black-crime/Black-culture connection that there is little outrage about the disproportionate number of Black men who have some connection to the prison or parole systems (Miller, 1996). Just as Chicagoans in the 1930s and 1940s failed to perceive double-shift schools as a form of racialized-education, so today many people do not view our current penal code as having racialized drug usage (Duster, 1997). National surveys have established that Blacks are no more likely to use illicit drugs than are Whites (SAMHSA, 1997), although crack cocaine is readily found in Black communities while powdered cocaine is found in White suburbs (Duster, 1997). The so-called war on drugs turns on the crack ver-sus powdered cocaine distinction, in that punishment is stronger for crack cocaine arrests than for powdered cocaine arrests, and therefore Blacksare arrested more, because crack is more readily available in Black communities. With the passage of drug laws in the 1980s, upwards of 90% of juvenile drug arrests have involved Blacks (Duster, 1997; Miller, 1996; Mauer, 1999; Tonry, 1996). Not only did the laws create an incredibly differential arrest ratio based on race, but also mandatory sentencing guidelines meant more Blacks would spend longer periods of time in prison. Before 1986, the average drug sentence for Blacks was 6% longer than for Whites, but four years later as the mandatory sentencing locked into application, the average sentence became 93% higher for Blacks (Tonry, 1996). In a few short years, the racialization of drug use and imprisonment became the norm. Duster (1992) points out that in 1983, 63% of the prison commitments for the state of Virginia involved Whites and only 37% involved minorities. By 1989, the pattern was reversed, with new commitments showing 34% Whites and 65% minorities, even though, as we need to keep in mind and as was pointed out earlier, drug usage by Whites and Blacks could not be differentiated, and in some instances it was actually higher for Whites. The pattern found in Virginia has been documented to be true for other states across the nation (Lusane & Desmond, 1991). Even after experts have explained to the general public that the drug laws are racially and socio-economically slanted, there has been little support for changing the laws at either the state or federal levels (Rep. Rangel [D-NY] introduced H.R. 2031, Crack-Cocaine Equitable Sentencing Act of 1997, but it failed to pass). It is as though people are saying that yes, maybe the laws don't help, but the real reason for all those folks in prison cannot possibly be the law itself. This likely echoes what was said back in the 1940s that yes, now that you point it out to me, double-shifting probably does not help matters, but there must be some cultural or genetic reasons why so many Black teens keep getting into trouble.

Conclusions

The scope of contemporary Black problems sometimes causes scholars to wonder whether the seemingly intractable problems reveal a crippled culture the origin of which was slavery. We explored the legacy of slavery concept and found it wanting. If anything, the evidence presented turns the legacy of slavery concept on its head, in that Blacks exited slavery with the type of social capital, family attitudes, and positive achievement motivation that could have readily facilitated their rapid acculturation into the mainstream of American society, had society wanted them.

If there is a message from this analysis it is that observers who are deeply immersed in the present and who sincerely want to find a way to both explain and solve certain Black problems should not assume that the legacy of slavery thesis is, to borrow a phrase from the study of law, "settled" history. Ogbu's attempt in 1991 to link contemporary Black achievement problems with slavery should never have seen the light of day because, by 1991, evidence to the contrary was abundant. The historical record is there but if it is not studied first hand, one begins the search for solutions to Black problems by committing violence against the history of the very people one professes to want to help. Finally, this analysis suggests that a group's disproportionate involvement in crime does not automatically bring into question the integrity of that group's culture. For example, our analysis confirmed the high rate of Black juvenile delinquency for Blacks living in Chicago, circa 1930 to 1940. However, as soon as it was revealed that for the time period in question, Black adolescents were spending upward to 40% less time in school because of a double-shift policy, then it became easy to comprehend that such a policy was essentially pushing Black youth toward mischief making and the streets, and no amount of Black cultural integrity could have prevented the trend. Consequently, the co-existence of Black crime rates and Black cultural integrity is not a contradiction, when systemic forces neutralize or undermine the *ameliorative potential* of Black culture (Mullings and Wali, 2001).

References

Anderson, J. D. (1988). *The education of Blacks in the South, 1860–1935*. Chapel Hill, NC: University of North Carolina Press.

Bullock, H. A. (1967). *A history of Negro education in the South, 1619 to the present*. Cambridge, MA: Harvard University Press.

Butchart, R. E. (1980). *Northern schools, southern Blacks, and reconstruction: Freedman's education, 1862–1875*. Westport, CT: Greenwood Press.

Butchart, R. E. (2002). Mission matters: Mount Holyoke, Oberlin, and the schooling of southern Blacks, 1861–1917. *History of Education Quarterly, 42* (Spring 2002), 1–17.

Butchart, R. E. (in press). Edmonia G. (1844–1870) and Caroline V. (1849–1926) Highgate: Black teachers, freed slaves, and the betrayal of Black hearts. In N. Mjagkij (Ed.), *The human tradition in American history.* Wilmington, DE: Scholarly Resources, Inc.

Clark, K. B. (1965). *Dark ghetto.* New York: Harper & Row.

Coontz, S. (1992). *The way we never were: American families and the nostalgia trap.* New York: Basic Books.

Dovidio, J. F., & Gaertner, S. L. (1986). *Prejudice, discrimination, and racism.* Orlando, FL: Academic Press.

Du Bois, W. E. B. (1935). *Black reconstruction.* New York: S. A. Russell Company.

Duster, T. (1992). Genetics, race, and crime: Recurring seduction to a false precision. In P. Billings (Ed.), *DNA on trial: Genetic information and criminal justice* (pp. 132–135). Plainview, NY: Cold Spring Harbor Press.

Duster, T. (1997). Pattern, purpose and race in the drug war: The crisis of credibility in criminal justice. In C. Reinarman & H. G. Levine, *Crack in America: Demon drugs and social justice* (pp. 260–287). Berkeley, CA: University of California Press.

Ehrenreich, B. (2001). *Nickel and dimed: On (not) getting by in America.* New York: Metropolitan Books.

Frazier, E. F. (1939). *The Negro family in the United States.* Chicago: University of Chicago Press.

Frazier, E. F. (revised, 1948). *The Negro family in the United States.* New York: Dryden Press.

Gibson, M. A., & Ogbu, J. (1991). *Minority status and schooling.* New York: Grand Publishing.

Goozner, M. (1990, September 3). Pay inequality grew in '80s, study finds. *Chicago Tribune,* p. 1.

Gutman, H. G. (1976). *The Black family in slavery and freedom, 1750–1925.* New York: Pantheon Books.

Harlan, L. R. (1958). *Separate and unequal: Public school campaigns in the southern seaboard states, 1901–1915.* Chapel Hill, NC: University of North Carolina Press.

Hill, R. B. (2001). *The strengths of African American families.* Lanham, MD: University Press of America.

Homel, M. W. (1984). *Down from equality: Black Chicagoans and the public schools, 1920–1940.* Champaign-Urbana, IL: University of Illinois Press.

Jaynes, G. D., & Williams, R. M., Jr. (1989). *A common destiny: Black and American society.* Washington, D.C.: National Academy Press.

Kluger, R. (1977). *Simple justice.* London: Andre Deutsch.

Lieberson, S. (1980). *A piece of the pie: Black and White immigrants since 1880.* Berkeley, CA: University of California Press.

Lusane, C., & Desmond, D. (1991). *Pipe dream blues: Racism and the war on drugs.* Boston: South End Press.

Mauer, M. (1999). *Race and incarcerate.* New York: New Press.

Miller, J. G. (1996). *Search and destroy: African-American males and the criminal justice system.* New York: Cambridge University Press.

Moynihan, D. P. (1965). *The Negro family: The case for national action.* Washington D.C.: Office of Planning and Research, U.S. Department of Labor.

Moynihan, D. P. (1996). *Miles to go: A personal history of social policy.* Cambridge, MA: Harvard University Press.

Mullings, L., & Wali, A. (2001). *Stress and resilience: The social context of reproduction in Central Harlem.* New York: Kluwer Academic/Plenum Publishers.

National Household Survey on Drug Abuse: Population Estimates. (1997). SAMHSA.

Newman, K. S. (1988). *Falling from grace: The downward mobility in the American middle class.* New York: The Free Press.

Ogbu, J. U. (1978). *Minority education and caste: The American system in cross-cultural perspective.* New York: Academic Press.

Ogbu, J. U. (1991). Low performance as an adaptation: The case of Blacks in Stockton, California. In M. A. Gibson & J. U. Ogbu (Eds.), *Minority status and schooling* (pp. 249–285). New York: Grand Publishing.

Patterson, O. (1998). *Rituals of blood: Consequences of slavery in two American centuries*. Washington, D.C.: Civitas/Counterpoint.

Payne, Y. A. (2001). Black men and street life as a site of resiliency: A counter story for Black scholars. *International Journal of Critical Psychology, 4*, 109–122.

Roner, R. (1992, July 5). Politics of welfare: Focusing on the problems. Rethinking welfare, part 1. *New York Times*, p. 1.

Scott, D. M. (1997). *Contempt and pity: Social policy and the image of the damaged Black psyche, 1880–1996*. Chapel Hill, NC: University of North Carolina Press.

Solinger, R. (1992). *Wake up little Suzie: Single pregnancy and race before Roe v. Wade*. New York: Routledge.

Spencer, M. B., Cross, W. E., Jr., Harpalani, V., & Goss, T. N. (in press). Historical and developmental perspectives on Black academic achievement: Debunking the "acting White" myth and posing new directions for research. In C. C. Yeaky (Ed.), *Surmounting all odds: Education, opportunity, and society in the new millennium*. Greenwich, CT: Information Age Publishers.

Steele, S. (1990). *The content of out character: A new vision of race in America*. New York: St. Martin's Press.

Steinberg, S. (1989). The ethnic myth: Race, ethnicity, and class in America (2nd edition). Boston: Beacon.

Stone, A. (1992, February 28). The recession's ripple effect. *USA TODAY*, p. 1A.

Swim, J., & Stangor, C. (1998). *Prejudice: The target's perspective*. New York: Academic Press.

Taylor, R. L. (1995). *African-American youth: Their social and economic status in the United States*. Westport, CT: Praeger Press.

Tonry, M. H. (1996). *Malign neglect: Race, crime, and punishment in America*. New York: Oxford University Press.

Wilson, W. J. (1978). *The declining significance of race*. Chicago: University of Chicago Press.

Wilson, W. J. (1987). *The truly disadvantaged: The inner city, the underclass, and public policy*. Chicago: University of Chicago Press.

Wilson, W. J. (1997). *When work disappears: The world of the new urban poor*. New York: Knopf.

Webber, T. L. (1978). *Deep like the rivers: Education in the slave quarter community, 1831–1865*. New York: W. W. Norton, Inc.

Woodson, C. G. (1919). *The education of the Negro prior to 1861*. Washington, DC: Associated Publishers.

WILLIAM E. CROSS, JR., is Professor of Social-Personality Psychology and he coordinates the Doctoral Program in Social-Personality Psychology at the Graduate Center for the City University of New York (CUNY). He is a cultural psychologist who links the fields of African American Studies and Social-Personality Psychology. His current research focuses on the structure, dynamics, variability, and life span dimensions of Black identity. His book, *Shades of Black*, is considered critical reading for those interested in the study of Black identity.

Journal of Social Issues, Vol. 59, No. 1, 2003, pp. 83–101

Negotiating Violence Prevention

Colette Daiute*, Rebecca Stern, and Corina Lelutiu-Weinberger

The Graduate Center, City University of New York

Evaluation research typically treats standards of violence prevention programs, like other curricula, as unquestioned values of a good society, while identifying youth as the problem to be solved. This article explains how the evaluative gaze can, in contrast, be critically fixed on the interpretations of various stake holders in the violence prevention enterprise, including curriculum authors, teachers, and youth, whose social values are often under-represented. In the context of a year-long literacy-based violence prevention curriculum focusing on racial and ethnic discrimination in 3rd and 5th grade urban classrooms, 5 teachers, their classes, and 36 individual students from these classes expressed contradictory and conforming values, suggesting to us the need to invite negotiation of social values as part of democratic education.

Theoretical Background

Like most social institutions, violence prevention programs are built upon stated and unstated values. We argue that evaluation research typically treats curriculum standards as unquestioned values of a good society, while identifying youth as the problem to be solved. The evaluative gaze can, however, be critically fixed on the interpretations of various stake-holders in the violence prevention enterprise. In particular, we illustrate how young people's values around issues of social conflict introduce important tensions across diverse socio-political interests represented by curricula and their implementation in public schools.

Our approach is to examine a violence prevention program through critical discourse theory (Daiute, 1998; Gates, 1992; Harre & Gillet, 1994), explaining

---
*Correspondence concerning this article should be addressed to Colette Daiute, The Graduate Center, CUNY, 365 Fifth Avenue, New York, NY 10016 [e-mail: cdaiute@gc.cuny.edu]. The authors are indebted to the teachers and students who participated in this curriculum study, all of whom are given pseudonyms to maintain their anonymity. We also thank the William T. Grant Foundation who generously funded most of the research reported in this paper, and we are grateful to Ellie Buteau and Martin Ruck for their assistance.

83

that children's everyday social interactions are contexts for understanding tensions in values across the school, home, media, and peer cultures in which they live. We also integrate Black identity theory (Cross, 1991) and social theory (de Certeau, 1984) with discourse approaches to explain how values are situated in socio-historical experience. This focus on the situated nature of social understanding extends developmental theory (Selman, Watts, & Schultz, 1997), which has been the foundation for numerous violence prevention programs (Aber, Brown, & Henrich, 1999; Johnson & Johnson, 1996; Weissberg & Bell, 1997).

Youth violence prevention programs can be analyzed for their guiding values about social relations from specific theoretical perspectives. Values are sometimes stated in propositions like "conflict resolution and peer mediation . . . [used for] integrative negotiation" (Johnson & Johnson, 1996, p. 477), "experiment with new and different ways of handling conflicts" (Samples & Aber, 1998, p. 228), "promoting self-esteem . . . so youth need not resort to violence . . ." and "teaching values . . . of love [caring]) and freedom [self-determination]" (Berkower, 1998, p. 1), but the values promoted in programs are sometimes implicit, such as the placement of programs in cities, suggesting that urban youth are particularly in need of this type of instruction. Analyzing values as they are interpreted by different participants in a violence prevention program could reveal the relativity of any particular set of foundational values and raise questions about the effectiveness and fairness of prevention programs in diverse societies. The nature of differences in values expressed in the context of a particular program offers insights, furthermore, about the kinds of values that vary and thus require attention in research and practice.

Evaluation studies have introduced research designs and related measures based on assumptions that problems occur in individual behavior or understanding, with only some programs relating these to social, environmental, or macro-social measures (Elliott, Hamburg, & Williams, 1998; Weissberg, & Bell, 1997). Analyses of program effectiveness have assessed children's aggressiveness, impulsivity, interpersonal negotiation strategies, cognitive capacities, and social deviance (Samples & Aber, 1998; Selman et al., 1997), and a few have identified symbolic processes such as aggressive fantasies and narrative representations of social conflict (Aber, Brown, & Henrich, 1999; Daiute & Buteau, 2002). To date, we have found no previous studies that make social values the focus of theory, practice, or assessment, and few studies that include extended reflections or interactions of program participants.

The consequence of evaluating whether participants master program values is that challenges to the program emerge as individuals' failures. Consistent with these ideas, our study is based on the concern that when mastery of program values is the goal, important differences across students' and teachers' social, cultural, and political lives are ignored—differences that have increasingly been shown to influence learning (Daiute, Campbell, Griffin, Reddy, & Tivnan, 1993). Although there may be universal agreement about the importance of eliminating physical and psychological violence in schools (Elliott, Hamburg, & Williams, 1998), our analysis of this previous research suggests that teachers and students interact with issues of violence from diverse positions of power, motivation, and experience, suggesting that curricula, like other institutions, should be examined from multiple points of view. Establishing theory and methods to interrogate foundations of social programs is important, we argue, for gaining insights about how young people understand social conflict and for assessing the contributions of such programs to social education in diverse societies.

Toward a Theory of Social Values

Previous research has shown how children are socialized to cultural beliefs and practices in educational, vocational, and social domains (Rogoff, 1990; Wertsch, 1991), but young people are also active constructors of social values in classroom contexts (Daiute, 1998; Guitierrez, Rhymes, & Larson, 1995). Tested here is the theory that when children draw on their experiences, they transform social values promoted by adults in their environments—in this case their teachers. Thus, we propose that in some contexts children may conform to educational agendas, while in others they may change, contradict, or reject them. We base our study further on the idea that the more heterogeneous the context, like urban public schools, the more dynamic the interplay of students, teachers, and broader institutional values, and the more important it is to consider diverse perspectives. Children working with knowledge about discrimination and poverty (Cross, 1991), for example, are particularly adept at shifting classroom discourse when given the opportunity (Daiute, Buteau, & Rawlins, 2001). The schools where we did our research provided contexts for the expression of diverse social values by participants from a range of racial and ethnic backgrounds.

We conceptualize "values" as culturally-specific ways of knowing, feeling, and acting in response to environmental, economic, and social circumstances—a definition based in socio-cultural theory (Rogoff, 1990; Wertsch, 1991). Individuals in heterogeneous societies interact with multiple cultures and diverse values systems, which may or may not overlap spontaneously (Guitierrez et al., 1995; Lee, 1993). Research on social development suggests that the ability to negotiate diverse perspectives comes with cognitive maturity (Piaget, 1968), yet diverse interpretations of the social environment, such as perceiving racist threats or not, are also the result of socialization (Cross, 1991) and instruction (Lee, 1993). Issues of power, rights, and responsibilities in social relations thus become paramount in the development of knowledge in educational settings (Walkerdine, 1984).

"Youth perspective" is, then, the set of values children express especially in their interactions with peers, where relatively equal power relations allow young people to voice a wider range of knowledge and practices than they do in the official curriculum of teacher-led discussions (Daiute et al., 1993). In this way, we conceptualize "youth perspectives" as formed in the multiple cultures where they live with peers, in school, at home, and cognitive processes flow from these contexts. The study described in this article is designed to identify the dynamic and situated nature of youth perspectives as expressed across diverse contexts, including full class discussions and peer group interactions. In class discussions, children may tend to conform to values expressed by teachers, such as their emphasis on empathizing with adversaries in conflicts. In peer interactions, these same children may express quite different values, such as the difficulty of resolving conflicts because of inter-group prejudices.

Social theory (de Certeau, 1984) explains that the relative under-representation of diverse student values in classroom settings is an issue of power relations. As representatives of the "will and power [in] . . . an educational institution" (de Certeau, 1984, p. 36), teachers' interactions are endowed as "strategies" controlling the educational enterprise, while students' interactions are relegated to more "tactical" responses, since they do not set the educational agenda. In large class settings, for example, children's discourse would be a "tactical" process, such as speaking out of turn, speaking too much, or not speaking enough in desired ways, rather than shifting substantive aspects of the discussion, while during peer interactions, children have extended the nature of task-related ideas more than when working with the teacher on similar class assignments (Daiute et al., 1993). Of course, the application of power relations in any given situation such as school would be moderated by historical and personal experiences—such that teachers who identify with discriminated groups might be put in tactical positions during interactions with administrators, even though they have strategic control in their classrooms. Our analyses explore whether and in what circumstances teachers and students exert strategic control as their expression of social values conforms—or does not—to those of the curriculum.

Focusing on the negotiation of social values in a violence prevention program, this inquiry addresses the question: What values tensions (consistencies, contradictions, complementarities) are revealed across curriculum materials and implementations of the curriculum by teachers and children in different situations? Addressing this question, we offer insights about the complexity and dynamics of social values in classroom contexts and consider implications of value negotiations for social issues instruction in educational institutions.

Analyzing Values in a Violence Prevention Program

The context of the study is 3rd through 5th grade classrooms in two public schools in a large Northeastern city where children and teachers introduced issues of racial and ethnic discrimination as a theme, and used high-quality children's literature as the point of departure for class discussions, peer group activities, and children's writing about social conflict (Walker, 1998). For example, one literary selection for 3rd grade was a story about verbal and physical discrimination involving a White boy (Raymond) and a recent immigrant Vietnamese girl (Hoa). A 5th grade literary selection was a story about a group of children in a Black community who had to attend a school serving mostly Whites when their school closed. A teacher's guide states the major values to be examined in relation to each novel through guided oral readings, class discussions, and a range of writing activities. The teachers' guides included discussion questions to identify central conflicts in the stories from different characters' perspectives about causes, resolutions, and consequences of conflicts.

Students wrote expository and narrative texts about social conflict, individually and with peers, about half way through the study of each book, to create an original ending to the story after a high point in the discrimination conflict. As an alternative to the teacher-led class discussion, this writing activity involved young peers in dyadic and small group interactions. The writing activity in relation to the novel *Mayfield Crossing*, for example, asked children to continue the story after the character, Clayton, said, " 'I'm the pitcher! Get off my mound! . . . You deaf or something, tar baby?' as he marched across the field with about twenty kids following him." This activity provided a context for role-playing conflict-resolution strategies promoted in the curriculum as well as leeway for introducing students' own values.

We used a systematic process to identify participants from a larger sample of nine classes, making this labor-intensive study feasible. Selection criteria included: (a) classes at each grade level with a full set of transcripts of teacher-led discussions and peer group discussions (research protocols involved audiotaping all the curriculum-related class sessions and as many small peer group sessions as possible), (b) teachers and students from a range of race/ethnicity groups and teaching experience, and (c) data from the 1997–1998 school year which maintained consistency involvement with the curriculum.

Participants in the study described here were five teachers and their students: 25 students per class in the three 3rd grades and 35 students per class in the two 5th grades. Student discourse was analyzed as a group in the teacher-led class discussions and individually in the peer interactions. Interactions by 36 students (10 male and 8 female 3rd graders, and 10 male and 8 female 5th graders) working on the peer writing activities were analyzed. Representing the range of race/ethnicity backgrounds in the schools, the five teachers included one identifying as African American, one as Latina (Puerto Rican), and three as European American. Of the five teachers, four were experienced teachers and one was a novice teacher. The 36 children whose peer interactions were examined included ten identifying as African American, six as Latino/a, five as European-American, three as mixed-race, two as Asian-American, two as other, and eight unidentified. The race/ethnicity pattern represents that of the broader school system.

Data collection sampled from curriculum activities in principled ways to capture social arrangements varying in power relations—represented here by teacher-student interactions and student-peer interactions. Data included 38 transcripts of teacher-led class discussions and 25 transcripts of peer interactions, selected from the beginning, middle, and end of the unit to ensure a representative range of interactions.

Data analyses involved examining values in conversations across contexts. With social values as the units of analysis, a taxonomy of values promoted in the curriculum grounds our examination of teachers' and students' expression of values. Our focus is children's peer interactions, based on our theory that children are especially likely to introduce diverse values when they interact in relatively equal power contexts. Providing contexts where children in multi-cultural urban settings can express their social values is important, in large part, because addressing problems like discrimination should rely on children's social histories. Identifying diverse social values, thus, is an opportunity to assess the potential for equitable social exchange.

Identifying Values

The values analysis proceeded in several phases, including (a) creating coding categories by compiling a list of stated and implied values in curriculum-related documents (an overview of the program, teacher's guides for focal literary selections, and notes from training sessions), (b) identifying values expressed by teachers as they led their classes in program lessons, (c) identifying values expressed by children in the teacher-led discussions and when working with peers, (d) computing percentages of social values expressed within and across contexts.

Eighteen values stated in the curriculum materials and the transcripts form the basis of the coding scheme. The researcher who compiled the list of values from the curriculum materials also wrote a definition for each value with examples. Since values are often implicit and draw on extended interactions, identifying values involved examining the broader context of interactions in a transcript and across interactions by a participant. Thus, while a code is assigned to a specific conversational turn, definitive assignment of that code might require reading beyond the turn, as mentioned in relation to some of the examples below.

The first group of values in the taxonomy includes *Love and freedom values.* *Love* values refer to establishing and strengthening relationships, understanding others, being kind, and making connections when relationships aren't smooth. An example of such a value as expressed by one of the teachers is, "These characters should find some way to get along, something in common."

Freedom values, on the other hand, have to do with an individual's or a group's self-determination, rights to respect, and ability to accept responsibility for problematic interactions. Teachers who stress freedom values might discuss that a newcomer to a classroom has the right to dress in whatever way he or she pleases without being teased. Also, a teacher who emphasizes freedom values might be likely to address social oppressions such as racism directly, stressing that conflicts must be identified and examined: "When you feel wronged, you have to defend yourself and your people." The difference between a love and freedom value in relation to a specific conflict comes about in a person's description of it, and, according to discourse theory, even certain seemingly minor differences in wording express social relational realities and govern action (Harre & Gillet, 1994).

Ultimately, the curriculum advocates a *balance of love and freedom values*, with this balance as the definition of "health." The following quote expresses such complexity: "You always have many different feelings, don't you? ... But there's always a mixture of feelings it seems to me, like you want to stick up for yourself but you also want to try again to talk to that person." Other statements balancing love and freedom values might mention respect for individual privacy as sometimes limited by the need to seek mutual understanding.

Several major values revolve around social conflict, including values about the *nature of conflict, conflict escalation, conflict resolution,* and *different participants in the resolution process.* A major assumption about conflict in the curriculum is that relationships don't always go smoothly, which means, in curriculum terms, that love and freedom might clash. One teacher, for example, who often used metaphors said, "There was ice existing between Raymond and Hoa, and what broke the ice?" to define conflict in terms of the cold feelings antagonists sometimes have toward each other.

The teacher's extension of this definition with the familiar expression "breaking the ice" expresses another major aspect of the curriculum: the analysis of interactions to determine how conflicts escalate, which is expressed in this quote by another teacher: "Now when some nasty things are happening and the conflict is building, steps are going up to a higher and higher level of conflict." The emphasis on conflict resolution is expressed well by the following quote: "Okay here's another thing you can do. With the person you're having the conflict with, you can agree on a rule."

The curriculum posits that perspective-coordination is a basic social-developmental skill required for resolving conflicts, as expressed in several curriculum values including *perspective-taking*, coordinating one's own perspective with that of others, and *expressing empathy and/or emotions.* According to theory underlying the curriculum, conflict participants must understand and value each other's points of view in order to resolve their conflict. Examples of these values include, "And the parents might look at it and say he's [been] hurting; the kids looked at it and thought something completely different," and "Someone want to tell us what it felt like?"

Mutual understanding also involves *valuing diversity.* Comments expressing diversity values express it as a given for many people and often as an obstacle, as in the following summary: "A newcomer to a community, a neighborhood, a school or a group, right—everyone has that feeling of not being sure if they're going to make friends or know the language or if they're going to fit in."

Four social orientations to conflict resolution expressed in curriculum values are (a) *individual orientation*, where personal needs, decisions, and qualities are depicted as central to conflict and resolution, (b) a *social/historical orientation* that appreciates cultural and other kinds of difference but does not necessarily emphasize the power differentials related to diversity, (c) a *social/political orientation* representing conflicts as processes of power relations, fairness, discrimination, or other justice criteria, and (d) a *universalist approach* which minimizes differences and emphasizes basic human similarities. An individual approach expressed in the quote "Somehow along the way that kid escaped racism by listening to his own heart and doing what he thinks is right" contrasts most sharply with the socio-historical approach in the following comment: "I didn't fit in because the Puerto Ricans in New York are raised a little differently." The universal approach, in contrast, emphasizes similarity rather than difference: "All mothers have expectations for their children."

Three other kinds of values emerged from preliminary analyses of the classroom implementation of the curriculum. They are: (a) *literacy*, which includes references to plot devices, character development, vocabulary, spelling, and literary conventions (chapters, headings, etc.), (b) *pedagogy/academics*, referring to discussions around the issue of "how to do school," such as how to work with a partner, (c) *classroom behavior*, such as waiting one's turn to speak.

Preliminary analyses of student interactions made clear the need to account for novel or *"unique" values*, including those that violated the curriculum values. Examples of unique values include two young partners' proposal that two characters' fight ended after a beating by the principal—a punitive approach that would not be tolerated in the curriculum. A different unique comment was made by a student who sided with a bully character saying "make me," belligerently rejecting another character's appeal that he stop teasing. Interaction processes were also coded against the curriculum values, such as participants' arguments and helping behaviors.

Coding Social Conflict Discourse

A coding manual refined through several phases of reading transcripts was the reference point for analyses. After preparing transcripts, coding identified values expressed per speaker turn, and then writing case summaries for each teacher-led class and student pair session. Categories were assigned as discretely as possible, but coding was not mutually exclusive, since a turn could, for example, express a perspective-coordination value and a pedagogy value. For each value, there was a set of defining features and a range of expressions. For example, perspective-coordination value expressions mention psychological state verbs ("think ... felt"; "feel ... made fun") for at least two persons, as in the following questions by two teachers: "How do you think Raymond felt when the principal broke up the fight?" and, somewhat differently, *"How would you feel if someone made fun of your clothes?"*

Coding reliability was addressed in several ways: (a) the three authors coded several of the same transcripts until they achieved 80% agreement on two transcripts, (b) then, one researcher coded the transcripts of teacher-led classes and another coded the peer transcripts, (c) to increase consistency across codings, researchers checked each other's codings, discussed and resolved any disagreements.

Identifying the curriculum values, as we described above, achieved one study goal of making explicit the value system underlying a particular educational violence prevention institution. Our second goal of identifying whether and how individual teachers and students participating in this institution expressed these or other values involved a qualitative analysis. With the values coding scheme as a guide, we created a case description for each teacher and student, via a process of identifying values in repeated readings of the transcripts and supporting those qualitative readings by computing percentages of turns per transcript (and mean percentages across transcripts) in which participants expressed each curriculum value.

With a general description of how the teachers implemented the curriculum values, we then turned to characterize the students' expression of values across the two contexts to reflect on theory about power relations and social values. In the teacher-led class discussion, we examined student comments in the transcripts as a combined student group, because they were not always identified and because class discussions tend to treat students as a unit (Guitierrez et al., 1995). In addition to describing whether and how students adopted the curriculum values as implemented by their teachers, this qualitative analysis identified students' preferred values expressions when they work in the relatively equal power situation with peers.

Procedures for the case description process involved responding to a set of questions with summaries and examples when reading through each transcript and when summarizing across the set of transcripts for a teacher/class. The questions guiding the case analysis were: (a) "What Voices of Love and Freedom (VLF) general values did the teacher (and the students as a group) emphasize, with what consistency and/or variation across the transcripts?" (b) "Discuss whether and how the teacher's (and students') orientation conformed to the VLF values (transformed them or differed dramatically) as discussed in the guides, modules, and overall philosophy." (c) "Summarize the teachers' (and students') orientation to the curriculum values by selecting several characteristic turns—expressions that capture the characteristic value expression of the curriculum—and display these on a chart with each value for each transcript, across participants, and contexts." These written summaries by at least two members of the research team were remarkably similar in terms of the values noted and the characteristic examples isolated. These descriptive summaries were accompanied by charts of percentages of turns (based on frequencies) expressing each value per transcript and per teacher. These percentages served to support the qualitative descriptions and to provide a basis for general descriptive (not statistical) comparisons.

Since these analyses are qualitative, we make no claims about the definitive or absolute nature of teachers' or students' values, nor do we imply any generalization beyond the five classrooms examined here. Instead, we open up typically unquestioned and unexamined values as they occur within and across teacher/student roles in five classrooms including teachers and students from a variety of backgrounds. Our inquiry thus involves a theory-based illustration of social value expressions.

Results: Contradiction and Conformity Around Social Values

Patterns of consistency and variation can be characterized as a value negotiation process. Of particular interest is the nature of children's values when they worked with peers and when they worked in teacher-led class discussions.

Teachers Embedded the Violence Prevention Institution Within the Educational Institution

Transcripts of the teacher-led class discussions revealed that the teachers all expressed the violence prevention curriculum values, albeit in different combinations. Close readings of each transcript in terms of the curriculum value categories indicated, also, that each teacher devoted considerable time to expressing educational values about pedagogical practices.

Table 1 presents the percent of turns in which the five teachers expressed each curriculum value. As shown by the percentages in Table 1, all the teachers emphasized pedagogy skills more than any other values, with the mean number of turns devoted to reinforcing pedagogical practices such as raising one's hand to speak, speaking loudly, using language precisely, etc., ranging from 16% to 34%. The two fifth grade teachers emphasized literacy values also, as did one of the third grade teachers, with 10% and 18% of the fifth grade teachers' turns devoted to literacy values and 10% of one of the third grade teachers' turns devoted to literacy values such as reading carefully, writing descriptively, and using characters' dialogue for insights about their beliefs.

Beyond those few common patterns, we observed some striking differences across teachers. Three teachers, Mrs. Smith, Mrs. Warren and Ms. Bates (European-Americans, as noted in Table 1) can be described as expressing values in patterns consistent with the curriculum, though they certainly brought their own inflections to the process. As illustrated in the pattern of turns expressing each value (Table 1), Mrs. Smith devoted 10% or more of her comments to values related to the issue of

Table 1. Percent of Turns Devoted to Social Values by Different Teachers

Curriculum Values	Third 1 Mrs. Smith Euro-American (Exp. Teacher)	Third 2 Mrs. Gates African-American (Exp. Teacher)	Third 3 Mrs. Morales Puerto Rican-Am (Exp. Teacher)	Fifth 1 Mrs. Warren Euro-American (Exp. Teacher)	Fifth 2 Ms. Bates Euro-American (New teacher)
Love Values	3%	5%	6%	7%	2%
Freedom Values	9%	2%	2%	11%	4%
Balanced Love/Freedom	1%	0%	3%	6%	3%
Nature of Conflict	0%	6%	0%	0%	2%
Analysis of Causes & Escalation	5%	1%	0%	6%	8%
Conflict Resolution	10%	1%	5%	10%	13%
Resolution Agents	1%	4%	6%	4%	6%
Expressing Points of View	17%	2%	1%	5%	6%
Expressing Feelings Can Lead to Understanding	6%	7%	15%	1%	4%
Analyzing Diversity	11%	7%	5%	1%	1%
Social/Historical Approach to Conflict	3%	8%	17%	4%	3%
Socio/Political Approach to Conflict	3%	4%	13%	7%	6%
Universalist Approach to Conflict	0%	3%	0%	2%	0%
Relating to Literacy Events, Artifacts, or Elements	4%	10%	4%	10%	18%
Pedagogy–Statements About How to Do School	20%	34%	20%	16%	18%
Behavior Comments	8%	4%	4%	8%	6%

Note. All teachers were experienced except for Ms. Bates, who was in her first year of teaching. Besides experience with teaching, another selection criterion was their race/ethnicity. Mrs. Smith, Mrs. Warren, and Ms. Bates were White teachers, while Mrs. Gates was African-American and Mrs. Morales was Latina. Both cultural background and teaching experience were thought to be relevant in conveying the multiculturalism of the curriculum. All percentages were rounded to nearest whole number, so totals may not equal 100.

conflicting points of view (17%), analyzing diversity (11%), and resolving conflicts (10%), with the expression of freedom values just behind (9%). Mrs. Warren
and Ms. Bates devoted 10% and 13% of their comments to conflict resolution
respectively. Thus, we see an emphasis by the three European-Americans on the
ultimate goal of the curriculum, which was to engage students in awareness and
practice of conflict resolution strategies (Walker, 1998).

Case descriptions revealed that Mrs. Gates and Mrs. Morales did not put much
emphasis on conflict resolution. Mrs. Gates devoted only 1% of her comments to
conflict resolution and Mrs. Morales 5%. Mrs. Gates' lack of focus on conflict
resolution was offset by her dramatic focus on pedagogy in 34% of her utterances. Mrs. Morales' orientation emphasized intergroup and interpersonal social
relational themes, including analyzing socio-historical aspects of conflict (17%),
promoting that participants express their feelings in conflicts (15%), and analyzing
socio-political aspects of conflicts (13%). These characteristic patterns by teachers illustrate the complexity of implementing a social issues curriculum and the
possibility of interesting diversity across teachers. Particularly intriguing for future study is the indication here that teachers from non-mainstream backgrounds
did not emphasize the conflict resolution value, which may indicate some critique
about curriculum assumptions about the causes of social problems. Minimizing
the focus on individual children's conflict resolution skills may imply more emphasis on society's role in promoting or allowing conflicts. This was explicit in
the instruction of Mrs. Morales, for example, who mentioned societal involvement
("They had a problem with us because we were Puerto Ricans from New York.").
On the other hand, Mrs. Gates' intense focus on appropriate school practices in
the absence of promoting specific conflict resolution practices was a more subtle
shifting of the violence prevention curriculum. Both strategies are interestingly
consistent with previous critiques by African American scholars (Delpit, 1988)
that explicit instruction in mainstream values is the business of school and not
instruction in social relations, which Black children already know.

While such descriptions of teachers' social values require further study to
establish their stability, they provide a backdrop for our analysis of the students'
values expressions.

Table 2 presents percentages of student turns devoted to curriculum values in
the teacher-led class discussions and in peer group interactions. Students' values
expressions in the teacher-led classes conformed to the curriculum value of conflict
resolution (12%) and also echoed the teachers' emphasis on general educational
values with expressions of pedagogy values (15%) and literacy values (14%). The
present study does not provide the means to do so, but it would be interesting in
future research to assess whether any different emphases across teachers' value
expressions were reflected in the students' orientations in the class discussions.
Particularly intriguing in this study, for example, is the issue of whether students in Mrs. Morales' class tended to emphasize, as she did, socio-historical and

Table 2. Percent of Turns Devoted to Different Values Used by Students in Teacher-Led Classes and Student Interactions

Curriculum Values	Mean Percentage Student Values with Teacher	Mean Percentage in Peer Interactions
Love Values	1%	1%
Freedom Values	1%	1%
Balanced Love and Freedom	0%	4%
Nature of Conflict	1%	4%
Analysis of Causes and Build-Up	7%	15%
Resolution of Conflict	12%	12%
Resolution Participants or Agents	4%	5%
Expressing Own/Others' Points of View	9%	16%
Expressing Feelings Can Lead to Understanding	9%	1%
Analyzing Diversity	3%	3%
Roles Played by Diversity	0%	3%
Individual Approach to Conflict	0%	3%
Social/Historical Approach to Conflict	8%	1%
Socio/Political Approach to Conflict	7%	3%
Universalist Approach to Conflict	1%	1%
Relating to Literacy Events, Artifacts, or Elements	14%	1%
Pedagogy–Statements About How to Do School	15%	7%
Behavior Comments	2%	1%
Unique Values	4%	19%

Note. Percentages were rounded to nearest whole number, so totals may not equal 100.

socio-political aspects of conflicts. Overall, the percentage of student turns locating social problems in groups and institutions was 8% and 7% respectively, which seems high for students the age of those in our study, so exploring whether this a general orientation or one more specific to individual teachers' orientations seems an important focus for future research.

Student Values in Peer Groups: Youth Transformation of Curriculum

Their expression of conflict escalation values (15% with peers, 7% with the teacher) demonstrated children's apparent penchant for playing out conflicts in detailed and sometimes exaggerated or playful ways, as in the following excerpt by two fifth graders: "Well they didn't play, they asked politely that they wanted to play? And they tried to be kind to them? But they didn't get a chance to play so they're getting' mad and start a, have an, after the argument they'll start a bigger fight." Children also sought understandings, sometimes persistently, about what all the trouble was about, such as a third grader, using "perspective taking" to criticize a character's actions, while also confronting his partner's misrepresentation of the character: "So why he hit, so why he hit Hoa? For no reason? Just like thaaaat?"

Children's expression of unique values was remarkable (19% in peer interactions and 4% in teacher-led classes), warranting discussion about how it illustrates issues of social values instruction and extensions of the curriculum. Unique values were not all the same, but we kept this as a single code to gain general insights about values extending beyond the curriculum.

Children's Strategic Work via Unique Values

Children's introduction of unique values is an appropriate use of peer contexts and, given that everyone has social experiences to inform their study of a curriculum focusing on conflict, it is not surprising that children would bring in some novel perspectives. The following discussion is a qualitative summary of the nature of transformations in children's values coded as "unique." Unique values often introduced novel orientations to conflict into the classroom. For example, one student introduced a value of "safety" when he stated that it didn't matter to him whether the conflict with a step-parent was resolved, just as long he "felt alright [because] his door was locked." Sometimes unique values were humorous or uncharacteristic of classroom discourse, such as a boy and a girl in a story solving their conflict by kissing each other.

Children's unique values sometimes contrasted dramatically from major as-sumptions in the curriculum and in teachers' interpretations of the curriculum. The curricular emphasis on peaceful resolution, which in some cases was an injunction against disagreement and fighting, emerged as somewhat controversial in the light of children's unique values, expressed as "we needed revenge" and the insistence that a person has to fight when being treated unfairly, or the mention of stereo-types. Young people's numerous physically and verbally aggressive interactions also challenge the taboo against conflict. For example, two boys were enticed to prove their physical strength to the group of girls accusing them of not knowing how to fight, or fighting like "a chicken." Gradually, children in a group all began challenging and threatening each other, with phrases such as: "I would like to smack her [a few unclear words] own sister," and "You need to be quiet 'cause you're scared of girls," and "I scared of her? I would knock her down!" Other unique value expressions were phrased as less violent threats: "You are getting on my nerves," or "Shut up," or "You're an idiot." Also, some unique points of view were developed around literary characters, such as when children excused the principal's hands off attitude because he was not aware of Raymond's behavior, when they proposed that Raymond was in love with Hoa, and when they created violent and confrontational story endings instead of resolutions with characters getting along.

Another assumption that children seemed to challenge implicitly in their peer interactions was the focus on the equality of all perspectives and thus the possibility for resolution. It is not surprising that children from family backgrounds that have experienced discrimination might question universalist explanations that "every-one is really the same and can get along." A powerful interaction by two immigrant boys, one of Arab descent and one of Western European heritage, illustrates how young people can critique mainstream society with some specific details that they do not express in the larger class discussion: "What a 'bad' country America is"; "America sucks, come on, America sucksa . . . it's not a good country, it has a lot of pollution, it does, I mean look at the manners they have"; and "the bad language they have"; and "yeah, the bad language, you can't even get used to them." This international perspective on treatment of newcomers is not only unique but also analytically complex in its detail and causal connections. Even though this, like other examples, is not stated explicitly as a critique of curriculum values, it is precise and strong, coming from nine-year-olds.

Children also uniquely raised questions around basic assumptions of school practice, such as the presumed need to embed the discussion of serious issues, like racism, in virtual contexts like sports literature. A pair of girls, one identifying as African American and the other as Latina, questioned the sense of taking away "baseball privileges" because of racism: "I don't think they're gonna beat each other up just because of baseball"; and "if they're racist, why they gonna beat each other up, 'cause of baseball?"

Analysis of conversations between two African American girls in the third grade class of a White teacher who focused on inter-personal comfort in cross-race relations, for example, shows that one girl in particular transformed and resisted teacher-expressed values. This young student recognized issues of diversity in herself, but brought in a *self*-stereotype (she wrote a lot as "an African person"). She also introduced profanity (repeated the word "bitch") and put herself in Hoa's situation, turning a scene into a violent event ("someone got killed in the nose"). She had an unusual resolution agent (lawyer), expressing knowledge of contentious and systematic aspects of social conflict. She implied physical aggression when threatening her partner (will pull her ear off), albeit in a joking way.

A similar value differing from those in the curriculum occurred when, rather than explaining that Raymond was wrong, as did his teacher, one boy stated that Raymond couldn't control himself—almost a justification for his bullying be- havior. Later, this same student placed negative consequences on Hoa (the actual victim) alone, when he suggested that she should get suspended. Whether these were positions of emergent sexism, racism, or playing devil's advocate, much of the two boys' discussion ran counter to the curriculum values.

In summary, the expression of values emerges as dynamic. In particular, chil- dren's use of the peer context to introduce values largely absent from the official space of the teacher-led discussions suggests that such negotiation can occur when classroom structure is varied. The same children who tactically seized the opportu nity of a teacher-led class discussion to chat with friends about lunchtime activities instead of listening to a story about the plight of young Black children caught in racial strife, used the peer context to introduce, strategically, novel values about issues of racism. In this peer context, a young Jamaican immigrant apparently drew on experience not elicited in the larger classroom when she passionately explained to her peer writing partner that people in their school acted in the same unwelcoming and unfair ways toward immigrant children as did the racist characters in the book. This child, moreover, wrote some conflict stories with resolutions conforming to the rules of conflict resolution promoted by the teacher and the violence prevention curriculum. In this way, a child who uses classroom contexts tactically and strategically to conform to and contest institutional values, raises questions to us about any absolute standards for conflict resolution processes and outcomes. Although the scope of this study did not allow for systematic comparison of values expressed by children across race/ethnicity groups, some of the most striking examples of strategic use of the peer context were by children identifying as African American and Latino/a.

Children's values expressions across the teacher-led and peer contexts underscore the need to conceptualize values as situated rather than absolute. The specific nature of the differences, moreover, suggests the importance, from young people's points of view, of consistently expressing values that differ from and sometimes contradict those in the curriculum. Certain curriculum values like resolving conflicts at all costs may cut short crucial deliberations that are germane to children's social develoment. Thus, rather than resisting values per se, we suggest that young people may be exerting control in their peer interactions to account for important unexamined aspects of the idealized social values in the official class discussion, such as when they express violence during an anti-violence curriculum and propose how the wronged character might be problematic or the bully misunderstood. Motivations for such strategic shifts would be the children's need to make sense of school work and their need to account for real life in contrast to the ideal life promoted in instruction, as well as, perhaps, to have a little fun. When violence prevention programs are placed in contexts where children are presumed to have experienced discrimination conflicts, it should not be surprising that they may need or want to express life experiences that the curriculum actually represses. The more socially relevant the curriculum, the more children may be positioned with no obvious option but to express contradictory values.

These observations about the intense negotiation of social values are consistent, moreover, with recent theory and research in moral psychology (Nucci, 2001). After many centuries of scholarship attempting to identify singular foundational grounds for moral decision-making (summarized in Nucci, 2001), researchers have begun to explore the context-dependent nature of judgments about human relations, welfare, and fairness (Nucci, 2001). Social developmental analyses have, thus, begun to consider the relevance of moral conventions to personal circumstances and goals, such as one's position in a social hierarchy and the salience of social mores to practicalities and interpersonal issues entailed in moral dilemmas. Accounting for moral openness in these ways Nucci (2001) offers further insight that children, who in some instances demonstrate mastery, good will, and maturity, when addressing issues of racial and ethnic discrimination, might readily shift to voice contradictory values when the discussion is personal, salient, and replete with true-to-life details lacking in a general discussion.

In summary, this analysis of youth perspectives on social conflict illustrates how children as young as seven years old negotiate social values in a violence prevention program. The patterns of conforming and unique values indicate, moreover, that social experiences contribute to establishing classroom-based knowledge and that young people use tactical opportunities from their relatively powerless positions to extend the curriculum as they challenge it. Even though young peers seem to re-construct the curriculum values more than adopt them directly, analyses from other studies in this curriculum context suggest that young people internalized some of the major messages (Daiute, Buteau, & Rawlins, 2001). Young people's values were thus, we argue, developed as an interplay between their participation in the violence prevention institution and their critical reflection based on attempts to make sense of the curriculum values in light of their own social and emotional experience. We propose that, when inviting young people to negotiate social values at their core, a curriculum could be an opportunity to develop the educational institution as well as individual children. These insights from diverse youth perspectives suggest that education can begin early to provide a forum for social discourse necessary in democratic institutions.

Policy to Open Values Negotiation

A critical approach to policy around violence prevention education would recognize that such programs are value-laden, and a major goal of each program should be to assist teachers and students in examining values rather than only conforming to them. Policy implications include, first, that open discussion about different values and the circumstances in which they apply should be an explicit and ongoing aspect of teacher training, student work, and research in violence studies. Children need to learn the legal and social rules of engagement in mainstream institutions and, indeed, how those relate and do not relate to everyday social interactions. Drawing on children's experience can, however, make the important point that those commonly-accepted values are open to examination and critique.

A second policy implication comes from our interpretation that curriculum-counter values suggest the need for a context where children can speak openly about concerns, fears, and reasoning that a curriculum designed from a mainstream perspective may suppress. Just as children can be socialized to express racist and sexist views or to express love and freedom values, they can be socialized to engage in critical reflection about social issues. We argue, thus, that an implication of this complex interplay of social values is that values *negotiation* should be part of the curriculum rather than treated as a precursor to it. Focusing on values in this way then challenges researchers and curriculum developers to examine how participants re-construct the program rather than how they re-produce it. Curricula are thus not stable entities but subject to interpretations from participants in diverse positions of power in an educational institution.

More action research is required as a basis for policy. Teams of clinicians, teachers, child advocate lawyers, parents, and children can share diverse experiences about hope in the face of racism, allowing, for example, a parent to require discussions about the limits on hope in the contemporary United States, so that her child is not made to feel responsible for the problems of society (see also Solis; Cross; and Hertz-Lazarowitz, this issue). If public schools are not sites for such conversations, then the need for alternatives is acute. A critical sociocultural model would involve all participants—including young students and their families—in expressing, examining, negotiating, and ultimately re-defining goals for social relations among persons and institutions.

References

Aber, J. L, Brown, J. L., & Henrich, C. C. (1999). *Teaching conflict resolution: An effective school-based approach to violence prevention.* (Research Brief). New York: National Center for Children and Poverty.

Cross, W. E. Jr., (1991). *Shades of Black*. Philadelphia, PA: Temple University Press.

Daiute, C. (1993). Youth genres: Links between sociocultural and developmental theories of literacy. *Language Arts* (September), 402–416.

Daiute, C. (1998). Points of view in children's writing. *Language Arts, 75*, 138–149.

Daiute, C., & Buteau, E. (2002). Writing for their lives: Children's narrative supports for physical and psychological well-being. In S. J. LePore & J. M. Smyth (Eds.), *The writing cure: How expressive writing promotes health and emotional well-being* (pp. 53–73). Washington, D.C.: American Psychological Association.

Daiute, C., Buteau, E., & Rawlins, C. (2001). Social relational wisdom: Developmental diversity in children's written narratives about social conflict. *Narrative Inquiry, 11*(2), 1–30.

Daiute, C., Campbell, C., Griffin, T., Reddy, M., & Tivnan, T. (1993). Young authors' interactions with peers and a teacher: Toward a developmentally sensitive sociocultural literacy theory. In C. Daiute (Ed.), *The development of literacy through social interaction*. San Francisco, CA: Jossey Bass, Publishers.

De Certeau, M. (1984). *The practice of everyday life*. Berkeley, CA: University of California Press.

Delpit, L. (1988). Other people's children. *Harvard Educational Review*.

Gates, H. L. (1992). *Loose canons: Notes on the culture wars*. New York: Oxford University.

Guitierrez, K., Rymes, B., & Larson, J. (1995). Script, counterscript, and underlife in the classroom: James Brown vs. *Brown v. Board of Ed. Harvard Educational Review, 65*, 445–471.

Harre, R., & Gillet, G. (1994). *The discursive mind*. Thousand Oaks, CA: Sage.

Johnson, D. W., & Johnson, R. T. (1996). Conflict resolution and peer mediation programs in elementary and secondary schools: A review of the research. *Review of Educational Research, 66*, 459–506.

Lee, C. D. (1993). *Signifying as a scaffold for literary interpretation: The pedagogical implications of an African American discourse genre*. Urbana, IL: NCTE Press.

Nucci, L. P. (2001). *Education in the moral domain*. New York: Cambridge University Press.

Olweus, D. (1994). Bullying at school: Basic facts and effects in a school-based intervention program. *Journal of Child Psychology and Psychiatry and Allied Disciplines, 35*(7), 1171–1190.

Piaget, J. (1968). *Six psychological studies*. New York: Random House.

Rogoff, B. (1990). *Apprenticeship in thinking*. New York: Oxford University Press.

Samples, F., & Aber, L. (1998). Evaluations of school-based violence prevention programs. In D. S. Elliot, B. A. Hamburg, & K. R. Williams (Eds.), *Violence in American schools* (pp. 217–252). New York: Cambridge University Press.

Selman, R. L., Watts, C. L., & Schultz, L. H. (1997). *Fostering friendship: Pair therapy for treatment and prevention*. New York: Aldine De Gruyter.

Walker, P. (1998). *Voices of love and freedom*. Logan, IA: Perfection Learning.

Walkerdine, V. (1984). Developmental psychology and the child-centered pedagogy: The insertion of Piaget into early education. In J. Henriques, W. Holloway, C. Urwin, C. Venn, & V. Walkerdine (Eds.), *Changing the subject: Psychology, social regulations, and subjectivity* (pp. 153–202). London: Routledge.

Weissberg, R. P., & Bell, D. N. (1997). A meta-analytic review of primary prevention programs for children and adolescents: Contributions and caveats. *American Journal of Community Psychology, 25*, 207–214.

Wertsch, J. (1991). *Voices in the mind*. Cambridge, MA: Harvard University Press.

COLETTE DAIUTE is Professor of Psychology at the Graduate Center of the City University of New York. A developmental psychologist focusing on children's social development, Dr. Daiute has been working for the past five years on a funded study on children's discourse and action around social conflicts in urban and suburban settings. Colette Daiute is author of *The development of literacy through social interaction* (Jossey-Bass Publishers) and *Computers and writing* (Addison-Wesley) as well as numerous articles.

REBECCA STERN is a student in the PhD program in Social/Personality Psychology at the Graduate Center of the City University of New York. She graduated from Swarthmore College with a BA in Psychology. Her major interests are in educational equity and social class identity. She is currently completing a project entitled "The Use of Personal Experience in Understanding Marxism."

CORINA LELUTIU-WEINBERGER is a PhD student in the Social/Personality Psychology program at the Graduate Center of the City University of New York. She graduated in 1999 from Hunter College, New York, with a BA degree, where she majored in psychology. Her main research interests concern: (a) ideology and discourse in post-Communist Romania, as represented in accounts given by young adults, and (b) inner-city life for youth and the functions of risk-taking. She is currently part of a large project, conducted under the supervision of Dr. Colette Daiute, regarding representations and understandings of conflict by pre-adolescents attending urban public schools.

Journal of Social Issues, Vol. 59, No. 1, 2003, pp. 103–119

Are Students Failing School or Are Schools Failing Students? Class Cutting in High School

R. Kirk Fallis and Susan Opotow*

University of Massachusetts Boston

In many urban public high schools today, students navigate their day by selectively cutting class leading to course failure and dropping out. Collaborative, qualitative research conducted with urban high school students indicates that cutting results from disengagement and alienation that students label "boredom." Focus group data (N = 160 in 8 groups) indicate that class cutting has not only an individual component that schools address, but also a systemic, conflictual component that schools do not address. These unaddressed, intransigent conflicts can foster moral exclusion and structural violence. These data suggest that rather than relying on standard punitive approaches, schools can respond to class cutting more effectively by taking students' concerns seriously, working collaboratively with students, and engaging in institutional self-scrutiny.

Class cutting (also called "skipping" or "ditching") is selective class attendance that occurs when a student comes to school, is marked present, but fails to attend particular classes without a legitimate reason. Decades ago cutting was a rare escapade for ordinarily compliant students or chronic behavior for a handful of students labeled "loafers" or "losers." Now, however, class cutting is neither rare nor characteristic only of miscreants. In many high schools today, particularly urban public schools that predominantly serve low-income students, more students navigate their school day by selectively cutting class than do not (Opotow, 1994; Opotow, Fortune, Baxter & Sanon, 1998). While it is tempting to view students who cut class as deficient in their academic capability, intelligence, motivation, or values, teachers dispute this stereotype and describe students who cut class as

---

Correspondence concerning this article should be addressed to Professor Susan Opotow, Graduate Program in Dispute Resolution, University of Massachusetts Boston, 100 Morrissey Blvd., Boston, MA 02125-3393 [e-mail: susan.opotow@umb.edu]. We thank Maurice Baxter, Pamela Hilton, Angela Khaminwa, Meenakshi Khanna, and Fredo Sanon for their vital support and insight.

intellectually and academically similar to their regularly-attending peers (Opotow, 1995a).

This paper describes the prevalence of class cutting, the way schools address it, and student perceptions of class cutting. Although class cutting seems prosaic rather than violent, our qualitative data indicate that class cutting is symptomatic of intransigent institutional conflict which, in turn, is fertile ground for *moral exclusion* (Opotow, 1990) in which some kinds of people are seen as outside the boundaries for fairness and, ultimately, for *structural violence* (Galtung, 1969) in which harm is gradual, chronic, and invisible. While class cutting has an individual component, it must also be acknowledged as an institutional issue with costly consequences for students.

Class Cutting

Students "cut" when they utilize breaks in the school day to selectively skip class. They do so to avoid classes they dislike, see as too hard or too easy, or for which they are unprepared; to avoid particular peers or teachers with whom they are engaged in conflict; to attend to personal matters; as well as for a variety of other reasons. While missing one class can be inconsequential, with even a few cuts, students lose a sense of continuity, class work becomes difficult to follow, homework becomes difficult to complete, and tests become difficult to pass. To cope, students cut test days. As grades suffer and students fail class, their academic progress slows. Students then become discouraged and drop out (Opotow, 1994; Khaminwa, Fallis, & Opotow, 1999). Overage students (16 or 17 years of age) can be discharged or transferred to an alternative program or to a high school equivalency program where low retention statistics suggest they may not graduate (Hoyle, 1993; Fine, 1991).

Class cutting is a slippery slope; once begun, the academic damage it does is difficult to reverse. In sequential courses, critical pieces of information needed to understand new material are missed, and students who return to class can face a cold welcome from overburdened teachers (Opotow, 1994, 1995a). Ultimately, short-term stress reduction gained by class cutting can lead to greater stress from academic difficulties. Rather than innocuous, cutting is the slow-motion process of dropping out made class-by-class and day-by-day in students' daily lives.

Prevalence

Although class cutting is particularly common in urban public high schools (National Center for Education Statistics, 1996), it is also problematic outside urban centers, occurs in schools throughout the world, and begins as early as fifth grade and continues into college (Lynn, 1995; Mulvany, 1989; Wyatt, 1992). Aggregate data on class cutting are scarce. Few empirical studies compare the characteristics of schools with high levels of cutting with those that have lower levels (but see Hofmann, 1991), but research suggests that students attending large urban schools have higher rates of class cutting than students in smaller schools (Bryk & Driscoll, 1988; Fine & Somerville, 1998), and that cutting has increased over the past two decades. In 1984, one-third of the students at an urban high school in the northwest United States cut at least one class a day (Duckworth & deJung, 1989), while ten years later, data from three large cities (Boston, Chicago, and New York) indicate that two-thirds of students at some schools cut at least one class a day (Boston Public Schools, 1999; Opotow, Fortune, Baxter, & Sanon, 1998; Roderick, 1997). System-wide effects of class cutting are evident in increases in within-grade retention, delayed graduation, and transfers and discharges of students (cf. New York City Board of Education, 1993, 1997; Hoyle, 1993). Thus, in many schools, particularly large, urban high schools, class cutting has become an acceptable *modus vivendi* for a substantial proportion of students and has proven itself an intransigent problem that is unresponsive to standard methods of intervention (Mulvany, 1989).

Intervention

Cutting interventions often begin with the classroom teacher who decides whether a student's absence is excused and the kind of follow-up that is indicated. If the absence is unexcused, a teacher might call home and/or notify administrators, deans, or guidance counselors. Many schools also utilize computerized flagging procedures to identify students who have accumulated a specified number of class absences over a given period. Regardless of specific procedures schools utilize to identify cutting, it is universally viewed as a disciplinary offense that triggers a variety of responses: parental notification, lowering of a course grade, failing a course, detention, suspension, and retention in grade. Staff and students report, however, that interventions designed to deter cutting—no matter how strict—are rarely effective. Some yield immediate but not sustained results; others are effective with some students but not all (Opotow, 1995a).

Although procedures for responding to cutting are often clearly specified, school staff typically respond in an *ad hoc* way, doing what feels right in the situation, and trusting their experience and intuition to guide them (Fallis, 2000). As a result, there are considerable within-school inconsistencies in meting out discipline and, given the high prevalence of cutting, punitive systems are sometimes not resorted to at all. Because cutting falls within the responsibility of teachers, counselors, deans, administrators, attendance staff, and others, each staff member can perceive others as responsible. In addition, following-up with each and every student who cuts class is virtually impossible in light of the pervasiveness of cutting. As one counselor stated: "I just do not have the time—I could not possibly call every parent when a student cuts class—besides, it is a disciplinary problem.

That is not our—it's not our job" (Fallis, 2000, p. 40). Students, aware of these limitations and inconsistencies in staff response, utilize them to cut class while avoiding detection and its consequences (Khaminwa, Fallis, & Opotow, 1999).

Surprisingly, given high proportion of students who cut class, schools do not identify cutting as a priority. Staff almost exclusively described cutting as an individual's problem and were unable to quantify cutting prevalence at their school or compare their school with others (Fallis, 2000). A staff member at one school said: "You see cutting itself is seen—it is not looked on—it is considered— ahhh—well, how can I say it?—it is almost like a pest—like a pesty thing. It is not considered that serious until there are other factors involved" (Fallis, 2000, p. 3). A staff member at another school said: "But it is funny you talk about cutting, because cutting—we have so many other serious issues. Cutting is kind of overlooked" (Fallis, 2000, p. 41). Not only can cutting be overlooked in schools, but responses to cutting tend to overlook students' understanding of class cutting. This paper focuses on students' perspectives and concerns to understand them and suggest their importance for practice.

Student Perspectives on Class Cutting

Methods

We studied class cutting in two cities in northeastern United States. Our primary research site in each city was a large urban public school (S1 = 3000 students; S2 = 1000 students). In each school, more than half the students were free-lunch eligible indicating low family incomes. Both schools had high dropout rates (22–42%), and although each school had considerable religious, ethnic, and national diversity, students were predominantly Black and Latino (94–98%).

In this paper, we report on data collected and analyzed collaboratively with two student researchers from S2 over a four-year period. In the first year the student researchers analyzed 10 interviews collected at S1. In the years that followed, student researchers collected qualitative data in focus groups (160 students in 8 groups) in which students described their perspectives on and reasons for class cutting. In this context, focus groups offer a number of benefits: they foster a collaborative atmosphere, students' comments create positive feedback loops, and students push themselves toward a deeper understanding of the issues at hand. This "spiraling effect" (Kahan, 2001) of focus groups is appropriately reported as products of the group rather than as comments attributed to particular individuals as would be the case for more individually-focused methods such as interviews.

Participants for focus groups were recruited by teachers in their schools and participation was voluntary. Student participants attended public high schools throughout the city, ranged from freshmen to seniors, and were members of ethnic and racial minority groups mirroring the demographics of cooperating schools. Student participants were told that our research examined students' views on class cutting. Following focus group sessions, student researchers worked collaboratively with university-based researchers to identity themes that emerged in focus group data. In reporting our findings we distinguish comments by student researchers Fredo Sanon and Maurice Baxter that emerged in post–focus group analytic discussions ("student researchers") from comments made by student participants in the focus groups ("students").

"Layered" collaborative research. Qualitative data analysis, the most labor-intensive of our research activities, evolved as taped discussions of puzzling or revealing statements in focus group transcripts. Because our topic garnered the interest of educators struggling with class cutting, we were periodically asked to present our research findings. Such dissemination efforts became part of our research process. In preparing for dissemination opportunities at conferences, for school committees, and in graduate education courses, the research process came alive. These dissemination opportunities challenged student researchers to become conceptually clear about their work. They prompted urgent, focused discussions (which were audio-taped) in which student researchers specified what they learned from their data and why it was important.

We describe this collaborative and cyclical research process as *layered* because each research activity—collecting, analyzing, and presenting research findings— led to new questions, additional data collection, analysis, presentations, and so on. Layering enabled the student researchers to acquire research and speaking skills while maintaining their interest during the slow process of qualitative analysis. Revisiting their data and findings, students' analyses became increasingly complex as they became aware of diverse perspectives and were able to identify contradictions in their own thinking around complex individual-institutional issues. Student researchers spoke with increasing clarity of what it meant to be a student in a large urban public school. Asked, "What was the research like?" Fredo Sanon said:

> It's like what we've been talking about. We were always talking about how cutting class did this or that. But when we started doing the surveys and the presentations we found out how and why. And it was real. It was there. Instead of us listening to what students in the transcripts were feeling, we got to feel it. I guess the research has helped us to come to understand a reality. It makes you understand that it is not just you—that there are other things going on.

Student-centered research. The student-centered research approach we utilized is more time consuming than qualitative analytic methods that center on the skills and knowledge of a social scientist. However, student researchers' knowledge proved to be a valuable resource. They were able to connect the research to the daily realities of urban students and their analyses yielded insight into subtle contextual issues that would have otherwise remained hidden in the data. Instead of viewing high school students as subjects, we worked alongside them. This approach is a paradigm shift that is consistent with a research methodology advocated by Kurt Lewin (1948): "we should consider action, research, and training as a triangle that should be kept together" (p. 211). Thus, to understand complex organizational life in schools, our research became a process "in which knowledge-getting and knowledge-giving are an integrated process, and one that is valuable to all parties involved" (Friedlander and Brown, 1974, p. 319; also see Cooperrider and Srivastva, 2000). Fredo Sanon described his engagement in the repetitive process of conducting research: "You got to learn a lot of things. We talked about some interesting topics. We really got into discussions and broke down why kids cut class. We were really committed. We wanted to know why." Students' commitment to knowing why provided us with the opportunity to understand class cutting as symptomatic of structural violence that claims so many students while remaining ineffectively addressed by urban public high schools.

Findings: Class Cutting and Boredom

In focus groups, students described class cutting as a reaction to educational structures that are sterile, bureaucratic, disrespectful of student's pedagogical preferences or goals, and that do not value student contributions. They also identified student, teacher, and staff burnout and the labeling of students as losers as additional causes of cutting (Sanon, Baxter, Fortune, & Opotow, 2001). A short-cut students use to label these alienating aspects of school is "boring."

Although the *Oxford English Dictionary* (1989) defines "boring" as tedious, wearying, and dull, it was only after talking with student researchers about boring for more than a year that we realized students use "boring" to mean this and more. For students, boring connotes a one-way, tops-down, unengaged relationship with a teacher whose pedagogy feels disrespectful because it is not designed to tempt, engage, or include students. In addition, for students, boring connotes something missing in their education, conveys a deep sense of disappointment, and casts class cutting as a coping mechanism for classes that fail to engage. Fredo Sanon said:

> Boredom is one person doing most of the talking. You are not doing anything. A lot of kids that we talked to said that the teacher makes it boring. Because if you know you are not getting good grades in that class and you know there is a chance you might fail then you're going to get bored because you don't want to do that work. I'm not going to do the work if I am going to fail anyway.

A student described classes as boring if they would not help her be productive now or in the future:

> Well, for me, it's like the learning. There's only like a few classes I actually care about. Everything else is, like, pointless, because I'll never use it in my life . . . If my teacher's not

teaching me anything, then I'm gonna go to work. I'm not gonna sit here and waste my time and twiddle my thumbs when I could be doing something more productive.

Boredom and school. In addition to seeing boredom at the individual level as the failure to meet an individual's pedagogical preferences or aspirations, students see boredom also at the institutional level, as the way things are done in schools, such as high staff turnover or excessive teacher absence:

> I do not go to that class. I cut that class everyday because it's like—okay the teacher's not there and we're just gonna sit here and watch TV and read the newspaper. I can do that at home . . . [or] if your teacher's not concerned about learning, you're not learning anything in that class, it's like a waste of your time. Why are you going to be there?

Students also see cutting as a coping response to lock-step pedagogy that does not work for everyone. Students see themselves as distinct and having their own motivators and skills. For some students, grades and doing homework are motivating; others care less about school or are more easily discouraged. One student said: "If the class is boring, I'm going to try only to a certain extent. If the class is real boring, I'm just going to say 'Forget it. Just give me the homework.'"

Students also noted that boredom in some classes resulted from the teacher's tendency to focus on a struggling student and ignore those who hunger for more: "They will cater to the people who don't learn, eh, who won't learn. They won't cater to everybody else." Another student said she cut because "every single day we're learning the same thing." She described her frustration with the painfully slow pace as a dialogue with her teacher: "Why can't you teach me something else?" "Because, oh, that other kid didn't learn it." "There's 35 kids in the room and one kid didn't learn anything; and you make us stay there and watch this kid learn?"

In addition to boredom resulting from a curriculum that does not challenge or interest students, students who want to engage can be further challenged by peers who have become disengaged, fallen behind, and become disruptive. Student researcher Maurice Baxter said: "It's not all the teachers' fault. Some students just act up so bad that the teachers after awhile just don't even care. The students who do want to learn, they just miss out on that." Fredo Sanon described boredom and disengagement as elicited and shaped by institutional culture:

> That's learned behavior. That's something that, you know what I'm saying, is instilled in you. . . . Kids who used to care are gonna stop caring because, it's like—"Well, I'm in this environment and nobody else cares, so . . . What am I gonna do?" You adapt to the environment. And if your teachers are just like, "forget it," you're like, "forget it" too. "I don't want to be here. I'm leaving."

Boredom and resources. At the societal level, students were keenly aware that pedagogical resources differed between schools and school systems. Comparing her school with an elite public high school, one student said: "That's another reason why people cut. 'Cause we don't have any, you know what I'm saying, anything—no reason to keep us here." She described attending a school that lacks resources not only as boring but also as a trap:

> You know, it's like going to the job where you work and you hate your job. Every chance you get to leave that job, you will leave. And there's nothing that we can do.... The difference between us going to school and having a job is you can quit the job and find another job. This school—we cannot go anywhere else. The only other school that offers things like that in [city] is [school]. And if you didn't get in in the seventh grade, then you know what I'm saying, all hope is lost for you unless you go to private school. But if your parents can't afford private school... then you get stuck going to a school like this and you're just not learning.

Another student commented that his school, unlike suburban public schools, does not offer course selection that he might need or enjoy, such as courses on specific aspects of literature, language choices in addition to Spanish, and advanced placement. One student, comparing what he sees in the media with his own educational reality, stated:

> You see TV and, like, do these schools really exist? Because we don't have them here. It's like—it's not like a real high school. We don't even have pep-rallies. We don't have homecoming. We don't have an honor society. They don't have anything in this school.

The lack of elective choices, extra-curricular activities results in school environments that students see as sterile, uninviting, and boring.

Discussion: Class Cutting as Conflict, Exclusion, and Violence

In these data, when students state that teachers, counselors, or administrators "don't care" and that students cut class because they prefer to "do something more productive," they appear to be fobbing off blame for cutting on others. Rather than taken as a serious institutional critique, students' explanations about class cutting can be dismissed as self-serving, one-sided, shortsighted, and immature (cf. Roman, 1996). Yet, our analyses suggest that students' reasons for class cutting are thoughtful. In contrast to school personnel who to tend to blame students and individualize the problem, students express a complex view that locates responsibility for class cutting in both individual behavior and its wider institutional context. Students described what they wanted and felt they deserved—caring and knowledgeable teachers they can count on to be there, a safe and individually-attuned learning environment, and resources that entice them. But they noted also that students have responsibilities. Reflecting on these data, Maurice Baxter said "kids have to motivate themselves instead of putting all the blame on teachers. It is a fifty-fifty thing from where I stand." Yet in spite of students' ability to articulate concerns connected with class cutting, their perceptions largely ignored at the institutional and system level in interventions design to deter cutting. This failure to take students' views seriously suggests that class cutting is behavior emerging from unaddressed intransigent conflicts, which have led to moral exclusion and structural violence.

Intransigent Conflict

Students describe class cutting as emerging in the context of conflicts, many of which concern institutional issues. Conflicts "exist whenever incompatible activities occur . . . An action that is incompatible with another action prevents, obstructs, interferes, injures, or in some way makes the latter less likely or less effective" (Deutsch, 1973, p. 10). School staff describe class cutting as occasionally leading to conflict involving students, parents, and the school, yet they also dismiss cutting as a "pesty thing" (Fallis, 2000, p. 3). In class cutting some conflicts were overt but many remained latent and unaddressed.

Dropping out among minority youth has been connected to latent conflict also (cf. MacLeod, 1995). Michael Apple (1996) describes, "student rejection of so much of the content and form of day to day educational life bears on the almost unconscious realization that . . . schooling will not enable them to go much further than they already are" (p. 99; also see Bourdieu and Passeron, 1990; Gison & Ogbu, 1991). Edwin Farrell (1990) describes student dozing as latent conflict, echoing students' descriptions of cutting as disengagement:

> One major manifestation of resistance, in behavioral terms, is dozing. Putting your head down on the desk is a visual signal. It is difficult to believe, because of the numbers who do it, that it can be attributed to depression or fatigue. The fact that my [student researcher] used it to define boredom to me implies that the behavior has a shared meaning for this population. It is socially constructed just as boredom is. And because it is passive resistance, there is often teacher compliance. (p. 23)

As we have discussed, class cutting has proven robust as an institutional problem. Intransigent conflicts that resist standard solutions are often characterized by misdiagnoses that miss deeper issues such as the basic need for consistency, security, respect, justice, and a sense of personal control (Burton, 1990; Fisher, 1997). Because what is at stake remains unaddressed, the conflicts persist and fluctuate in intensity. When interventions are ill-conceived or are not anchored within an empirical and theoretical foundation that can show the logical sequence of steps from identifying the conflict to achieving its resolution, they can increase frustration, deepen conflict, and lead to destructive outcomes (Rothman, 1997; Rouhana, 1995). In the long run, avoiding, renaming, and denying conflict rather than addressing it is rarely effective; often it leads to higher overall costs to institutions and individuals (Costantino & Merchant, 1996).

When school staff approach class cutting at the behavioral, manifest level or in an *ad hoc*, freewheeling way that overlooks or oversimplifies deeper, unaddressed issues, they may not only fail to stem class cutting, but can also exacerbate negative conflict dynamics and even cause harm. In the context of class cutting, focusing on individuals is not an inherently problematic approach; it can be warranted and helpful. However, focusing exclusively on individuals biases the intervention by protecting interests of the organization and those with institutional power while excluding the perspective of those with low power (Rouhana & Korper, 1996). Describing cutting at the individual level as a "discipline issue" means that institutional self-scrutiny is not warranted because institutional responsibility is not implicated.

Within institutions, admitting responsibility for harmful outcomes can be difficult because it threatens the core identity of school professionals who see their personal and institutional goals as promoting student well-being (Hicks, 1999; see also Janeway, 1980; Pratto & Walker, 2001). Therefore, conventional approaches to class cutting that locate blame exclusively in students protect the institution and its staff from scrutiny. Students, lacking voices and institutional influence, are the perfect repository for blame. Thus, for school staff it may not be enough to want to do *good*. It may even not be enough to have success at interventions on the level of individual symptoms. At the very minimum, school staff need to look more closely at structural contexts that give rise to the intransigent conflicts that foster cutting. Conflicts, when recognized and addressed, can promote constructive change, but conflicts can also be destructive. Destructive conflicts are those that foster moral exclusion and rationalize harms that others experience.

Moral Exclusion

Moral exclusion is viewing some kinds of people as outside one's boundary for fairness or "scope of justice" (Deutsch, 1974) so that considerations of fairness do not apply to them, they are not seen as worthy of effort or sacrifice, and they are not seen as entitled to community resources (Opotow, 1987, 1990, 1995b). Harm experienced by those who are morally excluded does not elicit remorse or a sense of injustice. Instead it is rationalized, normalized, and viewed as the way things are or ought to be. Thus, moral exclusion is a theory that describes how negative social categorizations give rise to moral justifications and allow those outside the scope of justice to be harmed. In its severe form moral exclusion justifies human rights violations and mass murder. In its mild form moral exclusion justifies disparate access to opportunity and resources. Whether mild or severe, moral exclusion fosters viewing those outside the scope of justice as psychologically distant, unworthy of constructive obligations, expendable, undeserving, and eligible for processes and outcomes that would be unacceptable for those within our scope of justice (Opotow, 2001).

In class cutting we see subtle forms of moral exclusion when students who cut class are depicted as deserving harsh outcomes. When students are caught cutting class, admonished, and persist, their fate—including failure, transfer, expulsion, and long-term negative outcomes—can be seen as the student's own doing. A school staff member, recognizing the systemic problems faced by his largely

African American student body, nonetheless said of students who "fall by the way-side" as the result of cutting: "Schools can not be everything to all kids. And they try to be—I think you have to have the, pardon my French, the *balls* to do what you tell them you're going to do. So if you cut you will get suspended" (Fallis, 2000, p. 48). Moral exclusion was also evident in the tendency of staff members to talk about students who cut class negatively and to frame students simplistically as "good" or "bad." One teacher said, "You as the class room teacher know in the first week or second week of class who is going to be good or who is going to be bad and who is going to pass" (Fallis, 2000, p. 54). This kind of thinking was also generalized from individuals to the student body as a whole. In explaining the make-up of his school, a staff member, sensitive to the institutional challenges his students faced, nevertheless disparaged them, saying: "I know what my particular situation is, we have, we're not getting the best at my school. Neither the best nor the brightest." At another school, too, a staff member stated "crack babies or the drug addicted babies—these are the kids that are at my school now" (Fallis, 2000, p. 55).

Students are painfully aware that they are struggling against these negative categorizations and they intrude on their interactions with school staff. One student said,

> A lot of teachers do make it seem like they do not like you. I mean they may not want it to come out that way, but a lot of teachers do make it seem like "I don't like you. You don't have to come to my class"—I mean they don't say it to you but the way they talk to you, you can see it. The way a teacher talks to one kid and then the way he talks to you. I have one teacher who will talk to one student with a soft tone, and then he talks to me he feels that he must bring some force deep inside of his voice, to make him sound all tough. I will think in my head, "Why are you putting this front up? Why are you acting this way...?"

Another student expressed skepticism about his institutions' interest in addressing class cutting constructively: "Nah, they would be like, oh you know, 'stupid kids' or 'they don't want to learn'—[or the administration] will go like, 'oh, just a bunch of Black kids. They don't want to learn nothing.' "

Several students who had discussed class cutting with peers reflected on the marginality and invisibility of students who cut class:

> S1: We went around asking questions, because there were a lot of kids just hanging out. Hanging out in the hall. Literally hanging out. They were, I think, it was like on the 3rd floor especially.
> S2: [We] knew where the hiding places were.
> S1: The smoking places and the makeup places.
> S3: They were like cockroaches; they did not care if anybody passed by.
> S1: If someone told them to move, they would just move to another area.
> S3: Even the teachers would not pay attention to them anymore.
> S2: Because they knew they were just going to go someplace else and it was just a waste of time.
> S1: And the teachers just didn't care.
> S3: Then they thought our interviewing them was just a joke, they were making fun, they were laughing, saying stupid comments—"Because we feel like it"; "Because the teacher does not give them work"—Which was a lie.

Not only were the students situated so that they were physically invisible to school staff, but they also internalized their invisibility. In hiding and joking, they concealed their desire for engagement in their schooling.

Framing class cutting with moral exclusion helps us understand how schools—trusted social institutions—can become locations of systemic violence in which a large proportion of students can be viewed as deserving invisibility, failure, and expulsion without eliciting a sense of injustice. Students are first seen as behaviorally, then as cognitively, and finally as morally deficient and therefore outside the scope of justice and, ultimately, the cause of their own debilitation. Moral exclusion, which flourishes in overt and latent conflict, can itself foster structural violence.

Structural Violence

The mismatch between the high prevalence and long-term costs of cutting for student and the ineffective, diffuse, and individually-focused responses of schools suggests that structural violence is a useful lens to understand class cutting. In contrast to direct violence which is committed by and on particular people, structural violence is gradual, chronic harm that occurs because of the way things are done, whose voice is heard or ignored, and who gets resources or goes without (Galtung, 1969). Structural violence debases people by treating them as irrelevant, but is difficult to isolate and examine. It remains invisible because responsibility for outcomes is diffused or denied by the way that institutions structure process and outcomes.

In class cutting, we see that injurious short- and long-term outcomes that accrue to students: (a) are not inflicted by any particular person; (b) are small, cumulative, hidden and institutionalized as the way cutting is and is not addressed; (c) occur for a substantial numbers of students who attend large public high schools in low-income urban communities; (d) are viewed as result of ill-considered student behavior rather than institutional process. We also see that: (e) issues and complaints by students are dismissed as groundless griping; and (f) in spite of the prevalence of class cutting and its injurious effect on students, responses are ineffective, maintain an individual focus, and blame the victim.

Conclusions

Implications for Moral Exclusion Theory

Our analysis suggests that moral exclusion is the alchemy that transforms intransigent, unaddressed conflict into structural violence. It does so by facilitating a critical figure-ground shift that situates responsibility for negative outcomes in victims rather than in those with institutional resources and power. In class cutting this shift is evident when the outcomes of unnamed and unaddressed conflicts fall more heavily on those who are relatively powerless in an institutional/political hierarchy. The full weight of dysfunctional institutional systems is then borne by the strata least able to influence those systems or even give voice to their negative impacts.

Our analysis of class cutting also reveals that violence results from both exclusion *and* inclusion. Violence can result from processes that exclude students from school justified by class cutting. While acknowledging that students are minors, young, and making shortsighted, counter-productive decisions, standard school interventions nevertheless treat students as competent, warranting such institutional consequences as transfer and expulsion. Violence also occurs as a consequence of *inclusion* of students in an institutional context in which they have no choice, in which they are exposed to forces over which they have no control, and as a result, have little chance of gaining what they want and need on their own terms. Thus, in schools that students find alienating and insensitive to their needs and goals, they have two choices. They can endure a dysfunctional system, succumb to systemic pressures, and suffer institutional systems that may psychologically debase. Or, as an alternative, they can take actions which may grant relief in the short term, such as cutting or dropping out, but suffer such long term consequences as decreased educational attainment and career opportunities. While either of these negative options are occurring, the complicity of the organization and its institutional processes that debase—clearly part of students' problems with schooling that leads to cutting—eludes scrutiny.

Implications for School Policy

Class cutting is an intransigent problem and capable of defying standard school interventions. In class cutting, we see structural violence flourishing when schools seek to preserve their sense of efficacy and worthiness by situating their problem in low-power individuals. Although small schools have the potential to positively transform educational environments (cf. Fine & Somerville, 1998), they are not the daily reality of most urban high school students. It is not the size of small schools that yields benefits to students, *per se*, but the opportunities they can offer students for engagement.

Our data and analysis suggest that, rather than getting tough and investing time and money in punitive interventions and security systems, school can approach class cutting with a stronger knowledge base by fostering student voice and engagement. When viewed as student critique and feedback, class cutting can be an opportunity to elicit student input to better understand students' experiences, perspectives, and hopes; to engage students as active members of the school community; and to utilize students' class attending choices to guide institutional change. Schools would benefit from student guidance in the design of institutional

interventions. As these data indicate, when students lack the opportunity to participate, offer their perspective, and have it acted upon, they may find themselves faced
with institutional conditions they find untenable. When schools fail to engage students in constructive forms of conflict resolution they miss an opportunity to teach
students appropriate and useful methods for dealing with conflict in institutional
life.

In contrast, when young people are provided with opportunities to expand their
conflict coping repertoires and negotiation skills, they will be able to deal with
life circumstances in ways that facilitate their physical and psychological health
and well-being rather than being debilitated by circumstances (Frydenberg, 1997).
Designing school processes and structures is an opportunity to elicit students' participation, encourage students to air their feelings and describe their experiences,
and for students to understand that they have been heard and have something to
contribute. This will not only help them learn how to express themselves effectively
but it will also give them opportunities to relate to the school staff in creative and
constructive ways. Inclusion, however, needs to be significant, and neither illusory
nor superficial. Students understand when they have real, transformative voice or
only expressive voice and the appearance of participation (cf. Sampson, 1993).

The collaborative, long-term research method that emerged in our efforts
to understand class cutting models the approach we suggest schools take. Maurice Baxter captures the way that the tedium and effort of research—similar to
schoolwork—can promote engagement, discovery, learning, conceptual integration, connection, respect, and personal growth:

> We were doing the same thing over and over. But in some way it always changed and
> we ended up somewhere different. Every time we talked we came up with some more
> elaboration or more detail. Every time we came in we had something different. We did get
> a lot out of the research: the patience, the reviewing things, just learning things, working
> with people, accepting other people's views, respecting their views, and trying to get one
> bigger or better view—trying to pull it all together.

References

Apple, M. W. (1996). *Cultural politics and education*. New York: Teachers College Press.
Boston Public Schools. (1999). *Boston Public Schools, Year Report 1999*. Boston: Boston Public School
    Committee.
Bourdieu, P., & Passeron, J. C. (1990). *Reproduction in education, society, and culture*. London: Sage
    Press.
Bryk, A., & Driscoll, M. (1988). *The high school as community: Contextual influences and con-
    sequences for students and teachers*. Madison, WI: National Center on Effective Secondary
    Schools.
Burton, J. (1990). *Conflict: Resolution and prevention*. New York: St. Martin's Press.
Cooperrider, D. L., & Srivastva, S. (2000). Appreciative inquiry in organizational life. In D. L. Coop-
    errider, P. F. Sorenson, Jr., D. Whitney, & T. F. Yaeger (Eds.), *Appreciative inquiry: Rethinking
    human organization toward a positive theory of change* (pp. 55–97). Champaign, IL: Stipes
    Publishing.

Costantino, C. A., & Merchant, C. S. (1996). *Designing conflict management systems*. San Francisco, CA: Jossey-Bass.

Deutsch, M. (1973). *The resolution of conflict*. New Haven, CT: Yale University Press.

Deutsch, M. (1974). Awakening the sense of injustice. In M. Lerner & M. Ross (Eds.), *The quest for justice: Myth, reality, ideal*. Canada: Holt, Rinehart, & Winston.

Duckworth, K., & deJung, J. (1989). Inhibiting class cutting among high school students. *High School Journal, 72*(4), 188–195.

Fallis, R. K. (2000). *An analysis of social influence in class cutting: Student-counselor negotiations*. Master's project, University of Massachusetts Boston, Boston, MA.

Farrell, E. (1990). *Hanging in and dropping-out: Voices of at risk high school students*. New York: Teachers College Press.

Fine, M. (1991). *Framing dropouts: Notes on the politics of an urban high school*. Albany: SUNY Press.

Fine, M., & Somerville, J. (1998). *Small schools big imagination: A creative look at urban public schools*. Chicago: Cross City Campaign for Urban School Reform.

Fisher, R. J. (1997). *Interactive conflict resolution*. Syracuse, NY: Syracuse University Press.

Friedlander, F., & Brown, L. (1974). Organization development. *Annual Review of Psychology, 25*, 313–341.

Frydenberg, E. (1997). *Adolescent coping: Theoretical and research perspectives*. London: Routledge.

Galtung, J. (1969). Violence, peace and peace research. *Journal of Peace Research, 3*, 167–191.

Gison, M. A., & Ogbu, J. U. (1991). *Minority status and schooling*. New York: Garland.

Hicks, D. (1999, June 22). *How functional aspects of identity become dysfunctional in protracted conflict*. Unpublished paper presented at the 12th annual conference of the International Association for Conflict Management, San Sebastian-Donostia, Spain.

Hofmann, W. P. (1991). The effects of computerized attendance systems on teacher attendance withitness and student attendance. (Doctoral Dissertation, University of Miami, Florida, 1991). *Dissertation Abstracts International*, # AAT 9214822.

Hoyle, J. R. (1993). Our children: Dropouts, pushouts, and burnouts. *People and Education, 1*(1) 26–41.

Janeway, E. (1980). *Powers of the weak*. New York: Knopf.

Kahan, P. (2001). Focus groups as a tool for policy analysis. *Analyses of Social Issues and Public Policy, 1*(1), 129–146.

Khaminwa, A., Fallis, R. K., & Opotow, S. (1999). Cutting in high schools. *Australian Journal of Guidance Counselling, 9*(1), 193–204.

Kipnis, D. (1976). *The powerholders*. Chicago: University of Chicago Press.

Lewin, K. (1948). Action research and minority problems. In G. W. Lewin (Ed.), *Resolving social conflicts*. New York: Harper and Row.

Lynn, P. (1995). *The 1993 Leavers: The Scottish School Leavers' survey*. Edinburgh: Scottish Office Education Department.

MacLeod, J. (1995). *Ain't no makin' it: Aspirations and attainment in a low income neighborhood*. San Francisco, CA: Westview Press.

Mulvany, J. (1989). Social control processes, activities and ideologies: The case of non-attendance in Melbourne. *Australian and New Zealand Journal of Sociology, 25*(2), 222–238.

National Center for Education Statistics (NCES). (1996). *NELS:88, National longitudinal study: 1988–1994; Data files and electronic codebook system. Third follow-up*. Washington, DC: U.S. Department of Education.

New York City Board of Education. (1993). *The cohort report: Four-year results for the class of 1992 and follow-ups for the classes of 1989, 1990, and 1991 and the 1991–1992 annual dropout rate*. New York: Division of Planning, Research, and Development, Board of Education of the City of New York.

New York City Board of Education. (1997). *The class of 1997: Four year longitudinal report and 1996–1997 event dropout rates*. New York: Division of Assessment and Accountability, Board of Education of the City of New York.

Opotow, S. (1987). Limits of fairness: An experimental examination of antecedents of the scope of justice. (Doctoral dissertation, Columbia University, 1987). *Dissertation Abstracts International*, DAI-B 48/08.

Opotow, S. (1990). Moral exclusion and injustice: An introduction. *Journal of Social Issues, 46*(1), 1–20.

Opotow, S. (1994, August). *"Breaking out": Class cutting in an inner-city high school.* Paper presented at the annual meeting of the American Psychological Association, Los Angeles, CA.

Opotow, S. (1995a, August). *The "cutting" epidemic: How high school teachers respond and adapt.* Paper presented at the annual meeting of the American Psychological Association, New York.

Opotow, S. (1995b). Drawing the line: Social categorization and moral exclusion. In J. Z. Rubin & B. B. Bunker (Eds.), *Conflict, cooperation, and justice* (pp. 347–369). San Francisco, CA: Jossey-Bass.

Opotow, S. (2001). Social injustice. In D. J. Christie, R. V. Wagner, & D. D. Winter (Eds.), *Peace, conflict, and violence: Peace psychology for the 21st century* (pp. 102–109). Upper Saddle River, NJ: Prentice Hall.

Opotow, S., Fortune, L., Baxter, M., & Sanon, F. (1998, June). *Conflict, coping, and class cutting: Perspectives of urban high school students.* Paper presented at the biannual meeting of the Society for the Psychological Study of Social Issues, Ann Arbor, MI.

Pratto, F., & Walker, A. (2001). Dominance in disguise. In A. Y. Lee-Chai & J. A. Bargh (Eds.), *The use and abuse of power: Multiple perspectives on the causes of corruption.* Philadelphia, PA: Psychology Press.

Roderick, M. (1997, July). *Habits hard to break: A new look at truancy in Chicago's public high schools.* Chicago: Consortium on Chicago School Research.

Roman, L. G. (1996). Spectacle in the dark: Youth as transgression, display, and repression. *Educational Theory, 46*(1), 1–22.

Rothman, J. (1997). *Resolving identity-based conflict in nations, organizations, and communities.* San Francisco, CA: Jossey Bass.

Rouhana, N. N. (1995). Unofficial third-party intervention in international conflict: Between legitimacy and disarray. *Negotiation Journal, 11*(3), 255–271.

Rouhana, N. N., & Korper, S. K. (1996). Dealing with dilemmas posed by power asymmetry in intergroup conflict. *Negotiation Journal, 12*(4), 353–366.

Sampson, E. E. (1993). Identity politics: Challenges to psychology's understanding. *American Psychologist, 48*(12), 1219–1230.

Sanon, F., Baxter, M., Fortune, L., & Opotow, S. (2001). Class cutting: Perspectives of urban high school students. In J. Shultz & A. Cook-Sather (Eds.), *Student voices: Middle and high school students' perspectives on school and schooling.* Lanham, MD: Rowman & Littlefield.

Simpson, J. A., & Weiner, E. S. C. (Eds.). (1989). *Oxford English dictionary* (2nd ed.). Oxford, UK: Oxford University.

Wyatt, G. (1992). Skipping class: An analysis of absenteeism among first year college students. *Teaching Sociology, 20*(3), 201–207.

KIRK FALLIS is a graduate student in the International Studies Program at the Golden Gate University School of Law. He has practiced law in Toronto, Canada, where he was called to the bar in 1992. He holds a certificate from the Canadian International Institute of Negotiation. He completed the master's degree in the Graduate Program in Dispute Resolution at the University of Massachusetts Boston, has participated in the Program for the Instruction of Lawyers at Harvard, the Program on Negotiation at Radcliffe College, and has served as a mediator in community programs in Toronto, Ontario, and in Boston. His research focuses on power asymmetries and implicit negotiations in organizational conflicts.

SUSAN OPOTOW is an associate professor in the Graduate Programs in Dispute Resolution at the University of Massachusetts Boston. She received her PhD from Columbia University in social and organizational psychology. Her research examines social psychological conditions justifying moral exclusion to understand the conditions that allow us to see others as outside the scope of justice and as eligible for exploitation and harm. Her work describes the implications of moral exclusion in schooling, environmental conflict, and public policy debates over fairness, such as affirmative action. She is associate editor of *Peace and Conflict: Journal of Peace Psychology*, and was issue editor for two issues of *Journal of Social Issues*, one on "Moral Exclusion and Injustice" (1990) and the other on "Green Justice: Conceptions of Fairness and the Natural World" (1994, with Susan Clayton). She edited, also, an issue of *Social Justice Research* on "Affirmative Action and Social Justice" (1992).

Journal of Social Issues, Vol. 59, No. 1, 2003, pp. 121–140

Black Youth Violence Has a Bad Rap

Jabari Mahiri* **and Erin Conner**

University of California at Berkeley

This research elicited and assessed the perspectives on violence of 41 middle-school students attending a unique school in a low-income section of a large northern California city. Through participation in and observation of instruction and other school-related activities, the researchers explored ways that these students experienced and reflected on violence in their lives and in popular culture. The researchers probed ways that these students' interpreted or reflected upon rap music and hip-hop culture, particularly its representations of violence, crime, and sex. This research provided insights into what these youth thought about violence in their lives including its depictions in electronic media. Additionally, it revealed ways that they resisted and/or critiqued some negative images and influences of hip-hop and rap.

In recent public discourse and media, youth, generally, and youth of color, particularly, have been increasingly represented as "dangerous others." In developing this idea, Conquergood (1992) noted that urban youth are inscribed by stigmatizing images of social pathology in the official discourse of the media and the legal system as well as in social welfare and public policy institutions (p. 3). Thus, he argued, other social forces and institutions are absolved of responsibility. Chomsky (1995) connected ways that people who are perceived as "dangerous others" are ultimately turned into scapegoats in society. He noted that, "The building up of scapegoats and fear is standard . . . . You don't want people to look at the actual source of power; that's much too dangerous, so, therefore, you need to have them blame or be frightened of someone else" (p. 134).

The image of youth, especially urban Black youth, as prone to violence and crime continues to persist with frequent references to negative influences of popular culture, often rap music and hip-hop culture, as partial evidence of "the

---

*Correspondence concerning this article should be addressed to Jabari Mahiri, University of California, School of Education, Berkeley, CA 94720 [e-mail: jmahiri@socrates.berkeley.edu].

problem" (Dyson, 1996; Koza, 1994; Mahiri, 1997; McLaren, 2000; Rose, 1994). This "evidence" is highly visible in electronic media despite the fact that commercialized hip-hop is not representative of the entire genre. Voices and perspectives that mainly are not heard in the discourse on violence and urban youth are those of young people themselves. Two key foci of our research were first to capture and represent perspectives of Black urban youth on violence in their lives, and second to explore their perspectives on and possible influences from hip-hop and rap with respect to violence. The central question for our research was what do the perceptions and reflections of these youth on violence in their lives offer to our understandings of the nature of Black violence, particularly in the context of ways that it is represented in the larger society?

This research utilized a number of strategies to elicit and assess perspectives of Black youth on violence. The youth were all students in a rather unique, charter middle school that operates in a low-income area of a large northern California city. The collection of data and artifacts focused on two classes in the school—the combined language arts/social studies class and the academic literacy class. In the first class, data collection centered on a curriculum unit on the book *Our America: Life and death on the South Side of Chicago* (Jones & Newman, 1997) written by two teenagers. Because of the nature and focus of this book and the kinds of learning activities and projects that were developed around it, this unit was extremely valuable for generating a variety of data and artifacts from the students with regard to their understandings and experiences with violence. Six students selected to represent higher, middle, and lower achievement levels in the class were formally interviewed to get additional insights into ways they linked considerations of violence in the curriculum unit to considerations of violence in their daily lives. In the second class, data collection centered on a unit developed around rap and hip-hop. This unit yielded a variety of data and artifacts on the students' perceptions and engagements with this music and culture with respect to issues of violence, crime, and sex. Student group dialogues as well as informal, conversational interviews with individual students were used in the second class to get additional insight into these students' engagements with and perceptions of hip-hop and rap.

Black Youth, Violence, and Rap

Influences of rap music and hip-hop culture on youth are pervasive. These influences are not only on Black urban youth, but affect many diverse youth groups nationally and globally. A number of researchers have heeded Baker's earlier call in *Black studies, rap, and the academy* (1993) to give rap more serious, scholarly study. For example, papers presented at the Modern Language Association Conference in 2000 with titles like "Global hip-hop youth culture," "The cultural politics of Afro-German hip-hop," and "Brazilian New Wave: Hip-Hop and the politics of intervention" reflect some of the new scholarship on hip-hop and rap while also reflecting their increasingly global natures.

Recent scholarship on rap also reveals many of its problematic aspects in local, national, and international contexts usually focused on its most acrimonious strain—gangsta rap. The core narratives of gangsta rap are extremely troubling in their glamorization of violence, material consumption, misogyny, and sexual transgression. Yet, as Dyson (1996) argued, the vulgar rhetorical traditions and practices expressed in gangsta rap are intricately linked to dominate cultural constructions of "the other" and market-driven strategies for rampant economic and human exploitation. Therefore, Dyson noted, the debate about gangsta rap should be situated in a much broader critique of how these narratives essentially mirror ancient stereotypes of Black identity and sexual proclivity through the society's circulation of "brutal images of black men as sexual outlaws and black females as 'ho's' " (1996, p. 178).

McLaren (2000) argued that moral custodians of U.S. culture have denounced gangsta rappers as prime instigators of juvenile delinquency. "Strutting apocalyptically across the urban landscape," McLaren wrote, "today's gangsta rappers have, for some listeners, become the new black super heroes invested with dangerous, ambiguous, uncontrolled, and uncontrollable powers" (2000, p. 240). According to McLaren, society's response to these dangerous, ambiguous, uncontrolled powers has been bi-modal—economic and iconographic exploitation on the one hand, and cultural denigration and containment on the other. For example, after analyzing all the articles about rap that appeared in the three most widely circulated news magazines in the United States and Canada (*Newsweek*, *Time*, and *U.S. News & World Report*) during the decade from 1983 to 1992, Koza (1994) made a compelling case that the vast majority of these articles "reinforced a link between rap and specific negative themes" (p. 183). Essentially, rap music had been made into a scapegoat. Koza further noted that the significance of these negative representations of rap should be seen in the light of theories "that negativity is a strategy of containment that tends to reinforce dominant ideologies" (1994, p. 184). Rose (1994) has additionally argued that strategies of containment associated with rap music and culture extended even into physical spaces in terms of the formidable obstacles of access to the venues in which rap concerts and associated events take place.

Although it is a problematic cultural practice, rap music does articulate and draw attention to complex dimensions of urban life. It often exposes, according to Dyson (1996), "harmful beliefs and practices that are often maintained with deceptive civility in much of mainstream society, including many black communities" (p. 177). Mahiri (2000a) noted that rap has also emerged as a powerful discourse that is able to effectively critique other discourses, including dominant ones. With respect to urban youth, Mahiri argued that this capacity of critique offered possibilities for counter-hegemonic perspectives and even actions in the social worlds of urban youth. He suggested that elements of hip-hop culture and rap music constituted a kind of "pop culture pedagogy" (p. 382) that extended, offered alternatives to, or challenged the pedagogy of schools.

In an earlier study focused on the use of "positive" rap texts, Mahiri (1996) analyzed a curricular intervention designed to help students become critical consumers of rap and hip-hop cultural texts and to develop their skills in writing similar texts. The goal was to see if the students could transfer these writing skills to the production of other literate texts. This study found that there were viable ways that rap and hip-hop cultural texts could be utilized in the classroom to facilitate writing development and to enhance learning. More recent, comprehensive, urban school studies by Morrell (2001) and Morrell and Duncan-Andrade (in press) found, also, that rap and hip-hop could be attuned in pedagogy and curriculum to motivate and facilitate student productions of academic texts as well as to generate heightened analyses of school sanctioned canonical texts. One of the classes under focus in this study attempted to use rap and hip-hop in its curriculum to promote learning.

Although Black youth are often socially constructed as perpetrators, violence in their lives (as with many other youth) is manifested in many forms. Polakow (2000) noted some of these forms as "the violence of poverty and homelessness, the violence of environmentally induced childhood diseases, the violence confronting children in schools and communities, the media and legislative 'criminalization' of children, and a national drumbeat of 'zero-tolerance' leading to the increasing confinement and incarceration of youthful offenders" (p. 1). Indeed, 15- to 30-year-old African American males are more likely to go to prison than to college (Cose, 2000).

Noguera (2000) reminds us that violence has always been central in the history and culture of the United States reflecting a national obsession that has been continually fueled by politics, media, sports, law enforcement, and the military. Some researchers have argued that the focus on Black youth as perpetrators of violence works to obscure other realities of violence and crime in this country. Males (1999) for example, suggests that Black youth and other contemporary youth are essentially being framed through the perpetuation of a number of societal myths about them. He used extensive Department of Justice and U.S. Census Bureau data and statistics to argue that it is really White adults in contemporary U.S. society, not youth, who are the "superpredators." The recent incidences of workplace shootings are one case in point where 95% of the perpetrators are White men (Fagan, 2001). According to Males (1999), "The truth, abundantly obvious from official crime reports over the last one to two decades, is that it is not minority teenagers, but adults over the age of 30—white adults, most specifically—who consistently display the largest increases in serious (felony) violent, property, and drug-related crime rates" (p. 5).

Context and Methods

Our research at Westwood Middle School (a pseudonym for the school) was predicated upon our prior involvement with some of its students, families, teachers, and staff as well as prior involvement in other activities in the larger Westwood community. This involvement began in a collaborative outreach project and intervention in an elementary school in this community. Over 90% of the students served by this intervention were African Americans from low-income families. Although most of these students were far behind their grade level academically, after the first two years of the intervention they made dramatic gains in reading, writing, and math as measured by the SAT 9, the key standardized test in the state of California (Mahiri, 2000b).

Approximately 15 students from this initial intervention went to Westwood Middle School. Through our involvement with Westwood Middle School at the beginning of the 2000–2001 academic year, it became clear that this particular site offered a special opportunity to explore our focus on Black youth perceptions of violence. We felt that our earlier involvement with some of the students as well as with members of the school staff would allow our informants to be more comfortable and more open in addressing the difficult issues of our research.

Community Context

In the 1960s the Westwood community was effectively severed from the downtown area of the city by the construction of a major freeway. The earlier closing of military installations and the closing of a number of large manufacturing plants also worked to severely weaken this community's economic base and to usher the departure of many of its working-class residents. This community now has very little in the way of businesses and services; there are no banks, pharmacies, hardware stores, or movie theaters and only one supermarket. There are, however, many liquor stores throughout the community. Recently, there has been some low-cost housing construction, but this development is now in tension with gentrification efforts in this community spurred by the catastrophic rise in housing costs in this region of northern California.

Westwood community's median household income is only 26% of median of this region in northern California. More than three-fourths of this community's residents live in poverty. Approximately 74% of the residents are African American while 11% are Latino, 9% Asian, 6% White, and less than 1% other ethnicities. Youth under the age of 18 account for one-third of the Westwood community's population making its median age around 28 years in contrast to 36 years for the surrounding region (Office of Economic Development, 1994).

School Context

Westwood is a small, charter school that had been in existence for two years at the time of this research. It opened in the fall of 1999 with 50 sixth graders. It took its name from the section of the city in which it is located and serves. It was founded by a volunteer working group comprised of parents, community leaders, teachers, and youth advocates who first met in 1996 to craft new approaches to the educational challenges facing African American students in this city. Recent statistics published by the city's school district revealed that African American students comprised 53% of the district's total enrollment, but 71% of students in its special education programs, 64% of students retained at their present grade levels, and 80% of students suspended.

All but three of Westwood's students were identified as African Americans. The school's mission statement noted that "A significant number of Westwood community youth are challenged by poverty, and very complex family circumstances. Some have been orphaned by AIDS and crack-cocaine or long-term incarceration of a parent. Some are being raised by foster parents or aging grandparents, or are essentially raising themselves." In many cases these youth are children of the "truly disadvantaged," a term that Wilson (1987) coined to define "individuals who lack training and skill and either experience long-term underemployment or are not members of the labor force, individuals who are engaged in street crime and other forms of aberrant behavior, and families that experience long-term spells of poverty and/or welfare dependency" (p. 8).

The school's committed teachers, staff, and community supporters believe that these children's complex lives required innovative solutions. Consequently, they developed Westwood as a small, charter, middle school (grades 6–8) in order to have a public school in which they controlled the curriculum and pedagogy as well as the budget and personnel. They also developed a number of after school services and an extended day program that provided additional academic and cultural activities for the students. Although they eventually plan to serve up to 150 students, a key tenet of the school is that it remains small so that every child can be known and treated as an individual. Also key to the school's approach was its focus on college preparation, leadership development, and African American history and culture. The school had high expectations for all of its students, and it also had high expectations and clear structures for parent participation.

Researcher Positions

Mahiri coordinates a longitudinal study that began with another school in the Westwood community. Approximately 15 of those students went to Westwood Middle School, and Mahiri got to know the teachers and staff in that site. At the request of the school's leaders, Mahiri provided some limited staff development.

Conner was one of the original mentors for several students in the longitudinal study. She continued her work with these and other students when they went to Westwood Middle School. During the second semester of the school year, she was asked to teach an academic literacy class at the school. Consequently, she and other teachers were able to create a number of class assignments that directly elicited the students' thinking and beliefs about images and influences of rap and hip-hop along with their perceptions and experiences regarding violence. Finally, Kim Bancroft, a colleague of Mahiri and Conner, helped with informant interviews and supported the research in several ways.

Research Questions

We framed two sets of questions to gain insight into our consideration of what the perceptions and reflections of Black youth on the violence in their lives could offer to our understandings of the nature of Black violence in the context of ways that it is represented in the larger society.

The first set of questions was directed to the combined language arts/social studies class, as they attempted to probe the student's experiences with violence. We wanted to know what were the students' actual experiences with violence? How did the students and their peers negotiate violent or potentially violent situations? The unit on *Our America* proved viable for addressing these questions with the students through their class work and projects for their teacher, Ms. Shanice Davis.

The second set of questions was addressed through the academic literacy class taught by Conner. Through this class we explored how the students understood the images and messages in rap music and culture and other forms of electronically mediated popular culture (some of which depicted violence and crime). We also probed if and how these images and messages personally influenced them.

Data Collection

Several forms of data were collected on the students in the two classrooms to capture their personal experiences with violence, to probe their reflections on violence, and to elicit their engagements with and perceptions about hip-hop and rap and the potential influences of its images and messages of violence. In Davis' class our data consisted of the following:

- Student projects and portfolios based on the *Our America* curriculum unit
- Observations and field notes on class discussions and activities around this unit
- Student class work, homework, and journals on this unit
- Interviews with the teacher and focal students

To provide a context for the nature of this data, a brief background on *Our America* is needed. It initially grew out of two radio documentaries, *Ghetto life 101* and *Remorse: The 14 stories of Eric Morse* that were created by the two authors. Journalist David Isay got the idea to have kids tell their own stories about growing up in public housing. The two boys he ended up getting were LeAlan Jones and Lloyd Newman who were 13 years old at the time. Jones and his sisters were being raised by his grandmother because his mother was mentally ill. Newman was being raised by his two teenage sisters because his mother had died and his father was an alcoholic. Isay decided "to equip them with tape machines and have them compose diaries of their lives, sound portraits of growing up in poverty" (Jones & Newman, 1997, p. 17).

Ghetto life 101 became the first of those stories. Isay found both boys to be "insightful, intensely curious, meticulous observers—a poignant mixture of little boys and adolescents wise far beyond their years" (Jones & Newman, 1997, p. 19). One evening after this initial collaboration, Isay got a call from Jones who told him that "A shorty [little boy] just fell out the window behind my house." The next day the story appeared in newspapers across the country. Five-year-old Eric Morse had been dropped out of a fourteenth-floor window of a building in Ida B. Wells by two other boys who were ten and eleven years old. These two boys became the youngest kids ever to be sentenced to prison in the United States.

Over the next year, Jones and Newman became the nation's experts on this tragedy and their investigations and interviews with people in the community resulted in an hour-long radio documentary that premiered on public radio in March 1996. Listener response was overwhelming and so were the forthcoming awards— one of which was the grand prize of the Robert F. Kennedy Journalism Awards which had never before been given for a radio program. These two poignant stories were combined with others to become *Our America* (Jones & Newman, 1997).

Davis, in conjunction with our colleague Bancroft, developed an extensive curriculum centered on this book for her language arts and social studies class. Because of the themes and foci of this book and the kinds of learning activities and projects that were developed around it, this unit was extremely valuable for generating a variety of data and artifacts from the students with regard to their understandings and experiences with violence. In addition to our observations and field notes on class activities and discussions on the book, we focused on several projects that the students did in conjunction with this unit. These projects were motivated by or modeled on some of the things that the young authors, Jones and Newman, did and/or reported on in their book.

- One project had the students research and document aspects of their own lives to create extensive self-portraits.

- Another project had the students learn about and interview a member of their community (like a senior citizen) to create "first-hand" biographies.

- A third project had the students take field trips and do individual research to document and assess the positive and negative aspects of the Westwood community in which they lived.

- A fourth project had the students keep journals on their responses and individual ideas that they had about their work and activities during this unit.

All of the texts and artifacts [like graded homework, portfolios, and journals] that the students created in doing these projects were available to us as sources of data.

To extend our understanding of how the students thought and felt about this unit and to learn more about its influences while it was in process, we conducted audio-taped interviews with six of the students in Davis' class. We balanced our selection of students for interviews with two who were doing well academically, two who were approximately in the middle of the class, and two who were struggling academically. We noted to the students that our study was attempting to look at their personal views on violence in the Westwood community. The six focal students were Tameka [a 12 year old girl] with low achievement; Sekou [a 12 year old boy] with low achievement; Alisha [a 12 year old girl] with middle level achievement; Stacia [a 12 year old girl] with middle level achievement; Mark [a 13 year old boy] with high achievement; and, Jason [a 12 year old boy] with high achievement.

Also, we had extensive discussions and conducted formal interviews with Davis to capture more of her perceptions of how the students were experiencing the unit and how they were generally dealing with violence in their lives.

With Conner becoming an instructor in the academic literacy class during the second half of the school year, additional learning activities and projects were developed around a unit on hip-hop and rap that yielded a variety of data and artifacts on the students' perceptions and engagements with this music and culture. One of the projects associated with this unit and one of the class activities that occurred during this unit were especially useful to the focus of our research:

- The students created their own rap albums complete with song lists, music themes, album covers, and the verses and choruses for one or more of the songs.

- Many of the students attended a funeral of the older brother of one of the students who had been in the school.

Like the unit on *Our America*, this unit also provided significant data that uniquely revealed the students' perspectives on violence through the lens of rap music and hip-hop culture and how the students felt they connected with considerations of violence and crime. Conner kept descriptive notes and reflective notes on student discussions and activities and informally interviewed students, usually in groups.

Data Analysis

Mahiri and Conner collaboratively coded and analyzed the data from the various sources and checked our codes and analyses with Davis, the focal teacher. We examined the data from the projects in Davis' class that linked to the *Our America* unit as well as the project in Conner's class that linked to hip-hop and rap. We looked for broad themes emerging in the student perspectives and personal experiences associated with violence that came up consistently in the data from these five projects along with discussions in class around aspects of the funeral. We used this same approach to examine data from our interviews and to analyze the descriptive and reflective note data from our observations of and discussions with the focal teacher and the students. Our analysis attempted to comprehend and represent the vantage points of our student/informants and their teachers on the ways that the students understood, experienced, and reflected on violence in their lives and through their music with an eye also on larger societal constructions of these youth around these same issues.

In responding to our initial research questions, we will discuss three of the broad themes that we found across all of our sources of data, and we will do so by drawing on a wide variety of the data to explicate each theme—interviews, student journals, self-portraits, student discussions on or about their field trips into the community, student created rap albums, etc. The students revealed that although their lives are saturated with violence ("It's like, shooting is like nothing to me no more."), they have considerable skills for dealing with or negotiating it ("I can walk away from violence."), they have more progressive values than are represented in the rap discourse that they are exposed to ("No More 'Proes'"), and they have cogent critiques of the discourse of rap and hip-hop.

Discussion and Results

"It's like, shooting is like nothing to me no more."

The above quote from Mark captured something of the intensity of violence and dissonance with which many Westwood youth have to contend. This and many other statements about violence by students at the school sounded like they could have been excerpted directly from *Our America*. During an interview, Mark talked at length about his personal experiences with violence in conjunction with his reading of *Our America* in Davis's language arts/social studies class. When asked what he thought of the book, Mark responded, "Yeah, I'm enjoying it, because like, it's, um, like I'll understand it more. Because like it was written by people around our age and stuff. So, I'm enjoying it more than I'm enjoying any other book" (personal communication with Mark, March 2001). Tameka appreciated the fact that "they talk about their neighborhood, and it's easy to read" (personal communication with Tameka, April 2001). Sekou told us that he had "never been into no books until he got it, [but now wants] to read it all the time" (personal communication with Sekou, April 2001). Both Sekou and Tameka have had some difficulty with reading and academic achievement in the past. Nearly every student in Davis' two classes echoed these kinds of sentiments about the book. The parents of one student, however, objected to the book and did not allow that student to read it.

Mark said that he could really relate to Jones and Newman and to many of the situations they described. For example, both authors grew up without a father in their homes, and Mark noted how this connected with his own life. "Like, uh, I don't know, like I can understand, too, because most of my life, seem like on and off I was growing up without a father. On and off and stuff" (personal communication with Mark, March 2001). Davis noted that issues described in the book like absent parents and/or parents with drug or alcohol addictions touched a personal chord with a number of her students. According to Davis, "a lot of the kids, who I know their parents to be drug addicts, were also discussing how you always love your parent in spite of the fact that they're not taking care of you. They (some parents) have problems with drugs. And some of them (students), when that part in the book came up, they sort of looked around like, is anyone looking at me?" (personal communication with Davis, March 2001).

Davis went on to tell a poignant story about how Sekou, one of her students, encountered his father on the streets while the class was on one of its field trips to document positive and negative aspects of the Westwood community.

[The students] discussed that . . . there were a lot of men who drank all day and were home all day. And that there weren't a lot of working men in the community. Because almost everywhere we drove, you saw groups of men just on the street, just doing much of nothing. And one of our students actually ran into his father that way. Um, so we stopped and talked to him. . . . It was in the middle of the day, and he reeked of alcohol. And he said, I don't deal with my father, because he's a crack addict. But he dealt with him that day.
Researcher: What was that like, for him to run into his father like that?
Davis: Well, we drove past, and then he got really quiet. And then he said, Ms. Davis, you see that guy over there? And I said, yes. He said, that's my father. And I asked him did he want to go back and talk to him? And he said, yeah. And his father, I mean, aside from just being [in jail], he kept saying he was out of town. . . . But he [the father] started talking about his mother. And that really upset Harold . . . . He was like, well, you know how your mother is. You know how women, they can be such . . . and he was about, you know, he was about to call her a bitch. And, and Harold was like, you know what, I'm ready to go. And he was like, come back around here and see me. You know I've been missing you. I've been calling you. You never call me back. And Harold got in the car, and he was like, yeah, right, he never calls me. And then he had the nerve to talk about my mother . . . . I don't come here to see him because he's not a good father . . . . And he was just, you know, he started talking about his grandfather having filled that role for him, and how his grandfather was the one that he looks up to and who supports him. (personal communication with Davis, March 2001)

The stories of students at Westwood read like stories in Jones and Newman's book, yet these students have complex understandings of circumstances that include drugs, crime, violence, poverty, delinquent parents, and extremely negative characterizations of Black men and women. They understand that they can love people who are significant in their lives without affirming or engaging in the negative behaviors of some of these people.

Jones and Newman's journalism strategies were used as models for a number of student research and reporting projects on aspects of life in Westwood. These projects created rich sources of data that revealed among other things the students' intricate (though evolving) understandings of the nature and causes of violence, crime, and poverty in their communities.

For example, in concert with Jones and Newman's work, students in Ms. Davis' class researched the Westwood community by interviewing some of its residents, writing their biographies, and creating community descriptions and maps that depicted positive and negative qualities. Students came to fairly sophisticated understandings of both the problems and some of the possibilities of Westwood. Tameka, for example, took pictures of things like burned out houses as well as really nice ones with satellite dishes and rose gardens as a part of her documentation of community assets and liabilities. Following is one of the conclusions she derived through this project:

> When I did my map, I said there ain't a lot of grocery stores in my community. There's only one grocery store and that's not a really good grocery store 'cause the prices too high and we gotta go to Pak 'n Save. So, we gotta go [to the east side of the city] or something like that. I think we shouldn't have to go outta our community just to go get some bread and some milk. (personal communication with Tameka, April 2001)

Students often interviewed older people in their families and in retirement homes to get more of a historical perspective on their community. Tameka spoke for most of the students when she said, "generally I like interviewing people, 'cause you get to find out a lot of stuff that you didn't know before" (personal communication with Tameka, April 2001). When asked whom she would interview if she could choose anyone, however, Alisha, responded that she would interview somebody who was homeless and somebody who was famous. She had a number of insightful questions for both the homeless person and the famous one, and she speculated that "the homeless person could have been famous or had a good job, and something happened to them, or the famous person could have been homeless until he got famous" (personal communication with Alisha, April 2001). She saw that the conditions of homelessness and poverty were not unconnected to desires for wealth and fame—that a person could achieve one status or slip back into the other because they were two sides of the same coin.

Interestingly, after reading *Our America* most of the students thought that life in Westwood was at least not as bad as it was depicted in the Ida B. Wells housing projects in Chicago. One of Sekou's conversations with us captured this sentiment, and while it revealed some limits of analysis, it also revealed some measure of hope.

> Sekou: We live in Westwood. And, I mean like [we have] shooting, uh, crack addicts, and stuff like that in our neighborhood. But we haven't really had no problems like people throwing people off the building or stuff. Just shooting going on, stuff like that . . . . I didn't even know Chicago was like that.
> Researcher: Shooting sounds like a problem.
> Sekou: Yes.
> Researcher: How do you feel about the shootings that go on?
> Sekou: Mm, I don't know. I can't do anything about it. But, I just pray that nobody gets hit.
> (personal communication with Sekou, April 2001)

The stark violence that Jones and Newman chronicled was in many ways reflective of the violence present in many Westwood students' lives. Sekou understood that these separate situations of violence were connected, yet still seemed to normalize the violence in his community. His normalization of violence might extend from a sense of helplessness as a young person to do anything about it. We will discuss later how many students did feel that there were things they could do to reduce and/or avoid violent situations, yet many of the students, like Sekou, felt that their communities were not as violent as what they had read about Ida B. Wells.

Yet, their school year was framed by three violent murders of youths that many of the students directly knew or knew of—Keith Williams, Lance Pryor, and Hodari Lockwood. All of the elementary and middle schools in the Westwood area feed into one high school which has some of the lowest achievement levels of any high school in the city and the state. At the beginning of the academic year in which we conducted this study, there was a horrific murder at this high school. A 17-year-old student named Keith Williams, a football star at the school, was shot and killed on the school's playground. Many of the students in Westwood Middle School either knew this young man or knew of his murder. There were many articles about this murder in local papers, and for months his picture was posted on six huge billboards all around this community under the bold caption, "Do You Know Who Killed Me?" At mid-semester a similar incident happened in a nearby Black community that also received national press coverage. Lance Pryor, after being shot in the neck across the street from his high school, stumbled back into the school building and died in the principal's office. At the end of the school year, the 20-year-old brother of one of Westwood Middle School's students was shot three times in the head and four times in the chest. He died on the sidewalk where he was shot. Like Keith, he had also been a football star at the same high school, and many of the children in the school knew him and attended his funeral.

"No More 'Proes'"

During the second semester of the academic year, Conner and another teacher at Westwood developed a unit for the two academic literacy classes that generated a number of student activities centered on rap and hip-hop. One of the projects in this unit was for the students to create their own rap albums complete with song lists, music themes, album covers, and verses and choruses for one or more of the songs. This unit provided significant data and artifacts that uniquely revealed aspects of the students' perspectives on and involvement with rap music and how they felt it was connected to violence, crime, and sex. Our findings from this data revealed how the students' understandings of violence and crime were expressed in their critiques of images and messages in rap music and hip-hop culture. A central feature of these understandings was reflected in the title of one of the albums created by one of the groups of students during this unit—"No More Proes."

"Proes" was a word this group invented by joining the words "prostitute" and "hoe." The work on these albums was done in the context of class readings and discussions on rap music with a focus on the portrayals of Black men and women. There were discussions about ways that Black men are portrayed as violent gangstas or drug dealers consumed by the pursuit of money and material things. Through discussions and examples from the music, students explored ways that Black women are frequently portrayed as promiscuous, superficial, gold diggers— essentially prostitutes or ho's. There were also discussions on positive aspects of rap music and hip-hop culture.

The students were told that they could create whatever type of album they wanted with whatever theme their group decided upon. The album assignments were complemented with student reflective writing in their journals. All of the groups except one created albums that critiqued rather than extended the negative discourse of rap. Following are discussions of three samples of these albums.

The cover that the group created for "No More Proes" contained two popular female rap artists: Lil' Kim and Foxy Brown. These women are notorious for their sexually explicit lyrics and provocative clothing. In their music, they often advocate dating men for their money and for the luxury that men can offer. All of the songs written by the students for this album had a similar theme that is partially captured in the following lines from one song titled "Pretty Black Sista": "Stop sellin' yo body to a man you don't know/Quit lyin' to yoself baby girl, You not a hoe."

Reflections in the student journals often extended the critique of the albums like in the following example that represented many that were handed in:

> I think the music industry needs to change some of their lyrics because they send negative thoughts to kids minds. For example the video Lady Mamalad. The song has . . . Lil' Kim and Cristina Angulara in the video half ass naked. When children see the video—they might want to keep seeing naked women on T.V. all the time. The other video that sends negative

thoughts to kids is Lil' Wayn's song Lil One. All they talk about through the song is selling drugs and making money. (Stacia's Student Journal, June 2001)

These students' critiques of the negative characterizations of men and women as gangstas and ho's suggests that they understand something of the larger cultural/political dynamics that generate these negative representations in rap music and in other areas of their lives (i.e., the way Harold's father characterized his mother in the situation noted earlier). Certainly, there could have been some attempts to reflect what they assumed was their teachers' perspective even though the teachers told them they could create any type of album that that wanted.

"Thugged Out," for example, was an album that was created by a group of girls with the intent of expressing very negative and oppositional messages and images. Although this album was consciously designed to counter the positive ones done by the rest of the class, there were ways that this group of girls as well as others in the class didn't dwell on the negativity. Some students, for example, noted that they listened to the music for the beat (and to dance to) rather than focusing on the lyrics. As one student wrote, "I like some negative and positive songs because I can dance to them" (Alisha's Student Journal, June 2001). The idea that students could see and hear negative images and understand that they are a part of a music genre that they can engage at a number of levels is of interest. They understood, for example, that they could be entertained by rap music and its representations and dance to its driving beats without adopting the values and behaviors so explicit in some of its genres. This perspective challenges the simple connections that the dominant public discourse and media so often draw between rap music and pervasive negative influences on Black youth. Interestingly, these simple connections are not made in the same way for other entertainment mediums like the violence on T.V. and in movies, and they are not made with respect to White youth who purchase 70% of rap music.

One final example of the kinds of albums that the students created was one that explored attitudes toward money. The title of this album, "Gain Green," was a clever way of illustrating money's destructive effects on the Black community. This group's work argued the pitfalls of an uncontrolled love of money. At one point in the lyrics, these student writers connected and critiqued money and violence: "Money make you go pound for pound [fight]/Money make you blast a couple rounds [shoot others]." Titles of other songs on this album were: "Money Makes the Ghetto Go Round," "Money Has Too Much Respect," "Money Has Chains," "Mr. Dollar Bill," and "Money Is a Mind Controller."

Another way that the students' critiques of issues like money, violence, and crime could be dramatically seen occurred towards the end of the academic year while this unit on rap and hip-hop was in progress. The event was the murder and funeral of Hodari Lockwood, the 20-year-old brother of Harold Lockwood who had been a student at Westwood for almost two years though he had recently moved to another city. Many of the students knew Hodari personally as he had often come to the school to pick up his little brother, and many of Westwood's students attended his funeral. It was fairly well known that Hodari supported himself by selling drugs in the neighborhood. Seeking a change in his life, Hodari relocated with his family and began attending college. Shortly after the move, he was involved in an altercation with a young man from Eastwood. He was shot three times in the head and four times in the chest. His murderer was himself shot less than a week later.

Hodari's funeral took place at a local funeral home. Later, in Conner's class the students wanted to talk about the funeral. They described the music that was played as extremely inappropriate. One of the songs sung by a male soloist depicted a man willing to "ride for his hood" or commit violence in the name of his neighborhood. While he sang this song, many people in the congregation used their hands to throw up gang signs from the neighborhood where Harold's family lived. Others walked up and down the aisles selling t-shirts and bandanas with pictures of other murdered youth from the area for ten dollars apiece. Westwood students who attended said the funeral resembled a party or club scene. They felt that people who were at the funeral drinking alcoholic beverages and smoking dope disrespected Hodari's death. Although the students are only in the seventh grade, other mourners offered them both drugs and alcohol. Hodari's body in the coffin was dressed very casually, in khakis and a t-shirt. The students described the funeral as low class or "ghetto," a term that does not so much designate a place as it does a mentality. The students perceptions and critique of the funeral suggested that it reflected very negative aspects of Black culture and music through the selection of music, the selection of clothes for the deceased and by many of the mourners, and the general creation of spectacle complete with foul language, liquor, and drugs. Yet, these young people were able to rise above this spectacle and not be adulterated.

"I can walk away from violence."

The quote that begins this section comes from one of the many student journal entries that showed additional ways these students have learned to mitigate negative influences while working to circumvent or ameliorate violence in their lives. This student wrote that "Violence is fighting, stealing, robbing, killing and being in gangs. I can walk away from violence and keep my distance as far as I can. I can also try to help others" (Mark's Student Journal, May 2001). The idea that these students felt that they could avoid violence themselves and also help others avoid violence was clearly reflected in their journals, as in the following example:

> What I could do to stop violence for myself is be aware of my surroundings and of the people who I hang around. I really can't do anything to stop violence in the community because there is always going to be violence wherever you go. The only thing that I could do is help others especially young people to be aware of staying away from violence and from doing violence. (Stacia's Student Journal, May 2001)

This recognition that the root causes of violence in their communities is much larger than they as individual students have the ability to change is important. They are beginning to understand that violence is caused by forces both inside and outside of their communities that are beyond their immediate control. However, they do see that some of the violence in their communities happens out of desperation. They see also a key role for adults in helping to control violent situations as the next journal entry partially suggests:

> What I can do about violent situations in my life is tell someone about the problem like the police or someone in authority. Well, I really can't tell anyone because I know if I do they'll either put me in a home with other people I don't want to be with and so I guess I'll have to deal with it unless I have someone that is a friend/adult. (Jason's Student Journal, May 2001)

Though this student was ambivalent about telling an adult, it is clear that the ambivalence was linked to whether there was an adult in this young person's life who could be trusted—a "friend/adult." From an earlier research project in this same community of Westwood, Noguera (2000) found that in contrast to a group of mainly White students in an affluent neighborhood, none of the students living in the Westwood community regarded telling an adult as a viable strategy for avoiding a violent encounter. However, the students in our study at Westwood School seemed to be developing the kinds of relationships that would allow them to see some adults and other authority figures as resources for helping them avoid violence. One more journal entry is provided to show that some of the students had good understandings of how to circumvent or ameliorate violence or potentially violent situations:

> When you get in a violent situation you try and solve it and not fight. The fight could result in losing someone's life. You could discuss the problem with the person. You could go to a teacher and tell them what happened between you and that person. If you see a fight in your neighborhood don't cheer it on, try to stop it. (Jason's Student Journal, May 2001)

Three main findings with respect to our research questions about the experiences and perceptions of these youth emerged across the various sources of data. These findings reflected three broad, yet highly related themes that clearly contrasted with the public discourse and media representations that construct Black youth as prone to violence and rap music as precipitating violence. Although we connect these findings only to the students at Westwood, it is important to remember that the circumstances of their lives closely correspond to the circumstances of many Black youth that U.S. society has characterized as "violent others." One difference, however, is the school that they were attending.

First, our data on these youth revealed that they had complex understandings of the nature and causes of violence and crime in their lives and communities. Second, their understandings often included critiques of negative aspects of violence and crime associated with things like gang and drug activities as well as critiques of negative images and messages of violence, crime, and sex in rap music. Third, their understandings and critiques of instances and images of crime and violence (along with the support of key adults) worked to mitigate negative influences from these sources and increased their desire to circumvent or ameliorate violent situations in their lives and communities.

Implications and Conclusion

Jones and Newman began *Our America* (1997) by noting that in this country Black children don't often get to speak their piece. In this study we tried to create a space for a group of Black students and their teacher to speak their piece on violence. Newman and Jones described a second America where the laws of the street, rather than the laws of the land apply. Though less than a mile from the downtown business center of the city, Westwood is located in that second America, and these students, like other members of this community, were subjected to the laws of the streets. Their voices, however, offered critical insights for research, policy, and practice related to violence.

First, the development of more culturally appropriate ways to get behind the blatant stereotypes associated with Black youth need to be developed. This was aided in our study by data being generated through some of the accepted processes of schooling. This meant that some of those processes had to be made flexible enough to accommodate different contents (like *Our America*). This flexibility also extended into different activities such as field trips through the community, class work that allowed for projects like the of rap albums that tapped more into the students' cultural competencies, and class communication formats and topics that allowed for difficult or traumatic issues to be discussed. For example, Davis noted that *Our America* worked through content that was very close to the students' lives, but they were able to have some distance through the text and were therefore more able to deal with things that could be personally very painful. The fact that these topics and activities were integrated into the accepted processes of schooling allowed for more authentic student voices to have frequent and varied opportunities to be heard.

Next, the dominant cultural narratives that assiduously work to connect and blame rap for violence, crime, and juvenile delinquency need to challenged and changed. Certainly, the vulgar images and messages of some kinds of rap music can be troubling, but often these images are no more than false exaggerations of Black life. On another level the scapegoating of rap works to obscure rather than illuminate its processes of cultural production and consumption. They need to be seen within the context of the much larger, global processes of the production and consumption of capitalism that commercializes and to some extent shapes what ultimately is experienced as rap and hip-hop. These complex processes require more sophisticated analyses as a part of understanding comprehensive questions associated with the development of youth including Black urban youth.

Additionally, a new look needs to be given to the roles of significant adults in the lives and development of youth, especially those youth that have the least access to societal resources. Davis, for example, noted that her students generally felt that adults in their lives should be better prepared to take care of young people's needs. This applies to adults in the communities, and it also applies to teachers in schools. Davis talked about how she herself had struggled to better understand and to better serve her students academic as well as other needs. She reflected on how long it took her to go into some areas of the communities where her students lived. "I know that my children are resilient," she told us, "but I had never really seen where it came from." When she finally did go, she found somewhat to her surprise that "there's a lot of beauty there."

Rather than coloring in the outline drawn by public discourse on Black youth violence, this research has attempted to document and explain aspects of the very human quest to struggle through and perhaps help ameliorate the stark conditions of disadvantage. It revealed the strategies these youth and their teachers construct to mitigate rather than perpetuate violence, and challenges the ideology and motives of societal perspectives and policies that don't reflect the complexity of violence in young people's lives. In looking at some of the violence and dissonance that was experienced and perceived by students at Westwood School, we hope that we have shared something of the beauty of their lives too.

References

Baker, H. (1993). *Black studies, rap, and the academy*. Chicago: University of Chicago Press.

Cose, E. (2000, November 13). The prison paradox. *Newsweek*, 40–46.

Chomsky, N. (1995). a Dialogue with Noam Chomsky. *Harvard Educational Review, 65*(2).

Conquergood, D. (1992, April). *On rappin' and rhetoric: Gang representations*. Paper presented at the Philosophy and Rhetoric of Inquiry Seminar, University of Iowa, Iowa City, IA.

Dyson, M. E. (1996). *Between God and gangsta rap: Bearing witness to Black culture*. New York: Oxford University Press.

Fagan, K. (2001, April 25). Suspect in shooting belies stereotypes. *San Francisco Chronicle*, p. A11.

Jones, L., & Newman, L. (1997). *Our America: Life and death on the South Side of Chicago*. New York: Pocket Books.

Koza, J. E. (1994). Rap music: The cultural politics of official representation. *Review of Education/Pedagogy/Cultural Studies, 16*(1), 181–190.

Mahiri, J. (1996). Writing, rap, and representation: Problematic links between text and experience. In P. Mortensen & G. E. Kirsch (Eds.), *Ethics and representation in qualitative studies of literacy* (pp. 228–240). Urbana, IL: National Council of Teachers of English.

Mahiri, J. (1997). Street scripts: African American youth writing about crime and violence. *Social Justice 24*(4), 56–76.

Mahiri, J. (2000a). Pop culture pedagogy and the end(s) of school. *Journal of Adolescent & Adult Literacy 44*(4), 382–385.

Mahiri, J. (2000b). Realizing the dream: Supporting literacy through mentoring. In N. H. Gabelko (Ed.), *Toward a collective wisdom: Forging successful educational partnerships* (pp. 71–79). Berkeley, CA: ECO Center.

Males, M. A. (1999). *Framing youth: Ten myths about the next generation*. Monroe, ME: Common Courage Press.

McLaren, P. (2000). Gangsta pedagogy and ghettocentricity: The hip-hop nation as counterpublic sphere. In K. McClafferty, C. Torres, & T. Mitchell (Eds.), *Challenges of urban education: Sociological perspectives for the next century* (pp. 227–270). Albany, NY: State University of New York Press.

McLaughlin, M., Irby, M. A., & Langman, J. (1994). *Urban sanctuaries neighborhood organizations in the lives and futures of inner-city youth*. San Francisco: Jossey-Bass.

Morrell, E. (2001). *Transforming classroom discourse: Academic and critical literacy development through engaging popular culture*. Unpublished doctoral dissertation, University of California, Berkeley, CA.

Morrell, E., & Duncan-Andrade, J. (in press). What they do learn in school: Using hip-hop as a bridge between youth culture and canonical poetry texts. In J. Mahiri (Ed.), *What they don't learn in school: Literacy in the lives of urban Youth*. New York: Peter Lang.

Noguera, P. A. (1996). Confronting the urban in urban school reform. *The Urban Review, 28*(1), 1–19.

Noguera, P. A. (2000). Listen first: How student perspectives on violence can be used to create safer schools. In V. Polakow (Ed.), *The public assault on America's children: Poverty, violence, and juvenile injustice* (pp. 130–156). New York: Teachers College Press.

Office of Economic Development. (1994). *Creating a community vision: Community goal statements and proposed implementation strategies*. City of Oakland: Author.

Polakow, V. (2000). Savage policies: Systematic violence and the lives of children. In V. Polakow (Ed.), *The public assault on America's children: Poverty, violence, and juvenile injustice* (pp. 1–20). New York: Teachers College Press.

Rose, T. (1994). *Black noise: Rap music and Black culture in contemporary America*. Hanover and London: University of New England Press.

Wilson, W. J. (1987). *The truly disadvantaged: The inner city, the underclass, and public policy*. Chicago: University of Chicago Press.

JABARI MAHIRI is an Associate Professor of Language, Literacy, and Culture, and is the Director of the Center for Urban Education at UC Berkeley's Graduate School of Education. His recent books are *Shooting for Excellence: African American and Youth Culture in New Century Schools* (1998), and *What They Don't Learn in School: Literacy in the Lives of Urban Youth* (in press, 2003).

ERIN CONNER is a doctoral student in the Division of Language, Literacy, and Culture and Coordinator of the Center for Urban Education at UC Berkeley's Graduate School of Education. Her research interests are minority language policies and alternative programs for youth development.

Journal of Social Issues, Vol. 59, No. 1, 2003, pp. 141–158

"Anything Can Happen With Police Around": Urban Youth Evaluate Strategies of Surveillance in Public Places

Michelle Fine*

The Graduate Center, The City University of New York

Nick Freudenberg

Hunter College Urban Public Health Program and the Graduate Center, The City University of New York

Yasser Payne

The Graduate Center, The City University of New York

Tiffany Perkins

The Graduate Center, The City University of New York

Kersha Smith

The Graduate Center, The City University of New York

Katya Wanzer

Hunter College Program in Urban Public Health, The City University of New York

In order to document urban youth experiences of adults in positions of public authority, including police, educators, social workers and guards, a broad based street survey of 911 New York City-based urban youth was conducted in which youth, stratified by race, ethnicity, gender and borough, were asked about their

---

*Correspondence concerning this article should be addressed to Michelle Fine, Social/Personality Psychology Program, The Graduate Center, CUNY, 365 Fifth Avenue, New York, New York 10016 [e-mail: mfine@gc.cuny.edu]. This research was funded by the Helenia Fund, Leslie Glass Foundation and Open Society Institute, New York City.

141

experiences with, attitudes toward, and trust of adult surveillance in communities and in schools. In-depth telephone interviews were conducted with 36 youth who have experienced serious, adverse interactions with police, guards, or educators. Findings suggest that urban youth, overall, express a strong sense of betrayal by adults and report feeling mistrusted by adults, with young men of color most likely to report these perceptions.

> Youth comments on police in New York City:
> "More police makes it less safe; anything can happen with police around."
> (Caren, 18, African American female)
> "More officers, less crime."
> (Tanya, 21, African American female)
> "Heavy police presence makes people feel more paranoid. I don't feel necessarily safer 'cause there is a police officer present."
> (Sarah, 20, White female)
> "Young people are scared of the police—more doesn't help."
> (Carlos, 18, Latino/Asian male)
> "More police may mean lower rates of murder but more police brutality."
> (Lin, 21, Asian American female)

In the past few years, incidents such as the assault of Abner Louima, a Haitian immigrant, and the shooting deaths of Amadou Diallo and Patrick Dorismond at the hands of New York City police officers have focused the attention of elected officials and the media on police practices in African American and Latino communities (Cooper, 1999; Kocieniewski, 1997; Rashbaum, 2000; Thompson, 1999). A report issued in 1999 by New York State Attorney General Elliot Spitzer found that the New York City Police Department stopped Blacks six times more frequently and Latinos four times more frequently than Whites (Spitzer, 1999; United States Commission on Civil Rights, 2000). A federal investigation by the Department of Justice urged New York City to take action to reduce citizen complaints about police behavior (Rashbaum, 2000). Several recent public opinion polls have showed that many New Yorkers, and especially African Americans and Latinos, believed that the New York Police Department unfairly targeted certain groups (Nagourney & Connelly, 2001).

One voice notably absent from the public debates on policing was New York City's young people. As the quotes above illustrate, young people hold diverse and complex views on policing. Although a primary rationale for aggressive policing was to reduce youth violence, policy makers, researchers and ordinary citizens rarely have the opportunity to listen to young people's views on this subject.

The present research, designed as an exploratory study, seeks to document how urban youth perceive agents of surveillance and protection such as police officers, security guards, teachers, and store and restaurant staff and to describe their reports of interactions with these adult authorities. We also examine how these interactions and perceptions vary by race, ethnicity, class, and gender (borough was included in the original analyses, for use in New York City, but not included in the current paper). Finally, we hope to understand better the consequences of these types of surveillance on urban youths' trust in adult society, civic institutions and democratic engagement.

To examine these questions, we conducted a survey of 911 New York City youth and young adults, recruited in public places, and we interviewed 36 of these young people in more extended telephone interviews. Our survey and interviews assess respondents' attitudes toward and experiences with adults in positions of public authority. As psychologists and public health researchers, we write with theoretical, practical, and political concerns. If urban youth perceive surveillance and intervention by police, security guards, personnel in retail stores and restaurants, and even their educators as evidence that they are perceived as untrustworthy, what are the adverse developmental and democratic consequences for our society as a whole?

Literatures Reviewed

The recent debates about policing in New York City and other urban areas are themselves part of several national trends: growing reliance on criminal justice to solve social problems—the United States now has more than 2 million individuals behind bars; an increasing concern about youth violence and school shootings, even in the face of declining crime rates; an increasing privatization of public spaces and a reliance on private security forces to maintain order in many urban areas; and a continued concentration of poor African American and Latinos in U.S. cities, even as these cities attract middle and upper class Whites (for further information see Fine et al., in press; Poe-Yagamata and Jones, 2000; Torre et al., 2001). Several bodies of literature which cross traditional disciplinary boundaries inform our work.

Views of and Interactions With Police

Several studies have compared the attitudes and sometimes the experiences of White, Hispanic and African American adults with police. In general, these studies show that Whites trust police more and have more positive interactions than Blacks, and that Hispanics fall between these two populations (Norris, Fielding, Kemp, & Fielding, 1992; Spitzer, 1976; Wilson, 1996). Norris et al. (1992) note that of all groups studied, Black youth tend to have the most "negative" and "hostile" feelings towards police (see also Anderson, 1994; A. Wilson, 1990; W. J. Wilson, 1996).

Heightened surveillance may breed this heightened suspicion. In an ethnography of 50 young urban Black men in gangs, Patton (1998) reported that these men perceived police as a force of oppression, not a force of community protection. Wilson (1996) concurs, stating that these young men often equate street level police officers with laws they are hired to uphold. The recent Quinnipiac University survey found that 64% of New York City Blacks, 52% of Hispanics and 21% of Whites rate police brutality as a very serious problem. (Quinnipiac University, 2001).

Wortley and Tanner (2001) have examined how race and ethnicity of youth affect the likelihood of being stopped and searched by police. In their study of over 3,300 Toronto high school students, they found that Black youth who were not involved with drugs or other delinquent activities were more likely to be stopped and searched by the police than those White youth who admitted involvement in illegal behavior. Demonstrating the frequency of racial profiling among adolescents, these findings suggest that even Black youth who do not participate in suspect behaviors suffer from police scrutiny.

Further, once youth are involved with the juvenile justice system, race and ethnicity dramatically influence outcomes. A recent study tracking youth through the United States juvenile justice system by race/ethnicity (Poe-Yagamata and Jones, 2000) found that 26 percent of young people who are arrested in the United States are African American, representing rates slightly higher than their representation in the general population. At every point in the criminal justice process, however, being African American increased the likelihood of more negative outcomes for youth. The most chilling finding of this analysis reveals that a full 58 percent of the youth who end up in state adult prisons are African American, more than doubling their original over-representation in the arrest rates.

School Surveillance

In schools, as on the streets, surveillance of youth, and youth of color in particular, appears to be on the rise. With media focus on school violence (Ferraraccio, 1999; Patton, 1998; Wilson & Zirkel, 1994) has come a corresponding proliferation of security guards, metal detectors, and zero tolerance policies in public schools (see Ayers, Ayers, Dohrn and Jackson, 2001 for educational, legal, and psychological analyses of the increased security measures within public schools; Hopkins, 1945). While most research in this area has not examined how youth experience zero tolerance, many scholars, educators, and activists across the United States have expressed the fear that heightened reliance on discipline, suspension, and expulsion, in the name of "zero tolerance," forces out large and disproportionate numbers of youth of color and conveys to youth that they are viewed as untrustworthy, suspicious, and potential criminals (Daiute, Stern, and Lelutiu-Weinberger, this issue; Fine & Smith, 2001; McCormick, 2001; Michie, 2001; Noguera, 2002). Indeed, the American Bar Association (2001) recently resolved that "the ABA opposes, in principle, 'zero tolerance' policies that have a discriminatory effect or mandate either expulsion or referral of students to juvenile or criminal court, without regard to the circumstances or nature of the offense or the student's history" (p. 2).

Urban Youth Perspectives on Surveillance

National anxieties typically attach to youth; moral panics have long targeted youth as the source of national troubles. Today, as in the past, concerns over crime, sexuality, and education focus on the "failures" of youth. In such panics, it is not unusual for a nation to construct technologies of surveillance, embodied in machines and people, often those very persons "entrusted" with public authority (see Ayers, Ayers, Dohrn & Jackson, 2001 for contemporary as well as historic analyses of youth as a target of national moral panics).

Foucault (1979) has argued that surveillance works "to impose a particular form of conduct on a human multiplicity" (p. 205). According to Foucault, surveillance is a strategy to discipline the public. Our study seeks to reveal the consequences, from an urban youth perspective, of aggressive policing and adult surveillance of young people in many corners of public space, with particular concerns about youth alienation and disengagement from adult society.

Recent research on youth in public and private spaces suggests that urban youth, especially low-income youth of color, are being squeezed out of public spaces and placed under scrutiny and threat of criminalization when they are in public sites, and even at home (e.g., Kerr and Stattin, 2000). Some have suggested that these policies may make it more difficult for young people to turn to teachers, police or other adults in positions of public authority for help (Freudenberg et al., 1999). Strikingly absent in this literature are the perspectives of young people, themselves, with a thorough analysis of race/ethnicity and gender. These are the empirical and theoretical holes that this research seeks to address.

Methods and Design

In order to assess youths' and young adults' perceptions and experiences of their interactions with police, security guards, and other adults in position of authority, we designed a "street survey" of 911 young people found in public places in New York City. In addition, we conducted open-ended structured telephone interviews with a sub-sample of 36 youth who reported, on their original survey, an instance of a difficult encounter with an adult in a position of public authority. A participatory action research model was implemented for this two-part, quantitative and qualitative study of New York City youth and young adults. In preparation for instrument design, the senior authors met with two focus groups of youth in two New York City high schools. Out of these discussions, four primary research questions evolved: (a) To what extent do urban youth experience adult surveillance as evidence of mistrust and harassment versus comfort and safety? (b) To what extent do race/ethnicity and gender differentiate youth experiences of adult surveillance, particularly by teachers, police and security guards? (c) Can we begin to identify the consequences of surveillance on urban youth? (d) To what extent does the perception of adult surveillance affect youths' trust in adult society, civic institutions, and democratic engagement?

Two dozen New York City youth and young adults, representing a racial, ethnic, and gender mix, were hired as coresearchers. Six 4- to 6-hour workshops were organized to train them on participatory action research (PAR) methodologies, quantitative design, and ethics, and to seek their wisdom, cautions, and language for instrument design. Over the course of these workshops, the youth and university-based researchers constructed a 112 item survey, "Young Adults and Public Spaces," a multidimensional measure developed to document the attitudes and experiences of New York City youth and young adults with adults in positions of authority (e.g., police, teachers, parents, store personnel, and security guards). Measures of trust, alienation, harassment, and help seeking were also included in the surveys.

In summer 2000, using flyers and street outreach, ethnically diverse teams of high school and college student interviewers approached and recruited respondents in public places throughout New York City: parks, street corners, outside schools, libraries and community colleges, and in other public sites. We sought a range of sites and youth, seeking to maximize generalizability for type of youth and type of setting in which they would be found. Interviewing sites were selected to enable us to fill each cell in our ideal sampling framework (calculated from the 1990 Census). The distribution by borough approximated the distribution by race/ethnicity of young adults (16 to 21) in the five boroughs of New York City. As we achieved our desired sample size in one group (e.g., Latino males in Manhattan), interviewers selectively sought participants to fill open cells (e.g., Asian females in Queens).

After determining that a young person was eligible (i.e., age 16 to 21 with residence in New York City), interviewers invited them to participate in the survey. Respondents completed an informed consent procedure (approved by the Hunter College Institutional Review Board), then filled out the survey, a process that usually took 20–40 minutes. Where necessary, interviewers read survey questions to participants. Those who completed the survey were given a free movie ticket at the end of the interview. All data were confidential and anonymous.

To gain insight into the complexity of and response to adverse interactions with police and other adults in authority, we interviewed, on the telephone, a sample of young people who had reported troubling interactions with police or other adults in the street survey and volunteered to discuss the incidents further. A total of 113 accepted this offer and we were able to reach 36 (32%) by telephone. This sample was 39% male and 61% female; and 75% were African American or Latino.

Street Survey Participant Sample

Comparing the characteristics of all young people in New York City with our street survey sample of 16 to 21 year olds, using U.S. Census data from 1990 for the New York City population, the sample was quite representative: 48% female,

Table 1. Percent of Sample Reporting Various Interactions with Police in Last 12 Months

Item	Male	Female	African Americans	Latinos	Whites	Asian/Pacific Islanders
Stopped	52	19	37	38	40	27
Frisked	32	6	18	23	23	19
Picked up in sweep	15	5	8	13	6	8
Detained	18	5	10	12	12	9
Arrested	16	2	14	13	11	6
Worried about being arrested (very much/all the time)			22	18	10	16

Note. Any respondent who indicated that she/he had been stopped, frisked, picked up, detained, or arrested at least once in the last 12 months is included in these percentages.

50% male: 23% White (compared to 30% White in NYC population under age 18), 30% African American (compared to 32% from the census), 30% Latino (compared to 32% from the census), and 10% Asian and Pacific Islander (compared to 7% from the census). It should be noted that our sample included 22% African Americans and 8% African Caribbeans. In addition, our sampling method was selected for young people who spent time on the street and therefore may be at higher risk for interacting with police (see Table 1). Thus, our findings may not be generalizable to adolescents who seldom leave their homes, although we selected a range of sampling sites (e.g., parks, schools, libraries, malls, basketball courts, beaches) to ensure diversity in the youth whom we did survey.

Instruments

Four scales were constructed using Likert-scale items taken from the survey.

Attitudes Toward Police. New York City youths' and young adults' attitudes toward police were assessed using this 12-item scale (potential scores range from 12–48), e.g., "Most police are just trying to protect the public," and "When I go out, my family worries that I may have problems with the police." Higher scores indicate more negative attitudes toward police. Cronbach's alpha is .79.

Comfort in School. This three-item scale was developed to assess youths' and young adults' comfort in schools, e.g., "I feel safe in my school." Higher scores (potential scores range from 3–12) indicate more comfort in schools. Cronbach's alpha is .63.

Trust Toward Adults. This scale assesses how youth and young adults trust adults in positions of authority, e.g., "It is comforting to know that adults around me care about me." Higher scores on the *Trust Toward Adults Scale* indicate more trust toward adults in positions of authority. Cronbach's alpha is .67.

Safe Places. This scale measures youths' and young adults' perceptions of safe and/or unsafe places in New York City. Youth were asked: "Think about the following 'places' in your life, and please tell us how safe they feel to you (from 1 [*not at all safe*] to 4 [*very safe*]), e.g., Church/Synagogue/Mosque, Local Park, the Subway." Cronbach's alpha is .77.

Findings From the Street Survey

On Youth Alienation

These urban youth narrated an ambivalence about police presence in their neighborhoods and a disappointment that police, guards, social workers, and educators view youth as suspect and untrustworthy, reporting considerable alienation in New York City. Data that illustrate this alienation include: 52% disagree (or strongly disagree) that New York City "makes young people like me feel welcomed," 54% feel "unsafe on subways," and 47% indicate that they worry about being arrested very much or all of the time. Further, many young people provide evidence of alienation from adults in general, with the important exception of their parents. For example, in response to the question, "If you were in a situation that would lead to your, or a friend, getting hurt, how likely is it that you would ask for help from the following people": 45% of the respondents said it was unlikely (or very unlikely) they would ask the police for help; 48% reported this for teachers or counselors; 60% for ministers, rabbis, or priests; 64% for social workers, and 61% for security guards. Indeed the only adults from whom a majority of youth were likely to seek assistance were parents (70%). While these data suggest that urban youth experience a narrow net of trustable adults, they also reveal that youth are not generally dismissive of adults. To the contrary, parents are appreciated as helpful by a large majority of the sample, and, as data below will demonstrate, youth in small schools are more likely to trust adults in varied positions of authority than youth in large schools.

Youth Attitudes Overall

A multivariate analysis of variance (MANOVA) was conducted to assess the relationships among gender, ethnicity, and the four scales. The overall model indicated: no main effect of gender, a main effect of ethnicity (Wilks' Lambda = .88, $p < .001$), and no gender by ethnicity interactions. Because the overall model depicts only a glimpse of the experiences of youth in New York City (via the four scales), the authors feel that the subsequent follow-up analyses, individual scale findings, and even responses to individual items will give the reader more insight into the overall perspectives of youth in New York City. Important findings are detailed below.

Attitudes Toward Police

The data for a single item may summarize the story of youth and attitudes toward the police. A contingency table was constructed to address ethnicity on the following item: "I feel comfortable when I see police on the street." Results indicated that 58% of African Americans, 53% of Latinos, 33% of Asian/Pacific Islanders and 33% of Whites disagreed or strongly disagreed with this statement. A contingency analysis illustrated that the proportional differences among ethnic groups are significant ($\chi^2 = 38.744$, df $= 18$, $p = .003$). Additionally, the follow-up univariate ANOVA of ethnic group differences and subsequent pairwise comparisons on the *Attitudes Toward Police Scale* indicated significant mean differences between ethnic groups: $F(6,836) = 2.26$, $p = .035$. The mean scores are as follows: African Caribbeans ($X = 32$); African Americans ($X = 31.3$); Latino/Hispanics ($X = 30.2$); Asian/Pacific Islanders ($X = 29.4$), and Whites ($X = 29.0$).

The means indicate that youth of African descent (i.e., African American or African Caribbean) have more negative attitudes toward the police than other ethnic groups. Specifically, the follow-up post-hoc analyses (LSD; for homogeneous variances) indicate that African Caribbean and African American respondents have significantly more negative attitudes toward the police than Asian/Pacific Islanders and White respondents.

A follow-up ANOVA indicated a significant gender difference on the *Attitudes Toward Police Scale*: $F(1,836) = 17.89$, $p = .001$. Specifically, men had higher scores than women. In other words, men have significantly more negative attitudes towards the police than women.

When the 36 youth in the sub-sample were asked about their views of local policing practices, they offered a range of responses. A content analysis of the 36 responses produced three categories: critics (50% of the sample), ambivalent critique (25% of the sample), and police supporters (25% of the sample). Critics expressed strong, negative views of the police, e.g., "More police means more fear of police," or "More police means more discrimination." Ambivalent critics expressed, also, substantial critical concern over police presence, but they voiced, as well, worries about crime, e.g., "More police may mean lower rates of murder but more brutality." Finally, police supporters cited only positive assessments of the increased police presence, e.g., "More officers, less crime," or "I feel safer." Females offered somewhat more positive assessments of the police than males.

Comfort in School

A considerable proportion of the young adults in this sample report that they do not feel psychologically or physically safe in schools: 21% feel unsafe (or very unsafe) in school; 45% see fights often or all the time in school; 50% believe police/security officers do not make school safer; and only 11% would report to a teacher if they witnessed a fight. With respect to the *Comfort in School Scale*, the follow-up ANOVA indicated significant gender differences: $F(1,628) = 19.48$, $p = .001$. Females ($x = 7.8$) tended to be more comfortable in school than males ($x = 7.0$).

Additionally, individual linear multiple regression analyses using the *Comfort in School Scale* as the predictor variable and each "position of authority" as the dependent variables indicated that comfort in school is a strong predictor of youth being willing to ask for help from various adults. Overall, 46% are comfortable talking with a teacher or a counselor in the event that help is needed. In fact, those young people who feel most comfortable in school are significantly more likely to ask for help from adults in positions of public authority, particularly teachers and counselors: $F(1,629) = 87.55$, $p = .001$, $r = .34$; but also from police: $F(1,632) = 44$, $p = .001$; and parents: $F(1,621) = 27.27$, $p = .001$, $r = .21$. In addition, school size correlates with students' willingness to seek help from adults. The larger the school, the less likely students are to seek help from an adult: $r = -.10$, $p = .011$. In particular, 57% of youth who attend a small high school (250–500 persons) vs. 43% of youth who attend a large high school (2000 persons or more) report that they would ask for help from a teacher/counselor.

Safe Places

The follow-up univariate ANOVA on number of places considered "safe" in New York City indicated a main effect for ethnicity only: $F(6,848)$, $p = .001$. African American and African Caribbean youth feel safe in fewer places in New York City than other ethnic groups. White youth feel safe in significantly more places. This research was conducted just after the high profile cases of Amadou Diallo, Patrick Desmond, and Abner Louima—all African or African Caribbean men assaulted by police—were in the media.

Interactions With Police

Our findings document that a significant proportion of urban youth experience problematic relationships with police and security guards. Nearly one in three respondents agreed that police often used abusive language against young people. A contingency analysis indicated a significant gender effect: On a four point scale of agreement with the statement, "Police in New York City unfairly use abusive language with some people," females are significantly more likely than males to report abusive language by police ($\chi^2 = 10.8$, df $= 3$, $p = .013$)

though the correlations were weak ($r = .09$, $p = .08$). Furthermore, more than half of all respondents (54%) reported that they disagree or strongly disagree with the statement "I feel safe when I see police in my neighborhood." More than a third (35%) of those enrolled in school said that police or security guards in their school did not make them feel safe. As Table 1 reveals, more than a third had been stopped by the police in the last 12 months; 20% had been frisked; 17% had been given a summons; and 11% said they had been arrested, with arrest rates slightly higher for African Americans and Latinos than Whites and Asian/Pacific Islanders.

Young men are far more likely than young women to report negative interactions with police. The results of the linear regression analysis using gender as the predictor variable and a composite variable of "interactions with police" as the dependent variable indicate that gender is a significant predictor of interactions with the police: $F(1,865) = 154.09$, $p < .001$, such that men experience significantly more negative interactions: $r = .40$, $p < .001$. Further, as Table 1 reveals, young men of color are somewhat more likely than Whites to be picked up in a sweep or arrested. Young men across racial and ethnic groups report frequent incidences of being stopped and frisked, with Latinos most likely to report being picked up in a sweep. It is noteworthy that while attitudes and interactions with police vary only somewhat by ethnicity, African Americans are more than twice as likely to worry frequently about being arrested.

Sexualized Harassment of Young Women by Police Officers

Quite unexpectedly, almost two-fifths of the young women surveyed indicated that in the past 12 months, male police officers had flirted, whistled, or "come on to them." By race and ethnicity, 51% of White females report they were "flirted with" by a police officer, compared with 38% of African Americans, 39% of Latinas and 13% of Asian/Pacific Islanders. One third of White and African American females reported being "whistled at" or that an officer "came on to me," compared with ten percent of Asian/Pacific Islanders. For many young women, the experience of street harassment by police was quite disturbing. Indeed, we had not even thought to ask about sexual harassment by police, but our youth researchers insisted. In the open-ended telephone interview, one young woman, Martha (African American female, age 19) explicated the psychological and social impact of police harassment: "They say they are protecting us, but they only make me feel more at risk." Susan (White female, age 20) explained, "So this is how I learned that the very people who say they are going to protect you sometimes make you the most vulnerable." This sexualized behavior may reduce young women's willingness to turn to the police in times of need, a problem that warrants further investigation and action.

Findings From the Telephone Interviews: Youth Reactions to Adverse Interactions with Adults in Authority in Public Places

While the street survey permitted broad based documentation of the frequency and response by youth to adult surveillance, the in-depth telephone interviews were designed to gather narratives from youths about incidents in which an adult in authority disrespected or threatened them. Of the original 113 identified as eligible for a follow up interview, only 36 could be reached and interviewed by telephone after four to six weeks due, in part, to changes in residence from summer to fall, inability to speak freely on the phone in apartments crowded with family, and school and work schedules that did not permit easy access to telephones.

We analyzed the data for key themes that emerged across the narratives collected in phone conversations, transcribed and analyzed for youth overall, by race/ethnicity and gender. Two readers (the first author and an assistant) reviewed all responses to the telephone survey, and generated six codes. These two readers then coded over half of the relevant narratives and calculated reliability ratings for each of the six codes: micro-aggressions (reliability .72), mistrust of adults/betrayal by adults (reliability .80), belief that adults stereotype because of appearance (reliability .82), empathy with adult perspective (reliability .80), anger/disappointment/fear (reliability .75), and belief that change is/is not possible (reliability .87). Reliabilities for these codes were between 72% and 87%. Details of the incident, attributions for the incident, and any emotion words used to describe the respondents' reactions were also recorded.

Overall, four findings emerged:

- Across the sample interviewed, most youth (30/36) report instances of "micro-aggressions." Everyday "micro-aggressions" of disrespect and suspicion (Boyd-Franklin and Franklin, 2000) by police, teachers and store staff toward youth are experienced as forms of interpersonal violence in schools, stores, and on the streets (on the variable "micro-aggression" two coders rated 20 transcripts and achieved an 85% reliability);

- Across the sample, more than half of the young people (19/36) interviewed perceived a fundamental mistrust of youth by adults, which often translates into a sense of betrayal and a vulnerable standing in the social community (on the variable mistrust, two coders rated 20 transcripts and achieved 80% reliability);

- Reviewing the interview data with an eye focused on race and ethnicity, despite the small numbers, there was a trend suggesting that African American youth were more likely to conclude that little could be done to change social arrangements or to grieve social injustice (coders rated 8 narratives on belief that something/nothing can be done, generating a reliability of .87).

While our numbers are too small to quantify, this suggests a psychological finding worthy of further investigation.

- Although youths across race and ethnicity seem to express some empathy even for adults whom they feel have betrayed them, they are worried that adults do not extend a reciprocal sense of empathy to them. That is, youths seem to be willing to see things from an adult's perspective, but feel that adults are not willing to listen to what it's like to be a young person (on the variable "seeking reciprocity/empathy from adults" two coders rated 15 transcripts, and reached 80% reliability).

The incidents which youths reported occurred on the streets with police or guards, in stores, or in schools. Stories of police harassment came largely from Black and Hispanic youth. Even the White female, Sharon (age 19), told of an incident in which she was "in a car with a Black kid driving and we got stopped because the cops thought we were selling drugs." In each instance the youth were "scared" or "shocked" at the behavior of the police, and report feeling as though it would be hard to trust police in the future. Across incidents, these young adults never reported the police misbehavior to authorities. A few spoke to parents, but did not report the problem because "people would take the side of cops, not a Hispanic kid" (personal communication, 2000, Jose, age 19) or "I guess they were doing their job . . ." (personal communication, 2000, Jimmy, age 19) or "I felt scared and *not* protected, didn't want to make it worse" (personal communication, Tommy, 2000, age 20). One African American female said it simply, "You get used to this, the pat downs, spread eagles . . ." (personal communication, 2000, Tasha, age 18).

Incidents in stores, too, typically involved youths of color. These stories reveal a shocking recognition of a social view that "I can't be trusted" (personal communication, 2000, Jimmy, 19) or "I might steal" (personal communication, 2000, Alfonso, 21) or "I don't have enough money to buy, so I'm gonna rob them" (personal communication, 2000, Malek, 17). The young women report that when they enter a store, they are quickly offered, "Can I help you?" (personal communication, 2000, Susan, Tasha and Carmita) while the men talk about security guards contacting sales clerks with walkie talkies (personal communication, 2000, Alfonso, 21), following them around or insisting that they purchase or leave (personal communication, 2000, Josh, 17, Walter, 17, Abdul, 20).

The stories from schools often involved teachers who "went off on me" (personal communication, 2000, Steve, 17), "stereotyped my people" (personal communication, 2000, Tyrone, 18) or "responded to me with an attitude" (personal communication, 2000, Victor, 19). Students typically spoke with the teacher, a friend, or another adult in the school, eager to have the behavior rectified. Yet in most cases the students indicated that "the teacher was having a hard day" or "sometimes it's just difficult to teach" (personal communication, 2000, Rosemarie, 17 and Sarah, 18) revealing a generous willingness to understand the dilemmas of educators today.

The youths typically attributed these interactions to adult stereotypes of urban youth of color. Although not queried about clothing or attitudes, almost 40% of those interviewed reported that adults in positions of authority often equate young persons who wear contemporary urban clothing (e.g., baggy jeans, du rags, etc.) with being a "thug" or criminally inclined (this emerged as we coded for "attributions to appearance"). Young adults of color were particularly likely to talk about the misinterpretation of their clothing as an act of disrespect and to remark on racial profiling by adults in positions of authority. One young man, Charles, explained, "officers . . . have the mindset that every Black male is some hoodlum, someone who is waiting to commit a crime."

Youth who report difficult confrontations with adults indicate that they were angry, scared, and discouraged, particularly with teachers and police (15/36). A number of Latino and Asian males (4) used words like "shocked" and "scared"; while quite a few African Americans (4) said that they were "used to it . . . it always happens," with a sense of bitter resignation to being reminded that they are not wanted in schools, stores, or on the streets.

Beyond fear and resignation, the youth expressed disappointment in their relations with police. Although 80% of this sample reported that they were in-volved in community service projects, 74% said they felt that increased police presence in New York City had worsened police relations with New York City youth—particularly with youth from communities of color and economic poverty (among the choices: improved relations, stayed the same, or worsened). These youths noted with regret a missed opportunity for collaboration between youth and police.

Overall, these young people were sensitive to the micro-aggressions of daily life, with youth of color far more likely to expect disrespect and feel they can't challenge such treatment. In their responses, they believe that youth should accept responsibility for their behaviors, and should participate actively and critically in civic life.

Discussion

This study, relying upon qualitative and quantitative methods, was designed with the deep participation of urban youth. The data reveal a multi-faceted youth perspective on aggressive public surveillance, with specific social, psychological, academic and civic implications of aggressive policing and adult surveillance of young people.

First, these data demonstrate that youth across race, ethnic, and gender lines report adverse interactions with and low trust in adults in position of public au-thority. While we cannot attest to the meaning of these experiences over time and cumulatively, James, an African American young man in a focus group, com-mented on this, as he replied to a young White man who reported being followed by a guard in a store: "Yeah, but I'm not going to grow out of it [being suspected] at age 21" (personal communication, 2000, James, 21).

Second, we found that using the lenses of ethnicity and gender can provide significant insights into differential interactions with police and adults in authority. Our findings confirm that African American and Latino males have the highest rates of adverse interactions and mistrust of the police and feel least safe in the city. These young men seemed most resigned to such treatment, unlikely to challenge the injustice. Young men across the board were more likely to have negative interactions with the police than young women and African American males were more than twice as likely as White males (22% vs. 10%) to worry about being arrested. Similarly, the data on perceptions of sexual harassment are probably the first to reveal the magnitude of these policing practices and to suggest an adverse impact on young urban women.

Third, most young people reported that the cumulative impact of adverse interactions with police, security guards, teachers, and store staff is that it makes them feel unwelcome in presumably "public spaces." The open-ended interviews reveal that adverse interactions with police, security guards, or teachers can leave youth with a sense of betrayal by adults, and powerlessness to challenge such behavior. The accounts of "micro-aggressions" by adults in authority, experiences far more frequent than police shootings or beatings, may erode youths' sense of belonging to public institutions for the common good. Youth who experience disrespect by adults in positions of authority may indeed experience higher levels of alienation from adult society and encounter more difficulty integrating into adult life. While further study is needed to assess the prevalence of this alienation, it may be that the long-term price of aggressive policing and other forms of surveillance is a less cohesive community, and a generation of youth who feel vulnerable and unwilling to seek assistance from adults and unable to grieve or challenge such treatment.

Since this study did not explore the long-term consequences of adverse interactions with police or other adult authorities we can only speculate about such outcomes. Based on our experience working with young people in New York City, however, we worry that aggressive policing may heighten racial tensions; move young people from public space into private space, thereby subjecting them to other dangers such as sexual abuse by adults, or risky drug or sexual behavior; or discourage young people from more active political or community participation.

Fourth, our study found that many youths who felt betrayed by adults in authority were, nevertheless, surprisingly empathic toward some of the very adults by whom they felt betrayed and disappointed. Youth recognized the benefits of reduced crime, admitted that they often acted in problematic ways, and accepted that in some cases, the police, guards, or educators were justified in taking action against them. However, they also recognized, and regretted, an adult unwillingness to suspend automatic judgements of young people, which further contribute to their sense of alienation and distrust.

Fifth, we find that school size may be an important predictor of young people's sense of trust in adults in general, as noted in the section on comfort in schools. Youth who attend small schools with caring educators report heightened trust in adults, which generalizes to social workers, police, and other educators (Fine & Somerville, 1998). These are the youth who are most likely to rely upon adults for support and seek assistance in times of need.

Finally, on a different note, our experience suggests that young people can be important partners in research. By using a participatory model, we were able to enlist young people in framing the research questions, developing instruments, finding and interviewing respondents, and interpreting the results (see Fine et al., in press).

In summary, the future of New York City and other urban areas depends on integrating our young people into adult society, having them believe that our public institutions will trust and respect them if they do not break the law and treat them fairly if they do. Our data suggest that police, security guard, and educator interactions with young men and women leave many of all races doubting these basic principles of a just society. Reduced crime rates benefit everyone but the costs of New York City's experiment with aggressive policing and privatization of public space have increased incarceration rates significantly and alienated a significant portion of future citizens and voters. Reassuring the city's young people will require establishing police practices that make all of New York's youth feel respected as worthwhile and contributing members of our communities.

References

American Bar Association. (2001). *Report to House Delegates, Recommendations on School Discipline.* New York: American Bar Association.

Anderson, E. (1994). The code of the streets. *The Atlantic Monthly, 273*(5), 80–92.

Ayers, R., Ayers, W., Dohrn, B., & Jackson, J. (Eds.). (2001). *Zero tolerance: Resisting the drive for punishment* (pp. 11–16). New York: New Press.

Boyd-Franklin, N., & Franklin, A. J. (2000). *Boys to men.* New York: Dutton Publishers.

Caine, R. D., Burlingame, M., & Arney, L. (1998). Off-duty police officers as school security guards in an inner city high school: An exploratory study. *The High School Journal, 82*(1), 11–23.

Cooper, M. (1999, February 5). Officers in Bronx fire 41 shots and an unarmed man is killed. *New York Times*, p. A1.

Devine, J. (1996). *Maximum security: The culture of violence in inner-city schools.* Chicago: University of Chicago Press.

Ferraraccio, M. (1999). Metal detectors in the public schools, Fourth Amendment concerns. *Journal of Law & Education, 28*(2), 209–229.

Fine, M., & Smith, K. (2001). Zero tolerance: Reflections on a failed policy that won't die. In R. Ayers, W. Ayers, B. Dohrn, & J. Jackson (Eds.), *Zero tolerance: Resisting the drive for punishment* (pp. 256–263). New York: New Press.

Fine, M., & Somerville, J. (1998). *Small schools, big imaginations.* Chicago: Cross City Campaign for Urban School Reform.

Fine, M., et al. (in press). Participatory action research: Behind bars and under surveillance. In P. Camic & J. Rhodes (Eds.), *Qualitative methods in psychology*. Washington D.C.: American Psychological Association. Also available: www.changingminds.ws

Foucault, M. (1979). *Discipline and punish: The birth of the prison*. New York: Vintage Books.

Freudenberg, N., et al. (1999). Coming up in the boogie down: Youth perceptions of violence in the South Bronx. *Health Education and Behavior, 26*(7), 788–805.

Hopkins, N. (1995). School pupils' perceptions of the police that visit schools: Not all police are "pigs." *Journal of Community and Applied Social Psychology, 4*(3), 189–207.

Kerr, M., & Stattin, H. (2000). What parents know, how they know it, and several forms of adolescent adjustment: Further support for a reinterpretation of monitoring. *Developmental Psychology, 36*(3), 366–380.

Kocieniewski, D. (1997, August 13). Injured man says Brooklyn officers tortured him in custody. *New York Times*, p. A1.

Lapsley, M. (1986). Moral judgment, personality, and attitude to authority in early and late adolescence. *Journal of Youth and Adolescence, 13*(6), 527–542.

McCormick, J. (2001). Aesthetics safety zones: Surveillance and sanctuary in poetry by young women. In Weis, L., & Fine, M. (Eds.), *Construction sites* (pp. 180–195). New York: Teachers College Press.

Michie, G. (2001). Ground zero. In R. Ayers, W. Ayers, B. Dohrn, & J. Jackson (Eds.), *Zero tolerance: Resisting the drive for punishment* (pp. 3–10). New York: New Press.

Nagourney, A., & Connelly, M. (2001, April 7). Guiliani's ratings drop over actions in Dorismond case. *New York Times*, p. A1.

Noguera, P. (2001). Finding safety where we least expect it: The role of social capital in preventing school violence. In R. Ayers, W. Ayers, B. Dohrn, & J. Jackson (Eds.), *Zero tolerance: Resisting the drive for punishment*. New York: New Press.

Noguera, P. (2002). Beyond size: The challenge of high school reform. *Educational Leadership, 59*(5), 60–64.

Norris, C., Fielding, N., Kemp, C., & Fielding, J. (1992). Black and blue: An analysis of the influence on being stopped by the police. *British Journal of Sociology, 43*(2), 207–224.

Patton, P. (1998). The gangstas in our midst. *The Urban Review, 30*(1), 49–76.

Philliber, W. W. (1977). Patterns of alienation in inner city ghettos. *Human Relations, 30*(4), 303–310.

Poe-Yagamata, E., & Jones, S. (2000, April). *And justice for some*. Washington, D.C.: Youth Law Center, Building Blocks for Youth Report.

Quinnipiac University. (2001, February 1). New York City Surveys. Connecticut: Quinnipiac University Public Opinion Polls.

Rashbaum, W. (2000, February 5). Undercover police in Manhattan kill an unarmed man in a scuffle. *New York Times*, p. A1.

Spitzer, E. (1999, December 1). *The New York City Police Department's "stop and frisk" practices: A report to the people of the state of New York from the Office of the Attorney General*. New York: Civil Rights Bureau.

Spitzer, S. (1976). Conflict and consensus in the law enforcement process. Urban minorities and the police. *Criminology: An Interdisciplinary Journal, 14*(2), 189–212.

Thompson, G. (1999, February 8). 1,000 rally to condemn shooting of unarmed man by police. *New York Times*, p. B1.

Torre, M., Fine, M., Boudin, K., Bowen, I., Clark, J., Hylton, D., Martinez, M., Missy, M., Roberts, R., Smart, P., & Upegui, D. (2001). A space for coconstructing counter stories under surveillance. *International Journal of Critical Psychology, 4*, 149–166.

United States Commission on Civil Rights. (2000, June). *Police practices and civil rights in New York City*. Washington, D.C.: Author.

Wilson, A. (1990). *Black on Black violence: The psychodynamics of Black self-annihilation in the service of White domination*. New York: Afrikan World Infosystems.

Wilson, J. M., & Zirkel, P. A. (1994). When guns come to school: Should you use metal detectors to search out weapons? Consider the legal issues. *The American School Board Journal, 8*, 32–34.

Wilson, W. J. (1996). *When work disappears: The world of the new urban poor*. New York: Vintage Books.

Wortley, S., & Tanner, J. (2001, February 14–17). *The good, the bad and the profiled: Race, deviant activity and police stop and search practices.* Paper presented at the 2nd Biannual Conference on Crime and Criminal Justice in the Caribbean, Kingston, Jamaica.

MICHELLE FINE is professor of social/personality psychology, urban education and women's studies at the Graduate Center, CUNY. Recent publications include *The Unknown City* (Beacon Press, with Lois Weis, 1998), *Speedbumps: A Student Friendly Guide to Qualitative Research* (Teachers College Press, 2000, with Lois Weis) and *Construction Sites: Spaces for Urban Youth* (Teachers College Press, 2000, with Lois Weis).

NICK FREUDENBERG is professor and director of Urban Public Health at Hunter College, CUNY and on the faculty of the social/personality psychology program at the Graduate Center, CUNY. He has written on HIV prevention among youth, urban health policy, youth in jail, and community organization for health. He is also a senior research fellow at the Hunter College Center on AIDS, Drugs, and Community Health.

YASSER A. PAYNE is a doctoral candidate at the Graduate Center, CUNY in social/personality psychology. His primary interests are in representations of poverty and African American males in popular culture and in the academy.

TIFFANY PERKINS is a doctoral candidate at the Graduate Center, CUNY in social/personality psychology. Co-author of *Keeping the Struggle Alive* (Teachers College Press, 2002), and the revised edition of *Building Community II: A Manual Exploring Issues of Women and Disability* (Educational Equity Concepts, 2001) Tiffany Perkins' writings focus on the conceptualization and analysis of the intersections of race, gender, class, and disability.

KERSHA SMITH is a doctoral student in social/personality psychology at the City University of New York Graduate Center. Her current research interests involve culturally relevant pedagogy and the role of culture in the academic development of students.

KATYA WANZER completed her master's in public health at Hunter College and now works at Mt. Sinai Medical Center.

Journal of Social Issues, Vol. 59, No. 1, 2003, pp. 159–178

Sowing the Seeds of Violence in Heterosexual Relationships: Early Adolescents Narrate Compulsory Heterosexuality

Deborah L. Tolman*, Renée Spencer, Myra Rosen-Reynoso, and Michelle V. Porche

Center for Research on Women, Wellesley College

In this paper, we explore how early adolescents' descriptions of their romantic relationships produce evidence of how precursors to violence are woven into the fabric of such relationships from the very beginning of their experiences of "heterosociality." We identified Rich's (1983) concept of compulsory heterosexuality as an interpretive framework for analyzing these relationship narratives, examining qualitative data from two samples (combined n *= 100) diverse in ethnicity and income to form a dialogue between youth perspectives and theory. We offer adolescents' descriptions, and our interpretations, of several themes, including the conceptualization of boys as sexual predators which normalizes such behaviors, girls' behavior in response to assumed male aggression, and boys' narration of their participation in relational processes which reproduce these beliefs and behaviors.*

The acknowledgment of violence in adolescent dating relationships has been a focus of growing concern among researchers, youth workers, and educators. This concern is justified by the rates of reported violence of various forms in adolescent dating relationships (e.g., experiencing verbal and/or physical abuse by a partner), ranging from 8.8% (Kann et al., 2000) to 40% (Sousa, 1999). Much of the research

---

Correspondence concerning this article should be addressed to Deborah L. Tolman, Center for Research on Women, Wellesley College, 106 Central Street, Wellesley, MA 02481 [e-mail: dtolman@wellesley.edu]. This research was supported by a grant from the Ford Foundation. We would like to thank Judy Chu for many contributions to the project, Kate Collins and Marta Allyson White for their assistance with preparation of the data, and Mary Harris for her assistance with preparation of this manuscript. Special thanks also to the teens who participated in these studies and to the staff and administrators at the research sites for their commitment and collaboration.

investigating this form of violence has targeted primarily college-aged adolescents, yet teens begin having romantic relationships much earlier, primarily in middle school during their early adolescent years (Furman & Wehner, 1997). In this paper, we explore how early adolescent girls' and boys' ordinary descriptions of their early romantic heterosexual relationships, obtained through qualitative inquiry, produce evidence of how violence, and the antecedents to violence, can weave into the fabric of such relationships *from the very beginning* of their experiences of "heterosociality" (Phillips, 2000). Through an iterative process of oscillation between theory and data (Maxwell, 1996), we identified Rich's (1983) conception of the institution of compulsory heterosexuality as an interpretive framework for analyzing youth's relationship narratives.

Neither of the two studies drawn upon in this paper was specifically about violence in these relationships. In inviting adolescents to describe both positive and negative aspects of their early heterosexual relationships, we noticed discomfiting intimations of expectations and experiences of male aggression and dominance punctuating the many tales of juggling peers, parents and boyfriends/girlfriends, hope and heartbreak, and emotional and sexual exploration. To expose possible roots of relational violence, we focus on these intimations in this paper.

Coming to the Lens of Compulsory Heterosexuality

In this feminist analysis of early adolescent romantic relationships, we examine and incorporate their sociopolitical context. Starting from a query about health and risk in these relationships, we began first to recognize and then to document recurrent scripted behavior which we identified analytically as enactments of compulsory heterosexuality. Rich conceived of heterosexuality as a universally pervasive *institution* organizing male and female relationships, not simply as attraction to and engaging in sexual behavior with the opposite gender. This institution of heterosexuality is comprised of unwritten but clearly codified and compulsory conventions by which males and females join in romantic relationships. Rich posited that heterosexuality is political in nature, rather than natural, functioning to serve the needs and desires of men within patriarchy, and therefore requiring various forms of male coercion of women for its production. She outlined how seemingly discrete social processes actually work synergistically to oppress women, including the socialization of women and men to feel that male sexual "drive" amounts to a right, the denial and denigration of female sexual pleasure or agency, and the objectification of women. Violence against women and the constant threat of it (including sexual harassment and rape), coupled with incitements for women to devalue their relationships with other women, sustain and perpetuate this institution to insure that it functions unconsciously and imperceptibly for most individuals.

Citing Black feminist theorists and novelists, Collins (1990) further illuminated this institution by identifying how several interlocking systems of oppression, specifically race, class, and gender, function so that compulsory heterosexuality is not merely the monolithic privileging of all men at the same kind of expense for all women. That is, race and class intersect with gender to generate hierarchies and concomitant horizontal processes of privilege and oppression within compulsory heterosexuality. For instance, Collins noted that within the United States, African American men encounter barriers to some of the privileges of power and dominance associated with norms of masculinity that compulsory heterosexuality confers on White men, while White women may take up positions of power and dominance over African American women. Other feminist writers, both of color (i.e., Asian United Women of California, 1989; Crenshaw, 1995; Hurtado, 1996) and White (i.e., Caraway, 1991; Furstenberg, 1996), have elaborated Collins' theory of how gender, race and ethnicity, and class function together to produce compulsory heterosexuality.

A cornerstone of Rich's analysis is the contested notion of a "lesbian continuum," which references and resists the prevention, disruption and generation of antagonism in relationships between women. We extend Rich's analysis by identifying how this institution also denigrates and encourages the erasure of *men's* strong feelings of emotional closeness to others, both women and men. Thus, another key component of the institution of compulsory heterosexuality is that male homosexuality, whether overt or suspected, be met with derision, humiliation, and violence, in line with the principle of denigrating anything feminine. That is, it is not only women for whom heterosexuality is "compulsory" but men as well (Connell, 1995). While it has been more and more frequently noted that boys police one another to conform to masculine norms (Connell, 2000; Dowsett, 1998), it is the *complementarity* to conceptions of women's behavior and treatment within compulsory heterosexuality to which we draw attention. Obviously, both men and women can and do resist participation in the institution of compulsory heterosexuality, creating alternative forms of being in heterosexual relationships or claiming identities and lives as gay, lesbian, bisexual, transgendered, or single. However, such departures incite significant and not infrequently severe ramifications and retribution.

A Revised View of Teen Dating Violence: Through the Lens of Compulsory Heterosexuality

We are particularly struck by how little research on teen dating violence inquires *why* there is so much violence. The lens of compulsory heterosexuality highlights the ways in which conventional norms of heterosexual relational dynamics produce and require male dominance and female subordination. Efforts to understand the phenomenon of teen dating violence have tended to conceptualize and research the problem as if it were only about girls and their individual pathology, for instance, as the result of girls' rejection sensitivity (Purdie & Downey, 2000) or history of child maltreatment (Smith & Williams, 1992). While the questions of gender differences and the gender of the perpetrator have consumed much of this research (i.e., Molidor & Tolman, 1998), there is a marked absence of a *gendered analysis* in research questions, designs, methods and interpretations.

The lens of compulsory heterosexuality also encourages us to examine various forms of male aggression and dominance as related and systematic. However, the teen dating violence literature does not acknowledge or recognize that the context in which much of teen dating occurs is school, and in so doing has not made or explored a possible link between sexual harassment in schools and teen dating violence. The pervasiveness of sexual harassment in schools has now been well-documented, with about 80% of girls in secondary schools reporting that they have been the victims of sexual harassment, naming both verbal and physical abuse from boys. While 60% of boys report sexual harassment, they cite more verbal than physical abuse, naming other boys as the more frequent harasser (*Hatred in the Hallways,* 2001; AAUW, 1993; Lee, Croninger, Linn, & Chen, 1996; Stein, 1999). Stein (1995) noted that the impact of adults failing to interrupt, or even respond to, harassment is to implicitly permit and silently encourage boys to engage in, and girls to accept, harassing behaviors. She leapfrogs over adolescent romance to the implications for adulthood in suggesting that this setup provides "training grounds for the insidious cycle of domestic violence" (p. 148).

Given the greater likelihood of sexual harassment among teens happening between students known to each other rather than among strangers (Fineran & Bennett, 1999), there may be a slippery slope from incidents of sexual harassment, which are normalized, to violence in simultaneously occurring early teen dating experiences. At a time when teens are just beginning to explore relationships and intimacy, girls and boys may have difficulty distinguishing between flirting and dominance and aggression. Sexual harassment may inadvertently function as a kind of dress rehearsal for heterosexual relationships. Our point about this theorized connection between sexual harassment and dating violence is its role in girls' and boys' psychosocial development in early adolescence. Fineran and Bennett's (1999) research provides evidence of a link between sexual harassment and beliefs about male power embedded in compulsory heterosexuality, which allows, even encourages, developing boys and girls to be socialized into the established hierarchy of males over females and to learn to grow comfortable with it.

Youth Perspectives on Early Romantic Relationships:
Foreshadows of Dating Violence

Description of Study 1

The 72 students (46 girls and 26 boys) we interviewed were chosen from among the participants in a longitudinal study in a Northeastern sub/urban middle school. This study of adolescent sexual health included both a survey and individual, semi-structured clinical interviews in which we asked early adolescents to share narratives about and descriptions of their experiences with romantic relationships and sexuality. The 72 students interviewed were part of a larger survey sample ($n = 244$) which included White (52%), Latina/o (23%) and bi-racial (17%) early adolescents from poor, working class, and middle class families (26% reported their families currently receiving public assistance) and who were all in the 8th grade. Of the entire sample, 78% of the girls and 85% of the boys reported having had some dating experience by the 8th grade and that their dating relationships lasted, on average, over two months.

The students we interviewed were chosen from among the students who expressed interest in being interviewed, reported having had some dating experience, and represented a range of beliefs about masculinity and femininity ideologies. Interviews were conducted at the school during school hours in a private space. They lasted from 1 to $1\frac{1}{2}$ hours and were tape-recorded and transcribed. Whenever possible, there was a match between the interviewer and interviewee in gender and race/ethnicity (as was the case for Study 2, see below). Spanish-speaking students who preferred to be interviewed in their native language were interviewed by a Spanish-speaking interviewer. The interviewers were guided by a protocol of open-ended questions such as "Could you tell me a story about something that's happened in your relationship, or about how it started or about a special time, which can help me understand what it's like for you?" They asked follow-up questions in response to the stories told, yielding co-constructed narratives about their experiences with romantic relationships (Silverman, 2000). Several questions about sexual harassment and dating violence were also included at the school's request.

We began our analysis by using the theoretical lens of compulsory heterosexuality to generate a list of scripted beliefs and behaviors that were narrated by the adolescents in the interview data (Simon & Gagnon, 1987), such as boys want sex while girls want relationships or girls need to protect themselves from boys' unstoppable sexual desire. First, a content analysis of participants' relationship narratives was performed to (a) verify that these scripted features were present throughout the database, i.e., not idiosyncratic and (b) collect a full range of examples of each of these features that appeared throughout the database. This process enabled us to choose quotes that were representative of the sample and also to cull out statements that were unusual, divergent or provocative, which invited complexity into the dialogue between theory and youth perspectives that is at the heart of this project. Several members of the research team looked at the same interview and independently identified themes reflecting scripted beliefs and behaviors present in that interview. We then met as a group and came to a consensus about the scripted features present in each interview, identified the most recurrent similarities and most notable departures from these features across all of the interviews. We then selected representative quotes for reporting findings. (Quotes are identified by pseudonyms chosen by the students themselves, including cases where girls selected boys' names.)

Then, using the Listening Guide method of narrative analysis (see Brown & Gilligan, 1992; Gilligan, Spencer, Weinberg, & Bertsch, in press; Tolman & Szalacha, 1999), we examined the ways these girls and boys were negotiating compulsory heterosexuality by listening specifically for their compliance with, neutrality towards, and open resistance to these scripts. The Listening Guide method involves a series of sequential readings of the same narrative in which the researcher "listens" for one specific perspective each time through. For this analysis, several members of the team read each interview five times, "listening" for (a) how the adolescents represented themselves in the interview, (b) how they experienced their own sexuality, and the ways in which they (c) enacted (d) did not enact, and (e) actively resisted compulsory heterosexuality. We then met together to come to a consensus about the interpretations we had developed on the basis of these "listenings" and then composed case summaries of how each of these adolescents managed compulsory heterosexuality. This work was done by an interpretive community (Fish, 1980) of a group of feminist women, diverse in their ethnic and economic backgrounds and sexualities. While our sample for Study 1 was diverse as described above, we chose to privilege gender in this analysis because there was not a sufficient number of cases of each racial/ethnic group to explore the multidimensionality of compulsory heterosexuality. In our discussion of Study 2, we will speak to evidence of how race and class oppression interplay with gender to produce variations in compulsory heterosexuality.

What We Learned From Study 1

Boys will be boys. One of the central tenets of compulsory heterosexuality that pervaded these young teens' descriptions of their romantic relationships was the belief that most boys are, *by nature*, sexual predators. This belief is exemplified by 14-year-old Juliana's statement "I think all relationships are like, like that. I think boys just get one thing and then they'll leave, ya know?" Such characterizations of boys and their interest in relationships as mainly a means to "get" sex were common in the girls' (and boys') interviews. Given this expectation of male sexual aggression, a priority for girls was learning to read and respond to it in ways that would allow them to participate in this new form of social relationship—while at the same time hedging to protect themselves from harm. Girls described the myriad ways in which they armored themselves against this anticipated sexual aggression, such as breaking up with boys in anticipation of being pressured for sex and setting firm limits with every boy around sexuality regardless of their experience with any particular boy. Will Smith, a 13-year-old girl, narrated how she set limits with her boyfriend before they ever even went out: "I was like, I was like 'Do you want to go out with me?' And then I was like, 'But, listen to this . . . so you can go out with me you have to realize that you're not going to have sex with me. The kissing is going to be done whether I like it, and if I don't like it, well then it's off.'" Her strategy to set firm limits up front leaves no space within which she can experience and explore her own pleasure and passion, suggesting that she does not feel the luxury of identifying or privileging her own need for space to explore a physically intimate relationship.

While girls' general statements about boys' dominance and aggression in dating relationships were exemplified by tough-sounding talk, such as Mallory's (a 13-year-old girl) declaration, "[t]hat would be like the first clue to get out of the relationship with someone—when they're mad all they do is hit," their actual descriptions of their own experiences highlight the complexities girls face. Several of these girls described boyfriends yelling at them, calling them names, and policing their social behaviors such as what clothes they could wear and when and with whom they could go out. While hitting might have been considered to be behavior that should not be tolerated, for some girls, other aggressive, and even abusive, behaviors seemed more acceptable.

Lisa, a 13-year-old girl, described frequent fights with her boyfriend in which he called her names. She labeled him "violent," giving an example from an incident just the day before—"I mean, yesterday he threw, he tried to throw a table at my friend because she was talking about me and we broke up"—and detailed how he yelled at her when they fight: "He calls me like, like, he says it so like, he says it like he means it, like, 'Oh, you're such a whore. You slut. You skank. Oh, you're such a fucking bitch.'" After relaying these experiences, she qualified her reports by explaining that he is not "real violent." She also reported his insistence on knowing her whereabouts at all times and his expectation that she be at home when not with him. Lisa's vacillation between viewing her boyfriend's behaviors as violent and not "real violent" seemed to hinge on whether the violence was physical or verbal. His violence seemed to be expected and was not itself problematic; it was when he went out of bounds of a "normal" range of expected aggression and domination that Lisa had a negative reaction. Lisa has already learned that she should be able to identify abusive men and "choose" normal men (Philips, 2000) and is having to hold the opposing realities that she is not supposed to tolerate mistreatment from boys and men while at the same time know and accept that "boys will be boys."

Sexual Harassment: A Pervasive and Normalized
Form of Gendered Violence

The acceptance of aggressive and dominating behaviors from boys was particularly noticeable in both the girls' and boys' descriptions of sexual harassment at school. While the school had clear policies, both girls and boys described regular occurrences of verbal and physical sexual harassment, primarily but not exclusively directed at girls by boys. They also indicated that this form of sexual harassment is expected and accepted by both boys and girls as simply a part of the school day. For example Ace Eagle, a 15-year-old boy, talked about boys making comments about girls in the hallways. He recited the names easily, "Gang, chickenhead, all you—all the above. All of it, everything." When asked about the reverse, girls making like comments about boys, he says "sometimes" and, like virtually all of the other interviewees, had difficulty coming up with any specific comments he remembered hearing, "Sometimes—I—I hear 'em, but I can't remember 'em right now." Dominique, a 13-year-old girl, told her interviewer "I mean, girls get called more names than guys do . . . . Cuz there's more names for girls." When asked why she thinks that is, she replies, "I don't know. I don't know. They were all invented before we were born, so, you know."

The most common way to deal with sexual harassment described by these girls was to decide not to care about it or to simply ignore it. Nicole, 13-years-old, said that she was frequently harassed by boys in school: "They just say stuff and stuff . . . . I don't know, they just irritate me like little bothering things like if you say something they will start mocking you and they never shut up and they bother me so bad . . . . Like when they grab my butt and stuff, that bothers me." While at first she "just wondered why they were doing it" and talked with a school counselor about it, at the time of the interview she said, "it's like no big deal . . . 'cause they always do it, I'm so used to it."

As other research has demonstrated, even when sexual harassment occurs in full view of adults in authority, intervention is far from assured (Stein, 1999). Mariah, a 13-year-old girl, indicated that she had been sexually harassed quite a bit in middle school, not only in the hallway but also in one of her classes in full view of the teacher. She said that when boys in her class made comments to her like "Oooh you look so fine. I wanta get [some of] this," the teacher merely responded by saying to the boys, "Oh guys, better stop saying that cuz you guys can get in trouble. If Mariah talks to someone here, you guys can get in trouble." Mariah quickly pointed out that this response, placing the responsibility on her to take action, did not make the harassment stop; in fact, she said, "They just start laughing and they don't pay attention to nobody." When asked why she did not report these boys, Mariah replied, "I don't know sometimes it's like I wanted to but sometimes I went like, oh, I can get them in trouble and they can't graduate for that." The teacher's response communicated to Mariah and the other students in the class that such behavior on the part of boys did not warrant further action on the part of the teacher (and therefore would continue), and that it is up to the individual girl to take action. She did, but she took action where she had the most immediate control—she changed her own behavior. She said that she tried to not get up in class and asked a friend to go to her locker to get things for her. While aware that her teacher's intervention was at best ineffective and at worst actually inappropriate in shifting the responsibility to her, her only other alternative was to file a formal report against these boys, action that she worried, perhaps induced or sustained by her teacher's response, was too severe.

Some girls did indicate that they did not fully accept this notion that boys are natural harassers or that they were obliged to tolerate such treatment. Kim, a 13-year-old girl, described frequent verbal and physical sexual harassment and while she had responded with come-back lines, such as a sarcastic "Good pickup line! You're good!" she said one day she just "couldn't take it anymore," so she kicked a boy who made a sexual comment to her. Despite her mother's efforts to defend her by going to the school and telling the officials that Kim "had a total right to do that" because the boy had been sexually harassing her, Kim did have to serve "one detention" (40 minutes after school) "for being violent." When Kim finally decided to resist the submissive response expected of her, she got in trouble, ironically being labeled violent, despite the fact she did so to counteract sexual harassment that had been ongoing. While Kim's resistance yielded sanctions, what distinguished her from other girls was the participation of her mother in backing up her story, her action and her outrage at having to tolerate violence from boys at school.

Notes From the Other Side

Listening to the experiences of the boys we interviewed about their early relationships, we were struck by their pervasive narration of constant and intense peer pressure to behave in sexually aggressive ways, particularly in front of other boys. Because we were inquiring about their romantic relationships, these data came to us "sideways," thus, *the pivotal role of how they relate to girls* in their process of establishing their masculinity and policing one another to do so became apparent. They described how dating and engaging in heterosexual behavior increases boys' status or popularity, and a few talked about being pressured to perform sexually in front of other boys, particularly by kissing girls, and voiced their concerns about being teased by other boys if they did not do so. Though few boys could name it, their stories, accompanied by their observations about their relationships, suggest that establishing oneself as heterosexual (i.e., *not* homosexual) was a crucial purpose of this behavior. Ace Eagle, a 15-year-old boy, in response to his interviewer's question about why he thought most boys his age want to have a girlfriend, replied simply, "So people don't think you're gay."

Ironically, some boys described engaging in such sexual assertiveness in the absence of their own sexual feelings. Doug, a 13-year-old boy, narrated this peer pressure when he said, "Yeah. Because most people have like girlfriends and boyfriends from like peer pressure. That's like a big thing in the eighth grade . . . . Well like the first couple of times you basically force—like you get used to it, like you might not . . . It depends like how much you like the girl." He described feeling pressure to kiss girls in front of his friends: "It was like people around me like oh, you should do that, you should do this, kiss and stuff, like in front of everybody. You know there'll be a group. It's just like sometimes you've got to like kiss her or whatever." Wayne, a 13-year-old boy, indicated that a boy does not always have to have a girlfriend, but he does have to have had at least one that everybody knows about, saying that "no one really cares" if you don't have a girlfriend, "It's only if you've never ever ever had a girlfriend." While Wayne had no conscious awareness that the point of this condition is to prove heterosexuality, he was keenly aware that not having a girlfriend has negative ramifications.

Boys described both public display of aggressive behaviors towards girls and talking about girls in a sexually explicit manner with other boys. LL Cool J, a 14-year-old boy, spoke directly about how showing that they can do sexual things with girls enhances boys' masculinity and hence their status among male peers. When asked by the interviewer why a guy would want to have a girlfriend he replied, " . . . to show other people . . . That he can have, let's say several girlfriends" which shows them "that you are macho or more of a man." For these boys the expectation that they should want sex all of the time with whomever they can "get it from" contributed to their engaging in sexual behaviors, without the space to pause to consider for themselves whether they were ready or even whether they themselves actually desired to do so.

One 14-year-old boy, Mattla, stood out in describing his growing dissatisfaction with this emphasis on sex as the end-all and be-all of relationships with girls and in narrating his developing sense of the kind of emotional intimacy, and its concomitant pleasures, that is possible in romantic relationships. Reflecting on this change in himself, he said "I used to like girls that would just like do stuff and everything [making out], just, but now I like girls that are more, I like to have a relationship with girls." Describing his current relationship he said:

> She kind of wanted the same thing I did for, with a relationship and . . . we started going out, I talked to her about it. She told me up front. She says uh, "I want to be really great friends," she said. "Still going out and doing stuff," she said. "But I don't want it to be like"—And she couldn't, she couldn't really find the word for it, and so I just said, "Like toying around and stuff." And she said, "Yeah." Like that. She said, "I don't want it to be like that." And I said, "I know I, that's the same thing that I want." So that was, it was good.

As Mattla began to recognize that there might be something more to romantic relationships than making out, he became interested in knowing what a girl wants from a relationship. Because he cared about her feelings as well as his own emotional response to her, interacting with her as a person with whom he felt connected rather than as a commodity for his sexual pleasure led to a willingness to shift his expectations to accommodate her needs. Yet even as we heard him begin to question and even reject several features of compulsory heterosexuality, we noticed how the "new" Mattla bumped up against *her* protective armor, delimiting emotional and intimate connection for them both.

Intersectionality: Contours of Racism and Classism Within Compulsory Heterosexuality

Description of Study 2

The second source of data comes from a series of six monthly workshops and focus groups conducted with a sample of 28 girls who were enrolled in an after-school program run by a grassroots feminist organization in the Northeast. The majority of the girls were early adolescents, although ages ranged from 11 to 19. Most of the participants were either Latina (Puerto Rican and Dominican) or African American, while others identified as White or Asian. All girls were from impoverished backgrounds, living in or near a downtown urban area. Many were referred to the program by school counselors or by parents or guardians.

The adults running this organization embrace a feminist perspective, and it is the hope that, as the girls participate in mentoring relationships, they will develop a critical analysis of how gender, race, and class are institutionalized to marginalize minority groups. The mentors, mostly middle-class professional women (White, African American, Latina), focus on teaching the girls about publishing and related job skills, as well as providing emotional support. These girls entered the program with an acute awareness of the effects of racism and classism, but with less concern about sexism or about the way these three forms of oppression work together. The goal of our workshops, conducted on site in an urban downtown setting, was to present a feminist model of female adolescent sexual health (Tolman, 1999) to them and listen to their thoughts, reactions, and insights.

Over the course of the workshop meetings, two facilitators covered various discussion topics: expectations for how girls should be, act, or feel in order to be feminine; experiences with dating and romance, including attention to sexual agency and sexual identity; and the impact that reputations have for risky and positive aspects of girls' sexuality. These groups were audiotaped. Workshops included short interactive activities; feedback from the girls to the program staff underscored the positive aspects of this experience for participants. Given the transitory nature of the participants, we were unable to do follow up groups with these particular girls. Material from these sessions will be used by the mentoring program to form the basis of a future teen publication (either printed or on-line) on heterosexual relationships and sexual health. Mentors will guide girls in the development of two- to four-page article on sexual health, using selections from transcripts and current research on girls' development.

To analyze data collected from these sessions, tapes of the focus groups were transcribed and integrated with field notes from the sessions and activities. First, we used an inductive method (Bogdan & Biklen, 1998) to see what would emerge about compulsory heterosexuality. Then we constructed conceptually-clustered matrices (Miles & Huberman, 1984) to identify examples of the most prominent emergent themes of male dominance and control, threat and danger, distrust of other girls experienced in the context of interactions with boys and men (in dating and casual relationships), and gendered behavior in relationships. An iterative process of analysis of matrices, transcripts and field notes revealed the degree to which these particular themes dominated the conversations across and within focus groups. Although the questions posed for each session were not designed to elicit these topics, these themes arose consistently in six out of the six focus group sessions.

What We Learned From Study 2

Boys as sexual predators. Echoing the interviews in Study 1, these girls spoke in vehement and outraged ways about how boys were primarily interested in getting sex and were willing to stay in a relationship only until they acquired it, as well as to utilize these sexual experiences to shore up their masculinity in the eyes of peers: "If [a girl] wanted to go out with a boy and they actually thought she was going to sleep with them, they'd just naturally go out with her 'cause just to have sex." A substantial section of the transcripts from each focus group reflected the consistent digression to talk about boys' control in relationships, suggesting that this theme was central to their experiences. While there was some dissension about whether this behavior was endemic to all boys, no girl could identify a specific boy who defied this norm. In one of the focus groups, where the topic was the risks of having relationships, the majority of the girls expressed their concern that once they had sex with their boyfriends, their boyfriends would leave them. They shared the sense that they were being monitored physically by boys and men in their communities who were trying to determine whether they were virgins based on characteristics such as how they walked or stood. One teen explained that she had a friend who was often approached by men because she stood with her legs "wide apart" and therefore was not only seen as no longer a virgin but also as having extensive sexual experience. The girls expressed discomfort and disgust with this practice and its purpose: "Once you start out, and they start out like, 'Are you a virgin?' And then you know, like she said, you know what they're about." Girls acknowledged the double bind of boys' interest in their status as virgins. On the one hand, "Dudes are mostly lookin' out for girls who are virgins, so they can take it," and on the other hand, "It's an issue for girls who are with dudes who are virgins too. Because they don't want to do it with someone with no experience."

While many of the girls reported that boys viewed girls in predominantly negative (i.e., disrespectful, exploitative) and sexual ways, it was also made clear to us that any attention from boys or men—however disrespectful or controlling or potentially dangerous—was better than no attention at all. These behaviors were accepted by the girls as a given hazard or gamble a girl has to take if she wants to have heterosexual romantic relationships. For instance, the girls described the way that boys would be "sweating" them, that is, being particularly attentive in the early phases of their relationships, until they "got them." It was apparent that the girls were savvy about the need of boys to establish their masculinity in front of peers, even if it meant disrespecting girlfriends. They recounted experiences at school where boyfriends would ignore them in front of other boys, then quietly slip over to say "hi." While the girls could reprimand their boyfriends "What, you know me now? You didn't know me 10 minutes ago!"—and critique this approach in the focus groups, they were shocked when we asked if that was a reason to break up with a boy, suggesting that it was an anticipated and normalized part of a romantic relationship.

Girls as Threats—Disconnection From the (Perceived) Enemy

A noticeable proportion of the focus group sessions were devoted to dealing with the consistent distrust among the girls. As often as not, the girls would criticize each other, engage in name calling including racial epithets, or outright refuse to work in small groups with particular girls. From our discussions with staff and our own observations, we determined that conflict within the group had multiple origins: racial/ethnic tensions, neighborhood affiliation and school loyalties, age disparities, and life experiences that fostered suspicion. These tensions contributed to a reluctance and even unwillingness to share their thoughts and experiences openly in the groups, in contrast to girls and boys in the context of individual interviews with adults in Study 1.

The girls ascribed this ubiquitous threat of wrongdoing and even violence from other girls, including girls they considered their friends, to perceived trespass into their heterosexual relationships. The boys were viewed in part as a commodity that provided certain resources (i.e., gifts, food) which the girls wanted or needed. Girls recounted stories about losing friends when they started a relationship with a boyfriend, because of other girls' jealousy. For instance, one girl explained: "Okay, let's say, ya'll are all cool and then someone gets a boyfriend. And then they're like, 'Yeah, my boyfriend does this for me.' And then they're like, 'Damn,' you know. 'Why can't I find somebody like that?' And then they start hating. Girls start hating." They also noted that girls called other girls the same derogatory names that boys use to refer to girls, such as "ho," in the service of competition for boys' attention: "I just had this girl call me a ho, because I had been out with this dude that she wanted to go out with. So she sittin' up here making up rules, calling me a ho." This moniker did not keep her from dating the boy; it was an anticipated part of a familiar process of engaging in a relationship with a desirable "dude."

On the other hand, some girls explained that if they saw their boyfriend being unfaithful and then they proceeded to fight with the "other" girl, they ran the risk of the boy concluding that he could control them, because they cared enough to fight over him: "If you fight a girl, okay, say I see my boyfriend kissing or whatever, and

I fight her—that's just going to let him know, 'Well, I got her like that.'" In this Catch-22, the girls have to wrestle with the dilemma of protecting what is theirs (i.e., their man, their relationship), while dealing with how this effort may make them vulnerable to further control and domination by their boyfriends.

They described girls being extremely calculating in finding ways to sabotage other girls' relationships, not denying their own participation in this practice. One girl had elaborated a plan whereby she and her friend watched over each other's boyfriends and for possible female predators: "I only have one friend that I let come around my boyfriend . . . . I know her boyfriend and she know my boyfriend. So we watch over each other." These girls spoke of a general mistrust of other girls and did not place much value on their friendships with girls, because they believed "friends don't stay forever." This sentiment stood in contrast to the girls in the more socioeconomically diverse middle-school sample, whose talk about boyfriends was not pervasively laced with the provision of needed material resources tied up in heterosexual relationships.

Absent Accountability of Boys

It was clear that the girls were aware of the double standard that boys could and should have a lot of sexual experience and not suffer negative repercussions, while girls run the risk of being branded with terrible reputations. Unlike the girls in Study 1, who stood in a primarily defensive posture towards this and other vulnerabilities, these more disenfranchised girls narrated a more active stance. They tried turning the tables on the boys by appropriating the very derogatory terms specifically and obviously reserved for them by putting the word "male" first. For instance, they called boys "male prostitute" or "male ho." Exemplifying how impervious to such outcomes boys feel by virtue of being male, one girl reported how a boy clearly stated to her: "Oh, I ain't a ho. Oh I ain't a female." However, her resistant view was, "You sleeping around, you a ho." This effort may possibly reflect how these girls had internalized sexism and the right of males to dominate by setting the terms (and in fact, may be viewed as a desirable moniker by the boys). However, it may alternately or even simultaneously be an effort to gain some control over boys by seeking to subject them to the humiliating experience of being categorized in a negative way as a result of open sexuality. In contrast, a girl who dates a guy who is labeled in one of these ways is then viewed in a similar manner, whether or not her behavior is similar to the boy's—"if they stupid enough to sleep around with him, then they a ho too"—while the reverse is not true for a guy who dates a girl who gets called these names.

The girls described how all of the boys would lie to their male friends about having sex in order to gain status. The language these girls report boys using to describe having sex had notably violent overtones. For instance, one girl mimicked: "Just to get props [respect] from their boys, like, 'Yeah. Yeah, I hit it. I hit it.'" We note the absence of positive words to describe intimacy and an absence not only of female sexual subjectivity but also of female humanity in this construction of sexual relations as "it." Fine, Roberts, and Weis (2000) suggested in their study with Latinas that young women acquiesced to the double standard "to 'protect' their men—both out of economic necessity, a blind 'respect,' 'embarrassment,' and the cruel mandates of heterosexual 'love'" (p. 102). Not only do boys have a lack of responsibility and accountability in these girls' stories, these girls carry the responsibility and suffer the consequences for maneuvering through boys' aggressive behavior—a heavier burden than armoring themselves from it, as the majority of the girls in Study 1 described.

A Moment of Possibility: Entitlement to Pleasure

In general, we interpreted a high level of compliance in girls' reports of being objectified by boys and men (see Bartky, 1990; Frederickson & Roberts, 1997). There was a focus on appearance throughout our sessions, valuing thinness, light-skin, and big breasts. This emphasis was also extended to the boys to whom they were attracted, and critiques of others' looks were often extremely harsh. Although the stories of these girls tended towards distressing enactments of compulsory het-erosexuality, there were also glimmers of resistance. In one session, a conversation about cultural and religious norms turned towards female genital mutilation, when one of the participants brought up a story she had just read in a magazine:

> *Interviewer: Do you know what happens to you when you do female circumcision?*
> Uh huh.
> You lose all feeling.
> *Interviewer: You lose all feeling.*
> You lose the feeling.
> Eewwww!
> There's no feeling.
> So you can have sex but it's not pleasurable.
> *Interviewer: Right.*
> That's wrong!
> That is wrong!
> That's something you should never do that to no little kids.

The girls were unanimous in their outrage over this practice, an exception to their usual disagreement and lack of support for one another. In a notable departure from how they referred to their own and others' female bodies, these girls conveyed their knowledge that sexuality can and should be pleasurable for them, that they have a right to the feelings in their bodies, and that denial of that right without consent and at such a young age is "wrong." Perhaps it is the extreme and egregious example of female genital mutilation that can illuminate institutionalized denial of female sexuality and subjectivity. This exchange suggests how these girls can reject seeing women, perhaps themselves, only as objects of others' desire. We were especially struck that girls named the theft of pleasure and desire, without consent, as the primary reason that genital mutilation is immoral.

Conclusions

The school in which Study 1 occurred was staffed by aware adults committed to ending teen dating violence, through classroom curricula and programs on dating violence, even including an annual performance of a play that depicts a girl who resists everyone's insistence that her boyfriend is abusing her and ends in her being murdered by him (which is followed by comments from a police officer and a social worker, as well as by classroom discussion). Some teachers were actively trying to stop it, sharing with us their feeling of swimming upstream and their frustration that the students didn't "see it," which was evident in such behavior as girls fighting over boys. While the message that dating violence is "bad" is clear, a critique of the larger systems which produce and perpetuate violence in intimate relationships was missing, leaving girls feeling scared and boys feeling unfairly accused. This approach bears an uncomfortable similarity to current overly simplistic tactics in abstinence—only education, such as AIDS education and "just say no" to drugs campaigns that gloss over the power dynamics of gender, race and class. This analysis suggests the need to re-evaluate and reengineer dating violence programs in schools that tend to focus on extreme outcomes rather than the more subtle, yet insidious instances of domination.

When asked to reflect on their observations of sexual harassment in their school, both boys and girls concluded that, although the gendered nature of these behaviors did seem "weird," it was simply *the way things were*. Despite separate curricular efforts to offset sexual harassment and dating violence, male aggression and dominance were naturalized and normalized by both the girls and boys. Information about equity and dating violence is woven into the reality of lived and observed relationships that is more powerful than the lessons of school. We would thus encourage schools to move beyond the defensive emphasis on legal ramifications of sexual harassment and re-center efforts on the emotional toll of compulsory heterosexuality for girls and boys as they build foundations for life-long relationships.

The lens of compulsory heterosexuality, modified to incorporate resistance to male homophobia, suggests that isolating dating violence and sexual harassment as independent phenomena, particularly given their implicit socializing functions during adolescence, may lead to largely unsuccessful attempts to treat the symptoms of a much larger problem that continues undiagnosed. The emphasis on "bad" behaviors which remains de-contextualized and unanalyzed is a missed opportunity for helping youth to develop critical perspectives, alternatives and alliances with adults and peers in relational spaces where resistance to the multiple axes of the institution of compulsory heterosexuality, rather than just its constituent parts, could occur. Yet at the same time, while these adolescents may be exposed to critiques of dating violence and sexism, we note girls' expressed sense, especially among somewhat older girls, of the lack of viable alternatives to these forms of gendered relationships, which contributes to the seeming inevitability of violence in and around their romantic experiences. Without new maps of other possibilities for a relational terrain in which boys are responsible, respectful and not having to prove their manhood by publicly kissing or "dissing" girls, such critiques in and of themselves may not provide much of a fit with girls' actual circumstances, choices, and lives.

The mentors of the girls in Study 2 all espoused strong feminist ideals and commitment to social justice through the structure of the program and through one-on-one relationships with the girls. The constraints of socioeconomic background and the daily insults of racial and ethnic prejudice the girls in the program experienced seemed to overwhelm the relevance of feminism—in particular as it pertained to their relationships with boys—in their current circumstances. Although the girls were able to "talk the talk" that one way for girls to be strong is to "be a feminist," they could not define what that meant, nor critique the system of gendered oppression, including male domination and aggression coupled with female betrayal or lack of support in which they as girls were embroiled. These girls reminded us that there are indeed some benefits to be gained by entering into scripted heterosexual relationships; as one of the girls pointed out, having a boyfriend is "something out of the ordinary." The tolerance for boys' dominance, even to the point of violence, in heterosexual relationships seemed to be relatively benign in comparison to other daily dangers. The vulnerability endemic in any focus group discussions, and perhaps even especially with regard to the topics we were covering, may have led to a glossing over of resistance or alternatives to the scripted behaviors they described. In contrast to the middle school study, we have only girls' perspectives on which to draw for this more disenfranchised group, and not that of the boys in their community. These findings underscore the importance of expanding the research agenda on adolescent sexuality from its exclusive focus on diminishing risk behaviors towards more developmental and gendered work on adolescents' romantic relationships.

By bringing the interpretive lens of compulsory heterosexuality to our understanding of girls' and boys' representations of themselves and their experiences, we examined their stories with a politicized perspective that they themselves did not evidence and/or may not have. This analysis of youths' perspectives on violence forces us to confront the tension between our worry that we are foisting this interpretive lens on them and our concomitant belief that in so doing we increase our ability to learn about how the institution of compulsory heterosexuality is placing seeds of violence in their adolescent heterosexual relationships. However, this analysis illuminates primarily invisible choices and constraints which adolescents negotiate with varying levels of consciousness and offers an alternative to the search for explanations of teen dating violence which dislodges and displaces a focus on individual pathology.

Finally, while we are not surprised to hear the variegated narrated acceptance of boys' aggressiveness and normalization of violence in these two samples, we are troubled by it and thus even more by the overwhelming attention paid to understanding why girls get themselves into or stay in violent dating relationships. This ongoing attempt to fix and fiddle with girls is coupled with a glaring lack of attention to understanding boys' aggression—how and why this way of being gets produced, or finding ways to intervene with, or interrupt and resist with, boys (see Sousa, 1999, for an exception). Research and interventions primarily geared toward the role of girls in (failing to) identify abusive behaviors leaves them with a "choice that is not a choice," does not assist boys in dealing with their anger and aggression, does not recognize boys' vulnerability or the lack of social/relational space for their emotional lives or for the development of possible critiques or (safe) alternatives to becoming men. At best, current programming tends to be focused on the teaching of identifying violence in relationships *after* they occur, and at worst pathologizing girls for entering these relationships. There needs to be greater emphasis on prevention for boys.

It is possible that, like the girls who lose their knowledge and voices in the face of dominant norms of femininity (Brown & Gilligan, 1992), some boys may lose track of their emotional responses to these externalized pressures or even their ability to notice them as they move through adolescence. While the emotional and relational difficulties of dominant norms of masculinity have been much discussed of late (i.e., Connell, 2000), the significance of how these phenomena fit together as complementary parts of the institution of compulsory heterosexuality needs to be understood. The complexity of boys' narrations of early romantic relationships, and, at least via the reports of the some of the girls in the focus groups, ongoing male dominant and aggressive behavior into adolescence, indicate that turning our attention to boys' experiences is not only necessary to understand the processes by which they become men but also a crucial component of the empowerment of girls.

References

American Association of University Women (AAUW). (1993). *Hostile hallways: The AAUW survey on sexual harassment in America's schools*. Washington, D.C.: Author.

Asian United Women of California. (Eds.). (1989). *Making waves: An anthology of writings by and about Asian American women*. Boston: Beacon Press.

Bartky, S. L. (1990). *Femininity and domination: Studies in the phenomenology of oppression*. New York: Routledge.

Bogdan, R., & Biklen, S. K. (1998). *Qualitative research for education: An introduction to theory and methods*. Boston: Allyn and Bacon.

Brown, L. M., & Gilligan, C. (1992). *Meeting at the crossroads: Women's psychology and girls' development*. Cambridge, MA: Harvard University Press.

Caraway, N. (1991). *Segregated sisterhood: Racism and the politics of American feminism*. Knoxville, TN: University of Tennessee Press.

Collins, P. H. (1990). *Black feminist thought: Knowledge, consciousness, and the politics of empowerment*. Boston: Unwin Hyman.

Connell, R. W. (1995). *Masculinities*. Berkeley, CA: University of California Press.

Connell, R. W. (2000). *The men and the boys*. St. Leonards, Australia: Allen & Unwin.

Crenshaw, K. (1995). Demarginalizing the intersection of race and sex: A Black feminist critique of antidiscrimination doctrine, feminist theory, and antiracist politics [1989]. In K. T. Bartlett & R. Kennedy (Eds.), *Feminist legal theory: Readings in law and gender* (pp. 57–80). Boulder, CO: Westview Press.

Dowsett, G. (1998). Wusses and willies: Masculinity and contemporary sexual politics. *Journal of Interdisciplinary Gender Studies, 3*(2), 9–22.

Fine, M., Roberts, R., & Weis, L. (2000). Refusing the betrayal: Latinas redefining gender, sexuality, culture and resistance. *The Review of Education/Pedagogy/Cultural Studies, 22*(2), 87–119.

Fineran, S., & Bennett, L. (1999). Gender and power issues of peer sexual harassment among teenagers. *Journal of Interpersonal Violence, 14*(6), 626–641.

Fish, S. (1980). *Is there a text in this class? The authority of interpretive communities*. Cambridge, MA: Harvard University Press.

Fredrickson, B. L., & Roberts, T. A. (1997). Objectification theory: Toward understanding women's lived experiences and mental health risks. *Psychology of Women Quarterly, 21*(2), 173–206.

Furman, W., & Wehner, E. A. (1997). Adolescent romantic relationships: A developmental perspective. In S. Shulman & W. A. Collins (Eds.), *Romantic relationships in adolescence: Developmental perspectives*. San Francisco: Jossey-Bass.

Furstenberg, R. (1996). *White women, race matters*. Minneapolis, MN: University of Minnesota Press.

Gilligan, C., Spencer, R., Weinberg, M. K., & Bertsch, T. (in press). On the Listening Guide: A voice-centered relational method. In P. M. Camic, J. E. Rhodes, & L. Yardley (Eds.), *Qualitative research in psychology: Expanding perspectives in methodology and design*. Washington, D.C.: American Psychological Association Press.

Hatred in the hallways: Violence and discrimination against lesbian, gay, bisexual, and transgender students in U.S. schools. (2001). New York: Human Rights Watch.

Hurtado, A. (1996). *The color of privilege: Three blasphemies on race and feminism*. Ann Arbor, MI: University of Michigan Press.

Kann, L., et al. (2000). *Youth risk behavior surveillance—United States, 1999* (No. SS-5). Atlanta, GA: Centers for Disease Control and Prevention.

Lee, V. E., Croninger, R. G., Linn, E., & Chen, X. (1996). The culture of sexual harassment in secondary schools. *American Educational Research Journal, 33*(2), 383–417.

Maxwell, J. A. (1996). *Qualitative research design: An interactive approach* (Vol. 41). Thousand Oaks, CA: Sage Publications.

Miles, M., & Huberman, A. M. (1984). *Qualitative data analysis: A sourcebook of new methods*. Beverly Hills, CA: Sage Publications.

Molidor, C., & Tolman, R. M. (1998). Gender and contextual factors in adolescent dating violence. *Violence Against Women, 4*(2), 180–194.

Phillips, L. M. (2000). *Flirting with danger: Young women's reflections on sexuality and domination*. New York: New York University Press.

Purdie, V., & Downey, G. (2000). Rejection sensitivity and adolescent girls' vulnerability to relationship-centered difficulties. *Child Maltreatment, 5*(4), 338–349.

Rich, A. (1983). Compulsory heterosexuality and lesbian existence. In A. Snitow, C. Stansell, & S. Thompson (Eds.), *Powers of desire: The politics of sexuality* (pp. 177–205). New York: Monthly Review Press.

Silverman, D. (2000). Analyzing talk and text. In N. K. Denzin & Y. S. Lincoln (Eds.), *Handbook of qualitative research* (2nd edition, pp. 821–834). Thousand Oaks, CA.: Sage Publications.

Simon, W., & Gagnon, J. H. (1987). A sexual scripts approach. In J. H. Geer & W. T. O'Donohue (Eds.), *Theories of human sexuality* (pp. 363–383). New York: Plenum Press.

Smith, J. P., & Williams, J. G. (1992). From abusive household to dating violence. *Journal of Family Violence, 7*, 153–165.

Sousa, C. A. (1999). Teen dating violence: The hidden epidemic. *Family and Conciliation Courts Review, 37*(3), 356–374.

Stein, N. (1995). Sexual harassment in K–12 schools: The public performance of gendered violence. *Harvard Educational Review, 65*(2), 145–162.

Stein, N. (1999). *Classrooms and courtrooms: Facing sexual harassment in K–12 schools*. New York: Teachers College Press.
Tolman, D. L. (1999). Femininity as a barrier to positive sexual health for adolescent girls. *Journal of the American Medical Women's Association, 54*(3), 133–138.
Tolman, D. L., & Szalacha, L. A., (1999). Dimensions of desire: Bridging qualitative and quantitative methods in a study of female adolescent sexuality. *Psychology of Women Quarterly, 23*(2), 7–39.

The authors were all affiliated with the Gender and Sexuality Project at the Center for Research on Women at Wellesley College during the course of this research.

DEBORAH L. TOLMAN is an Associate Director of the Center and a Senior Research Scientist; she is the director and founder of the project. Her book, *Dilemmas of Desire: Adolescent Girls Talk About Sexuality*, will be published by Harvard University Press in Fall, 2002. Her current research program on adolescent sexuality includes developing positive and comprehensive models of male and female adolescent sexual health, the relationship between adolescents' television viewing and their sexuality, including the role of gender ideology, and theorizing female sexuality development.

RENÉE SPENCER is Assistant Professor of Social Work at Boston University. As a clinical social worker, she developed and implemented psychiatric hospital programs for women based on feminist relational theories of psychological development. Her current research joins her interests in relational theories and adolescent development by focusing on the development of empirically based explanations of the often cited but poorly understood finding that a confiding relationship with at least one adult is one of the best protections against many forms of psychological trouble for children and adolescents.

MYRA ROSEN-REYNOSO is a doctoral candidate in the Developmental and Educational Psychology program at the Boston College School of Education. She is also a Fellow at Children's Hospital in Boston, MA. She is currently focusing on the employment outcomes and career development of women with disabilities which is funded by the National Institute on Disability Rehabilitation and Research. Her dissertation is a qualitative study of the work experience and vocational trajectories of Latinas with psychiatric disabilities.

MICHELLE V. PORCHE is a Research Scientist at the Center for Research on Women at Wellesley College. She is also a Research Analyst at Harvard University Graduate School of Education, working on a longitudinal project, investigating language and literacy development related to motivation and academic achievement for children and adolescents.

Journal of Social Issues, Vol. 59, No. 1, 2003, pp. 179–195

Producing Contradictory Masculine Subject Positions: Narratives of Threat, Homophobia and Bullying in 11–14 Year Old Boys

Ann Phoenix*

The Open University, Milton Keynes

Stephen Frosh

Birkbeck College, University of London

Rob Pattman

The Open University, Milton Keynes

This paper reports a qualitative analysis of data from a study of masculinity in 11–14 year old boys attending twelve London schools. Forty-five group discussions (N = 245) and two individual interviews (N = 78) were conducted. The findings indicate that boys' experiences of school led them to assume that interviews would expose them to ridicule and so threaten their masculinity. Boys were generally more serious and willing to reveal emotions in individual than in group interviews. A key theme in boys' accounts was the importance of being able to present themselves as properly masculine in order to avoid being bullied by other boys by being labeled "gay." The ways in which boys were racialized affected their experiences of school.

This paper reports a qualitative analysis of data from a study of masculinity in 11–14 year old boys attending schools in London. It first considers boys' experiences of feeling threatened by everyday practices in school. It then considers how

*Correspondence concerning this article should be addressed to Dr. Ann Phoenix, Faculty of Social Sciences, The Open University, Walton Hall Milton Keynes, MK7 6AA England [e-mail: a.a.phoenix@open.ac.uk]. The authors would like to thank the boys and the schools who made this study possible and the British Economic and Social Research Council, who funded this study in their *Children 5–16 Programme* (grant number L129251015).

boys are positioned in relation to the bullying associated with homophobia in many schools. The paper demonstrates that both these issues place boys in contradictory positions where they "police" their own (and often others') behavior in order to defend themselves against humiliation and being considered not sufficiently masculine (Eder, Evans, & Parker, 1995; Mac an Ghaill, 1994). In order to do this, we first briefly discuss positioning theory (Harré & van Langenhove, 1998) to conceptualize how boys position themselves as masculine. We then consider boys' accounts of how they expected interviews to be similar to their experiences of teachers and school lessons and, hence, to be threatening. The second empirical section of the paper explores how boys took up and/or resisted the violence they experienced as associated with homophobic name calling in their schools. It further indicates that the ways in which boys were racialized affected their experiences of school.

Subject Positions in Positioning Theory

Many researchers interested in identities and subjectivities use the notion of "positioning" (Davies & Harré, 1990) to emphasize that it is in social interactions that people create identity positions for themselves and others. Language is crucial to these identity positions because it is central to the setting up of expectations about how others and ourselves should behave as well as to how people buttress or resist these expectations. Identity positions are thus disputed or accepted in language as people have to explain, defend or abandon them in the face of others' resistance. For this reason, many theorists now see identities and subjectivities (which involve our reflections on ourselves and our emotions) as accomplished in talk and produced as we display (or perform) habitual forms of social interaction in particular situations with specific people (Butler, 1993; Davies & Harré, 1990; Riessman, 2001). It is thus possible for us to be positioned in contradictory ways because we routinely behave differently with different people, in different contexts, or at different points in the same interaction. This sometimes means that people find themselves in "troubled" subject positions if they have to face contradictions they have produced (Wetherell, 1998).

Masculinity and Subject Positions

In many countries it is now commonplace for researchers and media commentators to voice particular concern about two features of masculinity: young men's worsening record of academic attainment in comparison with girls and their propensity for violence (e.g., Ferguson, 2000; Gilbert & Gilbert, 1998; Katz & Buchanan, 1999). A substantial body of research analyses the place of these features in boys' lives and views them as, to some extent, interlinked. Thus, various studies have identified the forms of masculinity that gain most respect as involving hierarchies based on toughness, threat of (or actual) violence, casualness about schoolwork, "compulsory heterosexuality" and a concomitant homophobia (Epstein, 1997; Phoenix & Frosh, 2001; Martino, 1999; Skelton, 1996; Swain, 2000). As a result, boys and young men are forced to position themselves in relation to these issues, whether or not they wish actually to be violent or disengaged from schoolwork. While boys and men are positioned in different ways in relation to idealized conceptions of masculinity, they are constrained and/or enabled by what they consider to be the attributes of "real" boys and men (Laberge & Albert, 1999; Majors & Billson, 1992; Pollack, 1998). At the same time, they frequently produce contradictory masculine subject positions because they experience themselves as inhabiting a "culture of cruelty" that makes them feel sad and lonely, even as they routinely perform as if they are happy and cheerful (Pollack, 1998). As a result, many occupy defensive subject positions because they feel that they have to defend themselves against threat from other boys and from the possibility of failing to be properly masculine (Nayak & Kehily, 1996).

The Study of "Young Masculinities" in 11–14 Year Old Boys

In the study reported here, seventy-eight 11–14 year old boys from 12 London schools were interviewed individually and in groups during 1998 and 1999. In addition, we conducted 45 group interviews with groups usually of 4–6 young people (and a range from 4–8). Thirty of these group interviews were with boys in single sex groups and nine interviews were with mixed groups of boys and girls. This involved a sample of 245 boys and 27 girls. All were volunteers who had responded to a request, put out through their teachers, to participate in discussions on the topic of "growing up as a man" or, in the case of the girls, their "views on boys/young men their age." The study was approved by the ethics committee at the university administering the project and permission for young people to participate in the study was obtained through signed consent forms from boys and girls themselves and their parents. Four schools were in the private sector and eight in the public sector, ensuring a reasonable spread of social class groups and of ethnicities (since state schools in London are more ethnically mixed and contain many more young people from low socioeconomic status backgrounds than do private schools).

The main focus of the interviews was on the ways in which the participants experienced themselves and constructed their identities as young men in talk. The interviews followed a semi-structured format, but were geared towards encouraging the boys to express themselves in "narrative" terms—as freely as possible, elaborating on issues of importance to them. The interviews were "interviewee centered" with the interviewer (a White man) taking a facilitative role, picking up on issues the interviewees raised and encouraging them to develop and reflect upon these and to provide illustrative narrative accounts. These interviews addressed issues of self-definition as male/masculine, identificatory models, relationships with boys and with girls, intimacy and friendship, attitude towards social and media representations of masculinity, and so on. The interviewer saw his task as encouraging the boys to talk about themselves and worked hard to create a non-judgmental and affirming atmosphere. The 24 girls were interviewed once each by a female psychologist employed specifically for this purpose, with the focus being on girls' thoughts about boys their age.

According to many narrative theorists, we "make" our identities through our autobiographical narratives (Bruner, 1990; Finnegan, 1997; Hollway & Jefferson, 2000; Riessman, 2001). We were, therefore, interested in exploring the boys' narratives of their lives and how they construct masculinities in their accounts. For this reason we devised a qualitative study rather than contributing to the substantial literature that explores young people's identities using standardized measures (e.g., Ashmore & Jussim, 1997; Kroger, 2000; Marcia, 1994). All interviews were tape-recorded. Each individual interview and 27 of the 45 group interviews were fully transcribed (amounting to over 4000 pages of transcripts). In addition, the interviewer wrote very full summaries about each boy, each group and each school in the study, recording how interviews went and how he (the interviewer) felt about the interview and the boy(s) at various points in the interview. This summary allowed the interviewer to record impressions of the process of the interview (for example, whether it was "easy" or "difficult" and whether there were surprising aspects to it) and has been used to make preliminary connections across different interviews. Together with boys' accounts of what they expected interviews to be like and how they actually found them, the summaries have been used to analyze the ways in which the boys "co-constructed" their accounts with the interviewer in the interviews.

This paper is informed by a form of qualitative thematic analysis (see Denzin and Lincoln, 1994). This involves extracting the material relevant to considering how our interviewees found the interviews and what they had to say about their experiences of school in relation to homophobia and bullying. The material was qualitatively coded by identifying the themes to be found within it then analyzing the links between these themes. Close attention has been paid to young people's descriptions of their feelings and experiences. Since the analyses presented are qualitative, rather than statistical, no claims can be made that these findings are generalizable beyond the twelve schools studied and thus, relatively few quantitative claims are made about the findings. However, the three authors ensured the reliability and validity of the themes identified by comparing, checking and discussing codes throughout the study. Since they worked so closely together and codes were broad, qualitative ones, reliability rates were high, never being lower than 80% (assessed as agreement for all three authors). Those issues identified as important for the sample are ones that were produced by more than half the boys in the study. Where few boys produced particular kinds of accounts, this is mentioned. As in all qualitative analyses, the quotes presented are intended to allow readers to see whether or not they agree with the interpretations made.

Accomplishing Masculinity in Everyday School Interactions

Boys' Positioning of Themselves as Threatened by the First Interview

Before we interviewed boys, more than half of teachers warned us that they would not talk to us and that we would have difficulty controlling them and in five of the twelve schools particularly admonished the boys not to be too noisy, but to listen to the interviewer. This fear that boys would be "difficult" to control proved to be unfounded. However, while teachers portrayed boys as threatening, an important finding was that most boys (more than 70%) came to the interview situation with expectations that it would be threatening *to* them. Presumably because the interviews were held in schools and had some similarity to the structure of classroom work, they compared the interviews to school classes. They explained that they had (erroneously) expected the researcher to be like a teacher, not listening to them properly, but firing questions at them in oral examination fashion, evaluating their "performance" and possibly catching them out and so embarrassing them. Since being properly masculine entails not being humiliated, such fears are potentially also threats to masculinity (Nayak & Kehily, 1996).

> *Paul: It's like in class there's loads of people and it's like the teacher telling you what to do and you can't really speak like that.*
> *Maurice: It was good to talk about—like I can't really talk to teachers like this. They hardly listen to ya.*
> *Pete: . . . I prefer to do this rather than lessons.*
> *Matthew: I thought the questions were going to be a bit harder which I wouldn't know the answer to but it was fine . . . I thought if I answered something wrong then it would just ask me more and more about it and I wouldn't be able to answer them so it would be like getting harder and harder.*
> (Maurice, 14, White, state school; Pete, 14, White, private school; Paul, 11, White, state school; Matthew, 14, White, private school)

The extract below is from a group of mixed ethnicity run with 13–14 year old boys from a private school. It indicates that some boys misunderstood our introductory letter to them in which we stated our ethical position that, "if cases of abuse or extreme bullying are reported to us we shall have to report these to the school authorities." Contrary to our intentions, our letter contributed to making some boys feel initially that they were positioned in opposition to "authority"— in this case teachers and researchers. The boys explained that they expected the interviewer to be "weird" and expressed surprise that he did not ask about sex ("knowing girls") drink and drugs.

> *Hicham (Asian): I thought you were gonna be like our schoolteachers like [Andy: Really strict] 'cause like when I read the letter that you was erm (pause) doctor of something or something like that [giggle] yeah [laugh].*
> *Richard (White): Yeah in a dark room an' ask all these questions [loud laughter] [twenty questions]*
> *Hicham (Asian): Like my cousin did psychology for A level an' like she said all her erm*

(pause) professor like were really weird an' stuff like that. / . . . /
RP: So, I mean, what kind of questions did you expect that I'd ask?
Richard (White): I don't know. [several giggle]
Andy (White): Really, really terrible [Colin: do you know girls?] [laughing] . . .
Hicham (Asian): In the letter you said like you would report some stuff to the authorities,
school authorities.
Matthew (White): Yeah so [giggle] do you, smoke do you drink? Something like that.
Richard (White): I thought it would be you know, "Do you take drugs?"

For many boys, the interviewer's friendliness and openness allowed them to disrupt their initial positioning of themselves as threatened and him as threatening and to explore new subject positions. This explains why all the boys who expressed a preference for one interview over the other (14% vs. 18%) said that they liked the follow up interview better. They said that this was because of their familiarity with the interviewer and the sorts of questions he was likely to ask.

Jerry: I liked this one better than I did the other one 'cause I knew what it was going to be
like. I wasn't as nervous and things . . . now I know what it's like and it's quite fun.
Pete: I know what's going to happen now . . . it's just like me opening my big mouth for ages
speaking about my life stories.
(Jerry, 12, White, state school; Pete 14, White, private school)

It appeared that the experience of being positioned as social actors (rather than as passive) in the interviews helped some of the boys to reflect on social identities and relationships they tended to take for granted. This is a common finding in longitudinal studies that allow participants the opportunity to reflect on their lives (see, for example, Phoenix, 1994). In the extract below, Matthew (14, White, private school) said he preferred the second interview because the experience of the first interview had changed him, making him more observant and reflective:

Matthew: This interview was easier because I've had time to think about what I said last
time . . . .
RP: What have you thought about?
Matthew: Oh the people I hang around with, who I talk to sort of, I've sort of noticed a bit
more. [RP: Have you?] Yeah sort of I, I instead of just talking to someone I sort of realize
what I'm doing now. [RP: Oh right?] So sort of (.) also a bit more sort of self confident and
things.

It is noticeable that much of the boys' initial self-positioning in the group interviews was in relation to perceived threat. Their accounts indicated that, although they had volunteered and agreed to take part, they expected to be strictly controlled, inhibited and perhaps humiliated by a teacher-like interviewer. They were subsequently able to be reflexive about how they had changed their ideas on this once they encountered the researcher. However, such narratives also show that many boys experience schooling as threatening and restrictive, rather than facilitative. This is the context in which, we will argue, they construct masculinity as synonymous with "toughness," physical aggression and homophobia and antithetical to femininity and compliance with teachers (Ferguson, 2000; Parker, 1996; Skelton, 1996; Swain, 2000).

Defending Themselves Against Fears of Psychological Violence in Group Interviews

In this study, boys who were interviewed individually had all previously been part of the group discussions, so the effects of increasing comfort with the interviewer are, therefore, confounded with the effect of individual, as opposed to group, interviews. However, our analyses indicate that familiarity with the interviewer and type of interview both had an impact. From the accounts above, boys considered that increasing familiarity with the researcher enabled them to talk more openly to the interviewer. In addition, although they generally reported that they enjoyed the group interviews (and this was generally evident), they also explained in the individual interviews that there were some things they could talk about only in the individual interviews.

Research from many countries suggests that, while boys' relationships are characterized by joking and laughter, they generally do not want to be laughed at, particularly on issues that matter to them or that are important to establishing masculine status (Frosh, Phoenix, and Pattman, 2002; Jordan, 1995). In our study, almost a third (25, 32%) of the boys given individual interviews said that they preferred these to group interviews. They explained this in terms of having more opportunity to talk, including about "personal" things in a "serious" way without being constrained by fear of other boys "laughing" at them.

> *Michael: This [individual] one was more personal, and the one in the group was joking around having a laugh.*
> *RP: More personal?*
> *Michael: Like you telling about your family and everything and your views on issues.*
> *RP: That would have been difficult in a group?*
> *Michael: Yeah . . . I dunno it's like um if you said something like people might start laughing.*
> (Michael, 13, White/Greek, state school)

It was mainly in individual interviews that boys criticized other boys for being uncommunicative, thick-skinned, aggressive and uncaring. In the individual interviews, these boys produced "softer" versions of masculinity, in the sense of being less loud and funny and speaking about emotions and relations in ways which would be derided as "soft" and "wimpish" with a group of boys or even with adult males. This fits with Pollack's (1998) argument that the "Boy Code" requires U.S. boys to hide their vulnerable feelings if they are to survive in school. In a British study Katz and Buchanan (1999) found also that only 38% of the 1344 boys they studied said that they would talk to someone if they felt very upset, because they believed that "real men" do not show any feelings.

The contrast between what boys were like in the individual and single sex group interviews was especially apparent with the twelve boys (15%) who spoke, in the individual interviews, about being bullied. Only one of these boys elaborated on this in the group interview, in response to the other boys who were criticizing him for "grassing" on their friends. The other 11 boys did not mention in the group interviews that they were bullied at school. Recording how different one such boy, Chris (11, White, state school), was in the two types of interview, the interviewer noted in the summary of this interview:

In the group interview he seemed very different, bright, cheery integrated with the group . . . he said in a loud, jokey way that he was the "hardest." In the individual interview he was sad and serious and spoke about being bullied . . . for being small, weak and having a gap in his tooth. I wouldn't have imagined that a boy who was picked on for being "weak" could have been so noisy and cheerful when claiming, with tongue in cheek, to be the "hardest."

When asked if he could have spoken in the group interview about being bullied, Chris looked shocked as if this was completely out of the question. Asked why not, he said, *"Cause like they might laugh when they get out and tell people that were picking on you that I had told you."* In contrast to the group interview, in which he had joked with the other boys, in the individual interview he indicated he was afraid of other boys laughing at him. This gives us an indication of how aversive for boys was the possibility of being the object of derisive laughter and, hence, the lengths to which they would go to defend themselves against it. It does not seem far-fetched to think of boys' experiences of this sort of derision as violent.

Forearming against possible attack in reaction to what one says is a common defensive strategy in everyday talk, where the dilemmas raised by self-positioning in discourse leads to the use of defensive formulations such as: "I'm not prejudiced, but . . . ." (Billig, 1991; van Dijk, 1992). The anxiety about the possible negative consequences of self-revelation in the group interview led boys to defend themselves against the "troubled" subject positions that could result (Wetherell, 1998). This defensiveness sometimes allowed us to see how boys positioned themselves in contradictory ways in the individual, compared to the group interviews. For example, Oliver (12, White, state school) enthused with the others in the group interview about gory films, blood and guts, producing a version of himself very much as "one of the boys." However, in the individual interviews he spoke about being bullied by boys for mixing with girls instead of playing football. When he was asked in the individual interview if he thought he had been different in the group interview he said that in the group interview he could not speak "freely," whereas in the individual interview,

No-one knows except me, you, and the tape. Like when I said that I hate boys, about playing football and that, all the people who play football would gang up on me and beat me up. When I said that I act like a girl, that I like girls better than boys, they'll gang up on me and beat me up for that.

Oliver's contention that he could speak "freely" in the individual interview assumes that he is basically the same in both contexts, only more able to express himself in one than the other. Yet, whereas when interviewed individually he provided rich narrative accounts of befriending, mixing and identifying with girls, in the group interview he was deeply engaged in stereotypically boyish discussions. Our suggestion is that it was inconceivable for Chris, Oliver and other boys to talk about being bullied in the single sex group interviews not just because of their fear of reprisals, but because they were constructing different versions of themselves in different interviews. Oliver, for example, used the group opportunity to position himself within canonical narratives of masculinity as tough, interested in weapons and different from girls—and hence as not the sort of boy who should be bullied.

Appropriating and Resisting Bullying and Homophobic Subject Positions

Much recent research in schools has noted that homophobic name-calling is frequently used as a means of "policing" what boys are allowed to do (Epstein, 1997; Eder & Evans, 1995). Jordan (1995) suggests that boys who cannot position themselves as "superheroes" when they start school struggle to compare themselves favorably with boys who are seen as "the most masculine." To establish their masculinity, therefore, they have to differentiate themselves strictly from girls. Policing relationships with other boys and vilifying other boys as "gay" all serve this function. There is some evidence that there are social class and racialized differences in the importance of heterosexual performances in boys' lives. For example, Laberge and Albert (1999) found that, because of their relative powerlessness, working class boys were more likely to suggest that masculinity was about being able to demonstrate unequalled strength, attract girls, and look "cool." Similarly, Majors and Billson (1992) argue that the widely admired heterosexual "cool pose" of African American men is a defensive strategy which serves to protect them from being overwhelmed by racism and by their lack of social power. Sewell (1997) found also that British African Caribbean schoolboys—much admired as particularly masculine—are viewed as particularly heterosexually threatening.

There are a few noteworthy exceptions to general rules that boys cannot have close physical relationships with other boys and still be masculine. Rudberg (2000) identifies a "clan" of intellectual boys who dominated their school in Oslo, Norway without being tough or sporting. These boys occasionally hugged and kissed each other (although never in the public setting of the school). Yet, their confident physicality with each other does not challenge "compulsory heterosexuality." "[T]he [few] boys who claim that there is such a bodily intimacy among boys also underline that this only goes for the ones who are self-confident enough, and where there is no doubt whatsoever about their 'actual' straightness" (Rudberg, 2000, p. 12). There is, however, some evidence that some older boys can "come out" as gay provided they have won respect from their peers, for example, by being tough and sporting (Epstein, 1997).

Despite these exceptions, the ubiquity of homophobia not only affects those derided as gay, but also impacts on the identities and experiences of boys in general, regardless of their social class or ethnicity (e.g., Epstein & Johnson, 1998; Mac an Ghaill, 1994; Nayak & Kehily, 1996). Why are boys so homophobic and what are the effects of this on their identities? Drawing on the work of Butler (1997), among others, this research has suggested that popular masculine identities are produced through homophobic performances. For example, Nayak and Kehily (1996) analyze boys' homophobia as a set of activities through which they publicly and repetitively assert their "normal" masculinity through heterosexuality. Concomitantly, because of its status as "not masculine," homosexuality is associated with femininity and the construction of masculinity is partially underpinned by projecting this "femininity" onto particular boys who are singled out as gay or not sufficiently masculine. Nayak and Kehily suggest that the compulsive and repetitive way in which boys assert their masculinities through homophobia shows how fragile these identities are. Boys' homophobic performances may thus be understood as readily available defensive ways of shoring up their masculinities by constructing the feminine other as threatening and distancing themselves from boys constructed as "not properly masculine."

Although we did not introduce the topic of homophobia ourselves, about a third of the seventy-eight boys we interviewed individually spontaneously mentioned that some boys were called "gay," as well as "woosie" and "girl." The boys labelled as gay were seen as possessing the same characteristics that were denigrated in girls. Hence, homophobia was intertwined with misogyny. As Epstein (1997) found when interviewing gay men about their experiences and identities at school, homophobia was expressed "towards non-macho boys and was in terms of their similarity to girls" (p. 109). In the study reported here, boys had to be careful about what they did or said for fear of being called gay or effeminate—both of which they invariably found upsetting. In this sense their identities were "policed," in that they were scrutinized for lack of conformity to a core, heterosexual notion of appropriate masculinity and "deviations" were punished through name-calling and/or ostracism. Part of the boys' self-positioning was, therefore, designed to defend them against being called "gay," resulting in boys "policing" of themselves and others by repudiating versions of femininity. The research available suggests that there are a variety of practices involved in such policing, including not just blatant homophobia, but also more subtle strategies for constructing "non-hegemonic" masculinities as "feminine" (e.g., Martino, 1999; Parker, 1996). These have the dual effect of alienating boys who transgress the hegemonic norm too obviously, and confirming the received boundaries of "masculinity" for those who do not.

The idea that mixing too much with girls is evidence of being non-masculine was widespread among the boys we interviewed. While having girlfriends was taken as a sign of masculinity, boys who hung around with girls as friends were liable to be constructed as effeminate (especially boys like Oliver, quoted above, who was subordinated because he was fat and neither played, nor liked, football). Boys who did have friendships with girls presented these as exceptional and longstanding and not as signaling a preference for the company of girls over boys. Thus, Donald (12, White, state school) was highly critical of boys like Oliver for hanging around with girls out of preference.

> Donald: You're silly for hanging around with a girl. You should be hanging around with big boys, you should be part of us playing football, not walking around with girls speaking about 911 [US teenage programme] and all that, stuff like that.
> RP: If boys have girlfriends are they called woosies then?
> Donald: Not really... if one of us went out with a girl that was 14 or 12—our age, and good looking and stuff, they'd say "Oh nice girlfriend," and then they'd go when people touch like that [demonstrates by patting himself on the shoulder] they pat you on the back and stuff like that.

Boys who were considered to have "nice girlfriends" gained approval, but boys who went round with girls as friends were constructed as "woosies" who engaged in "girly" conversations about boys' bands rather than playing football with "big" boys.

Disavowing Homophobia as "Just Cussing"

Boys generally disavowed homophobia as serious intent when constructing their identities in interaction with the interviewer. Almost all (nearly 80%) suggested that homophobia, although extremely common, was insignificant, claiming, for example, that calling a boy gay was "just" a cuss or "just" a joke. Only six of the 78 boys interviewed individually, however, insisted that they themselves were not in any way homophobic. The passage quoted below comes from a mixed ethnic group of boys at a single sex school. The boys (like all the others we interviewed) said they did not know of any gay boys and revealed their intense homophobia. Then when asked if they ever got called gay they said they did and illustrated how this was "just" a joke.

> RP: Are, are there any boys here who are gay then d'you think (.) in this school?
> Several: I don't know I don't know [inaudible].
> Neil (White): I don't know and I don't wanna know I swear.
> Adam (Black): They, they, they wouldn't show their faces in this school [laughter].
> Sadam (Asian): Yeah, come down with pellet guns ain't it.
> Paul (Black): Especially in this school cause if they're gay (.) erm (.) people will like (.) beat em up and (.) bully em.
> RP: Would they yeah, yeah. [1] Do any of you ever get called gay (.) at all?
> Several: Yeah, yeah everyone gets yeah called like—
> Adam (Black): Like I call these lot gay sometimes.
> Neil (White): Like I could be having a cussing match yeah.
> Several [inaudible] [RP: Why, why do, do you call them gay?] that's a laugh it's just a joke.

Tom (White): . . . Like his surname's Ray and mine is May [Sadam: that's right] and some-times they say Sadam Ray is gay with Tom May [raucous laughter].

Simply asking the question of whether there were gay boys in their school introduced the possibility that there might be, and caused the boys to distance themselves from gays in emotionally charged ways. The intensity of the homo-phobia displayed by the boys in the above group contrasted with their relaxed and jokey manner when discussing how they cussed each other as "gay." For this was "just a joke." The implication here was that there was no one near them at school who really was gay, and that if there was, it would certainly not be a laughing matter. Similar tensions are produced when White boys negotiate the boundaries between racialized "just joking" and accusations of racism (Back, 1996).

This kind of joking is likely to have prevented many boys from becoming too close. It helped also to "police" boys' behavior, reminding them of the unaccept-ability of close relations between boys and men, as well as making it difficult for them to be serious with each other. Furthermore, there was a thin line between jokey and serious cussing, with unpopular boys being cussed aggressively as gay, even though no one thought they were actually gay. The fact that they claimed that "gay" was "just" a cuss did not help them and was sufficiently threatening for boys to work hard to avoid being cussed in that way.

Racialization of Sexuality: Black Boys as Different

Although most London state schools are ethnically mixed, there are tensions between ethnic groups (e.g., Back, 1996). We found in this study that boys from different ethnic groups were racialized and ethnicized in ways that are specific to the British context. For example, in one state school, several boys identified two Turkish boys, reported to work hard and to spend all their time together, as "gay." The following extract from a 14 year old White boy makes this clear.

Ahmed and Ali, they are sort of, like everybody think they are gay yeah (2) and they cuss them too . . . because they . . . talk in Turkish and you like and you think they are cussing you but probably they are not yeah and still get cussed.

Asian boys in the study were similarly constructed as not powerful or sexually attractive and so were liable to be subjected to homophobic name-calling. By way of contrast, Black boys of African-Caribbean descent were less likely to be called "gay." They could spend a lot of time with girls and still be considered to be of high status because they were seen as strongly heterosexual. There was some evidence that teachers' reactions to this were racialized. For example, Mervyn describes being sexually attracted to girls, and reports that some teachers suggest that he is transgressing gender boundaries. In the group interview with 12-year-old Black boys, from which the quotation below comes, it is clear from the response of Stewart that the scenario Mervyn describes is familiar:

Mervyn: Some teachers say to me if I like being with girls so much why don't I join them? I think what's the point of saying that? I'm not going to be gay when I grow up . . . .
RP: What do the teachers mean by that?
Stewart: That means why don't you be a girl if you enjoy being around them so much?
RP: Meaning what?
Stewart: They're trying to say if you're with the girls if you like a girl yeah why don't you join them, that means go and talk to them on the table, they mean why don't you be a girl so you can associate with them?
Mervyn: One teacher called me a "male whore." I find that term abusive.

Mervyn was a tall, powerful and popular boy who was confident, articulate and outspoken about racism. Because of this, he said some teachers perceived him as a threat: *"When they get a strong Black boy like me, it's like a challenge to them."* Recent ethnographic research confirms the view that teachers tend to construct Black boys as more rebellious and threatening, often linking this with perceptions of them as physically large and as heterosexually mature and attractive (Sewell, 1997). Mervyn was proud of being a "strong Black boy" who could stand up to teachers, but was also highly critical of teachers for constructing him as a threat and picking on him in class.

British and U.S. research suggests that Black young men of African-Caribbean descent are viewed in some ways as "super-masculine." They are seen as possessing the attributes that are constructed by young men as indicative of the most popular forms of masculinity—toughness and authentically male style in talk and dress. Paradoxically, while they are feared and discriminated against because of those features, they are also respected, admired and gain power through taking on characteristics which militate against good classroom performance. (See Ferguson, 2000 and Majors & Billson, 1992 for discussion of similar issues for African American boys and men in the U.S. context.) In Britain, Sewell (1997) found that many of the 15-year-old Black boys he studied were both positioned by others, and positioned themselves, as superior to white and Asian students in terms of their sexual attractiveness, style, creativity and "hardness." They are, "Angels and Devils in British (and American) schools. They are heroes of a street fashion culture that dominates most of our inner cities" (Sewell, 1997, p. ix). At the same time, however, they are the group of pupils most likely to be excluded by teachers from schools. In this study too, the ways in which boys of African-Caribbean descent were racialized gained them the admiration of other boys, but the censure of their teachers.

Conclusion

Although interviews are often considered to be self-contained, it was clear that boys in this study brought their histories of previous positioning and their expectations of the interviewer and the interview to the research situation. The accounts produced by most boys indicated that they enjoyed and valued as "different" the experience of being interviewed about themselves. The interviews thus contradicted their usual experience of school as a potentially threatening situation that, by exposing them to ridicule, could threaten their masculinity. By way of contrast, they explained that they were surprised to have an adult treating them as social actors, rather than testing them, problematizing them, firing questions at them and embarrassing them. The boys' accounts indicated that they positioned themselves differently as they became familiar with the interviewer and his questioning, and as the interviewer got to know them and could identify and discuss issues important to them. The boys' behavior and disposition also varied between individual and group interviews. For example, in the individual interviews boys were more serious, more critical of boys in general and more willing to talk about things which might be derided as "wimpish" or "soft" if other boys were present. The different kinds of interviews thus provided opportunities to analyze various ways in which the boys constructed themselves as masculine in their talk and how anxiety provoking this was for them. This allowed us to see contradictions between how boys produced their subject positions in the group interview context in comparison with the individual interviews. The methodological implications of these findings suggest that both group and individual interviews are important to research on identities. Researchers therefore need to be clear about what aspects of identities they are likely to tap with each—as well as that accounts may change as interviewees become more familiar with the interviewer.

"Compulsory heterosexuality" is a cultural imperative in most schools in many countries, including the UK and the United States (Eder et al., 1995; Hey, 1997). We found that homophobic name-calling provided a quick, easy way for boys to claim masculinity. For that reason, many boys are invested in using homophobic abuse to confirm and strengthen their own masculine status (Nayak & Kehily, 1996; Redman & Mac an Ghaill, 1997; Swain, 2000). We also found that homophobia was linked with the counterposing of masculinity and femininity (Epstein, 1997; Jordan, 1995; Swain, 2000) and boys went to great lengths to avoid being labeled "gay." There were indications that boys were racialized differently in relation to sexuality and that teachers derided Black boys who liked girls' company. Boys who called others "gay" tended to deny homophobia in favor of maintaining that they were simply joking and employing a "cuss" whose use was not punished within schools. At the same time, it reduced their vulnerability by positioning them as "not gay" and, so, masculine. Part of boys' self-positioning was thus necessarily contradictory in order to defend themselves against the anxieties raised by being called "gay." While adult men have similarly been found to "police" each other, and to construct masculinities through homophobia (Connell, 2000), the intensity of interactions within schools and boys' vulnerability to charges of not being masculine enough makes this an important source of distress for many boys.

Policy Implications

There is a burgeoning literature that aims to identify ways in which boys should be treated in order to improve their school performance and their behavior (e.g., Ferguson, 2000; Pollack, 1998). The findings from this study fit with many of the recommendations made in that literature. It is clear from what boys said about their expectations of the interviewer, that they experience schools as threatening places. As a result they are primed to be tough and unwilling to display emotion in order to protect themselves from humiliation and unsympathetic treatment that will threaten their masculinity. Teachers, parents, and policy makers thus need to find ways of treating boys sympathetically and allowing them to talk about emotions without being teased or belittled so that their expectations soften. In addition, the significance of homophobic name-calling needs to be recognized. Boys in this study reported that teachers in the schools in which we worked did not define homophobic name calling as bullying and so did not impose sanctions on those who engaged in it. Yet, this way of performing masculinity is powerful because it helps to buttress versions of masculinity that have a negative impact on many boys and girls. It requires to be taken seriously as a common and painful form of bullying.

References

Ashmore, R., & Jussim, L. (Eds.). (1997). *Self and identity: Fundamental issues*. Oxford, UK: Oxford University Press.

Back, L. (1996). *New ethnicities and urban culture*. London: UCL Press.

Billig, M. (1991). *Ideology and opinions*. London: Sage.

Bruner, J. (1990). *Acts of meaning*. Cambridge, MA: Harvard University Press.

Butler, J. (1993). *Bodies that matter* New York: Routledge.

Connell, R. (2000) *The men and the boys*. Berkeley, CA: University of California Press.

Davies, B., & Harré, R. (1990). Positioning: The discursive Production of selves. *Journal for the Theory of Social Behavior, 20*(1), 43–63. (Reprinted with modifications as Ch. 3 in Harré, R., & Langenhove, L. Van (Eds.), *Positioning theory: Moral contexts of intentional action*. Malden, MA: Blackwell.)

Denzin, N., & Lincoln, Y. (Eds.). (1994). *The handbook of qualitative research*. London: Sage.

Eder, D., Evans, C. C., & Parker, S. (1995). *School talk: Gender and adolescent culture*. New Brunswick, NJ: Rutgers University Press.

Epstein, D. (1997). Boyz' own stories: Masculinities and sexualities in schools. *Gender and Education, 9*(1), 105–115.

Epstein, D., & Johnson, R. (1998). *Schooling sexualities*. Buckingham: Open University Press.

Ferguson, A. (2000). *Bad boys: Public schools in the making of Black masculinity*. Ann Arbor, MI: University of Michigan Press.

Finnegan, R. (1997). "Storying the self": Personal narratives and identity. In H. Mackay (Ed.), *Consumption and everyday life*. London: Sage.

Frosh, S., Phoenix, A., & Pattman, R. (2002). *Young Masculinities*. London: Palgrave.

Gilbert, R., & Gilbert, P. (1998). *Masculinity goes to school*. London: Routledge.

Harré, R., & Langenhove, L. Van. (Eds.). (1998). *Positioning theory: Moral contexts of intentional action*. Oxford: Blackwell.

Hey, V. (1997). *The company she keeps*. Buckingham: Open University Press.

Hollway, W., & Jefferson, T. (2000). *Doing qualitative research differently*. London: Sage.
Jordan, E. (1995). Fighting boys and fantasy play: The construction of masculinity in the early years of school. *Gender and Education, 7*(1), 69–85.
Katz, A., & Buchanan, A. (1999). *Leading lads*. London: Topman.
Kroger, J. (2000). Ego identity status research in the new millennium. *International Journal for the Study of Behavioral Development, 24*(2), 145–148.
Laberge, S., & Albert, M. (1999). Conceptions of masculinity and of gender transgressions in sport among adolescent boys: Hegemony, contestation and social class dynamic. *Men and Masculinities, 1*, 253–267.
Mac an Ghaill, M. (1994). *The making of men: Masculinities, sexualities and schooling*. Buckingham: Open University Press.
Majors, R., & Billson, J. (1992). *Cool pose: The dilemmas of Black manhood in America*. New York: Lexington.
Marcia, J. (1994). The empirical study of ego identity. In H. Bosma, T. Graafsma, H. Grotevant, & D. de Levita (Eds.), *Identity and development: An interdisciplinary approach*. London: Sage.
Martino, W. (1999). "Cool boys," "party animals," "squids," and "poofters": Interrogating the dynamics and politics of adolescent masculinities in school. *British Journal of Sociology of Education, 20*(2), 239–263.
Nayak, A., & Kehily, M. (1996). Playing it straight: Masculinities, homophobias and schooling. *Journal of Gender Studies, 5*(2).
Osborne, P., & Segal, L. (1997). Gender as performance: An interview with Judith Butler for radical philosophy. In K. Woodward (Ed.), *Identity and difference* Milton Keynes: Open University Press.
Parker, A. (1996). The construction of masculinity within boys' physical education. *Gender and Education, 8*(2), 141–157.
Phoenix, A. (1994). Researching women's lives: The practice of feminist research. In J. Purvis & M. Maynard (Eds.), *Researching women's lives from a feminist perspective*. London: Taylor and Francis.
Phoenix, A., & Frosh, S. (2001). Positioned by "hegemonic" masculinities: A study of London boys' narratives of identity. *Australian Psychologist, 36*(1), 27–35.
Pollack, W. (1998). *Real boys: Rescuing our sons from the myth of boyhood*. New York: Henry Holt.
Redman, P., & Mac an Ghaill, M. (1997). Educating Peter: The making of a history man. In L. Steinberg, D. Epstein, & R. Johnson (Eds.), *Border patrols: Policing the boundaries of heterosexuality*. London: Cassell.
Riessman, C. K. (2001). Analysis of personal narratives. In J. F. Gubrium, & J. A. Holstein (Eds.), *Handbook of interviewing* (pp. 695–710). London: Sage.
Rudberg, M. (2000, January 19). *Boy bodies—The question of intimacy*. Paper presented at the Masculinity and Boyhood Studies Seminar: The Royal Danish School of Educational Studies, Copenhagen.
Sewell, T. (1997). *Black masculinities and schooling: How Black boys survive modern schooling*. Stoke on Trent: Trentham Books.
Skelton, C. (1996). Learning to be "tough": The fostering of maleness in one primary school. *Gender and Education, 8*(2), 185–197.
Swain, J. (2000). "The money's good, the fame's good, the girls are good": The role of playground football in the construction of young boys' masculinity in a junior school. *British Journal of Sociology of Education, 21*(1), 95–109.
van Dijk, T. (1992). Discourse and the denial of racism. *Discourse and Society, 3*(1), 87–118.
Wetherell, M. (1998). Positioning and interpretive repertoires: Conversation analysis and post-structuralism in dialogue. *Discourse and Society, 9*, 387–412.

ANN PHOENIX is a Senior Lecturer in Psychology at the Open University. Her research interests include the social identities of young people, particularly those associated with gender, "race," social class and consumption. Her publications include *Young Mothers*? (Polity Press, 1991); *Black, White or Mixed Race? Race and Racism in the Lives of Young People of Mixed Parentage* (with B. Tizard; Routledge, 1993, 2nd ed., 2002); *Shifting Identities Shifting Racisms* (Ed. with Kum-Kum Bhavnani; Sage, 1994); *Crossfires: Nationalism, Racism and Gender in Europe* (Ed. with Helma Lutz and Nira Yural-Davis; Pluto 1995); *Standpoints and Differences* (Ed. with Karen Henwood & Chris Griffin; Sage, 1998); and *Young Masculinities* (with Stephen Frosh and Rob Pattman; Palgrave, 2001).

STEPHEN FROSH is Professor of Psychology and Director of the Centre for Psychosocial Studies in the School of Psychology at Birkbeck College, University of London. His numerous academic publications include *For and Against Psychoanalysis* (Routledge, 1997), *Sexual Difference: Masculinity and Psychoanalysis* (Routledge, 1994), *Identity Crisis: Modernity, Psychoanalysis and the Self* (Macmillan, 1991), and *The Politics of Psychoanalysis* (Macmillan, 1987; 2nd ed., 1999). He is co-editor, with Anthony Elliott, of *Psychoanalysis in Contexts* (Routledge, 1995) as well as co-author of *Young Masculinities*.

ROB PATTMAN is a researcher in the Faculty of Education at the Open University. He has taught sociology in Britain and southern Africa and published articles on Whiteness, gender identities, sex and AIDS education, and social theory. He is co-author of *Young Masculinities*.

Journal of Social Issues, Vol. 59, No. 1, 2003, pp. 197–211

On (Not) "Coloring in the Outline"

Linda C. Powell*

Resources for Change, Inc.

This article provides an overview and analysis of 10 studies on violence and injustice from the perspective of youth. These articles are contained in the issue of Journal of Social Issues *entitled* Youth Perspectives on Violence and Injustice *and, in the articles, the authors offer a unique opportunity to go far beyond the current discursive terrains of youth and violence. Through a reinterpretation of what is conceptualized as normative, an expansion of the conceptualization of "youth" and an exploration of a broad range of topics, contexts and methods, the issue explores five provocative and significant critical themes. These themes are:* methodology is critical; youth as subject, not object; gift and danger of a clinical approach; centrality of school? *and* at the intersection of social justice and development. *The impact of popular culture on youth and violence and the importance of examining what adults value as "entertainment" are discussed also.*

Adding a new voice to a conversation, a new point of view, does more than just increase the content in a linear way (Walkerdine, 2002). Including a voice that has previously been excluded contains the potential for changing the entire discussion. "Facts" and other notions once taken for granted are opened to scrutiny. "Natural" connections and causalities yield to new ways of organizing ideas and relationships. Notions assumed "settled" lead to new questions and implicate new players. In scientific terms (Kuhn, 1962), science moves forward not by careful and gradual research programs, but by huge new ideas that replace old ones. The action of moving youth voices toward the center of the study of violence is such a paradigm shift.

Daiute and Fine (this issue), the editors of this issue, report 10 studies that go beyond what Mahiri and Conner (this issue) describe as the public discourse

---

Correspondence concerning this article should be addressed to Dr. Linda C. Powell, President, Resources for Change, Inc., Philadelphia, PA [e-mail: linda_c_powell@hotmail.com]. The author would like to acknowledge the thoughtful comments and suggestions for revisions by the editors and reviewers of the article and Rosemarie A. Roberts for her assistance with preparation of this manuscript.

about Black youth violence or "the outline" which sets boundaries of a somewhat proscribed conversation that adults have about young people and violence. Daiute and Fine (this issue) echo Mahiri and Conner's desire to go beyond this kind of "coloring in the outline" (Mahiri and Conner, this issue, p. 139). This issue offers an opportunity to color far beyond the lines of the currently overlapping terrains of youth and violence. The 10 studies featured reinterpret what counts as normative, expand the conceptualization of "youth," and explore a broad range of topics, contexts and methods. The editors and contributors to this issue assume that there are ongoing, multiple systems that influence the lives of young people, that these systems can interact in paradoxical and counterintuitive ways and that when we listen, young people can describe their experiences in ways that are multi-layered and complex. As the studies report, listening to these stories can dramatically enlarge our sense of and the nature of the "problem" of violence and the "meaning" of youth. In taking an important theoretical turn—that young people have something to say about their own lives, and these young people do not disappoint—this issue creates the possibility of shifting the conversation and public discourse about youth and violence.

Lewin (1951) and Fallis and Opotow (this issue) remind us that social behavior is a function of both persons and their environments. From a youth-based perspective, this issue's ambitious task is to begin to make the function of both individual and contextual elements of youth and violence clearer and more precise. Youth narratives and experiences map in detail and in color the connections between their internal lives and their environmental context—looking at interactions, relationships, causality, and influences between the multiple ways they describe their experiences, and their life contexts and behaviors and the impact of social institutions. In many of these studies, the authors have, as Phoenix, Frosh, and Pattman (this issue) describe it, "gotten out of our way," giving us the actual words of young people. They let us decide whether or not we agree with the researchers' interpretation. In others, the authors (e.g., Cross, this issue) have carefully interwoven history with present day realities so we may re-view youth and violence.

Coloring outside of the line is not simply about the shape of the boundaries, but also about the hues and textures around the boundaries. The authors offer not just studies of "kids of color" but they enter the more dangerous area of seeing the experiences of kids of *all* colors through the prisms of race, gender and class. We begin to see the ways in which social identity matters in the social construction and attributions of behavior and the development of identities. In particular, young people have different experiences of similar stimuli and different consequences of their behavior depending on race, ethnicity, gender, or class (Bailey, 1992–93; Giles, 2001; Style & Powell, 1995; Wellesley College, 1992). These "embodied" studies give us additional insights into the experiences of youth that are always influenced by status, history, and position. For instance, we learn that violence is not something that "Black young men do," but violence becomes a phenomenon affecting all young people, but with potentially differential impact and consequence based on race and class. In this issue, we hear the voices of girls and of boys; of young people from elementary school through adolescence and early adulthood; of young people living in and migrating to the United States, Israel, and Britain. We meet these youth in their classrooms, in community organizations, on the streets, and in history. We see them through the lenses of psychology and sociology, through feminism, and through antiracist analyses. Some of these young people live in circumstances of war, racism, or tremendous social dislocation. Some studies dare to ask youth about "violence," itself. And they respond by telling us about their relationships, their homes, and their schools. More frightening, when they are asked about their relationships or about school, we learn how violence and the antecedents to violence weave into the everyday fabric of friendships, romance, and learning. Conducting research that surfaces youth perspectives in an authentic way requires a cognitive shift, a move away from the idea of "youth as problem" to an empathic entering into and with the experience of young people themselves. Making this cognitive shift leads to a set of theoretical and methodological "taken for granteds" that are provocative, significant, and subtly understated. In the following section, I discuss these shifts as critical themes that run across these papers.

Critical Themes

Methodology Is Critical

The studies are explicit in generating methods that allow researchers to "hear," theorize, interpret, and analyze critically what youth say about violence and how they say it. This may require some departures from more typical research methods. These methodological investments and innovations come in many forms and at every stage of research. Writers such as Phoenix et al. (this issue) and Tolman, Spencer, Rosen-Reynoso, and Porche (this issue) create research situations in which adults must listen deeply to youth, following their lead in inquiry and interpretation. Daiute, Stern, and Lelutiu-Weinberger (this issue) designed their project so that youth talk to adults could be contrasted to youth talk with peers, while studying the values of adults and students. Fine et al. (this issue) build research and survey questions *with* young people, turning over unexpected rocks in the differences between adult and youth experience. Using historical and sociological methods, Cross (this issue) excavates and examines the myths that generate and potentially pervert approaches to youth problems today. Spencer, Dupree, Cunningham, Harpalani, and Munoz-Miller (this issue) use a specific theoretical framework that "integrate[s] salient issues of context and development" (p. 34). In exploring young people's experience with victimization via their thoughts, fears, and physical symptoms they attempt to "[capture] the meaning-making processes underlying foundational identity development and outcomes" (Spencer et al., this issue, p. 35). Hertz-Lazarowitz (this issue) applies concepts from a model of Social Drama (Harre, 1979) that seems uniquely useful in understanding the action and intergroup dynamics on a university campus.

These approaches are a far cry from the traditional approaches to studying youth violence. First, these studies investigate the experiences of "normal" kids, those not officially identified as violent or "at risk" for violence. In this way, these are truly studies "of" violence from the perspective "of" youth. Secondly, these studies care about development as a dynamic. Violence is not conceived as a one time event. Rather, it is viewed as an experience that will influence what occurs next in their lives, coming at a vulnerable time in the lifespan and having impact on learning, relational development, feelings of engagement/alienation, etc. Finally, each of these studies comments in some way on the "essentialist versus systemic perspective" (Cross, this issue, p. 68). For instance, Cross (this issue) states that observers essentialize problems when Blacks (or youth) are involved and those same problems are perceived as more systemic when Whites and other social groups (like adults) are studied. Most of these studies are interdisciplinary, including the methods of social, developmental and clinical psychology, sociology, history, public health, and education. Fine et al. (this issue) worked with young people at the outset of the research to generate questions, discovering a vein of experience that the adults could not access. Most of the studies used multiple methods, including clinical interviewing. Phoenix et al. (this issue) remind us that since "we 'make' our identities through our autobiographical narratives" (p. 182), we can learn from young people by having them tell rich, complex potentially contradictory stories about their experience. Tolman et al. (this issue) describe this process as creating a "... dialogue between theory and youth perspectives ..." (p. 163). Solis's (this issue) theoretical framework holds that violence is "a dialectical process that is constantly unfolding between social structures and individuals" (p. 27). Therefore, for her, violence has social, rather than natural or individual, origins. Fallis and Opotow (this issue) included dissemination as a critical part of their data analysis; this phase challenged student researchers to become conceptually clear about their work and allowed each stage of the project to generate new questions.

Youth as Subject, Not Object

What each of these studies indicates is the potential for empowerment and, hence, new results when young people are involved as subject and even researcher, rather than simply objects of someone else's inquiry. As Hertz-Lazarowitz (this issue) sums up, "... we sought to document young people in conflict and confrontation using events of injustice and surveillance to develop critical and political thinking" (p. 54). The phenomenology of meaning making rather than remaining object in someone else's study requires new kinds of supportive and interpretive research environments. The results of these studies suggest (not counterintuitively) that young people tell different stories when they trust that their authentic experiences are genuinely valued and respected. This may be an inadvertent "meta-finding" of these studies. Wells (1985) has usefully given us the "radio" metaphor for thinking about multiple levels of analysis, and how to think usefully about group-level variables. Daiute and Fine (this issue) state that youth today are growing up with a sense of adult betrayal and alienation. If we imagine that many stations are playing all the time, it becomes possible to "tune in" to a single station and listen. This is not to say that no young people have good relationships with adults, but that when we tune in on the "youth station" we hear the absence of sufficient holding environments constructed and honored by adults for youth.

Group relations theory (Rioch, 1975; Shapiro and Carr, 1991; Wells, 1985) uses psychoanalysis and social psychology to build complex understandings of individuals, groups, and social systems. It can help with the interactions between institutional and personal factors and how these influences conspire to create identities and connecting individual lives, personal narrations and institutional effects. Fallis and Opotow (this issue) introduce the notion of multiple levels of analysis (individual, interpersonal, and institutional) when identifying what gets addressed and what remains latent within a system. They offer a sophisticated interpretation of school cutting, an activity they conceive of as challenging the authority of the school to avoid conflict or direct challenges of systems and processes they see as alienating. A purely behavioral and individual focus protects the system from investigating its own contributions, dynamics, and interests. Systemic failure (disengagement, alienation due to the nature of school) is handled by individual interventions. As long as we see only individuals, the systemic or group level problem will persist, unfettered and unaddressed.

Fallis and Opotow's (this issue) complex definition of "boring" as a reason to cut class is instructive as we think about young people and violence. When students describe something as boring, they are not just describing the absence of something or being disinterested. Upon investigation, they mean something very specific: a one way, top down, unengaged relationship with a teacher whose pedagogy feels disrespectful because it is not designed to "tempt, engage or include" them. From a youth perspective, boring is not a naturally occurring phenomenon. It is the predictable outcome of specific decisions and actions of the teacher and school.

The third major assumption of these writings, again refreshing and understated, is that *the social world is not necessarily neutral* for young people. Researchers must be willing to suspect that some young person isn't personally troubled or some issue isn't just "pesty . . . ." We have to be willing to look at institutional structures that contribute to youth behavior. Fallis and Opotow (this issue) note that "moral exclusion is the alchemy that transforms intransigent, unaddressed conflict into structural violence [and] . . . situates responsibility for negative outcomes in victims rather than those with institutional resources and power"

(p. 114). This notion indicts our adult, researcher attention, spotlighting what it emphasizes or what it doesn't seem to notice.

Institutions cannot be taken as helpful or supportive simply because adults intend for them to be. Young people develop a variety of ways of navigating their complex social world. These studies document how much can be learned by listening to the experiences of young people as they challenge public institutions. From the perspective of young people, history, schools, and communities can oppress and create inequity. As an example, many policing programs are allegedly designed to protect citizens. However, Fine et al. (this issue) discovered that young people experience themselves as a population at risk of police targeting. That is a youth perspective on adult surveillance.

What is the impact on identity development when receiving a constant message that you are untrustworthy, suspicious and potential criminals and it "shows" on you—your look determines your criminality, not your behavior. As Fine et al. (this issue) note, even good behavior does not protect Black youth from police surveillance. Similarly, the voices of young people have rarely been heard in discussions of police violence, despite being a target of more aggressive policing initiatives.

Finally, these essays recognize *that adult definitions of social problems can be social defenses* (Jaques, 1955; Menzies, 1975; Powell, 1994) against the anxiety stirred by youth perspectives on social problems. Why is it still an unusual idea to take students' concerns seriously when planning school reform efforts or to work with them collaboratively in creating youth policy? This avoidance of authentic engagement serves as a psychological defense for adults. For example, what happens when we look beyond cutting class as an individual issue to the systemic issues giving rise to cutting? What happens when we consider youth behavior as data and even a critique, not just as individual errant behavior (Fine, 1991)? When teachers see cutting class as a disciplinary matter, it protects them from the hypothesis that it is a comment on their teaching.

Gift and Danger of a Clinical Approach

The authors of these studies honor young people's experiences with and explanations about the risks of violence to their physical and *psychological* well-being. For the purposes of this issue, youth violence is not a "disease" and violence against and by young people must be addressed as a social and political problem. This moves beyond individual behavior, into the realm of phenomenology, or the meaning making systems that young people employ to understand and organize their experiences. These studies require stepping back from individually framed behavior and looking at the big picture of affective experiences of young people. This issue assumes that youth *do* have internal worlds that are products, reflections, and defenses against their experiences.

Across these essays we hear a psychoanalytic or clinical language through which researchers stretch to recognize the relation of adult fetishes and youth behavior; adult anxieties and our projections onto youth. Further, the researchers seek to move into the internal world which inevitably brings us into the world of clinical dynamics. For example, Daiute and Fine (this issue) note that "Research in the field of youth violence . . . rarely reports from the standpoints of youths themselves who may look at the world around them as problematic. . . . Adults *project* onto youth our growing concerns about violence [emphasis added]" (p. 2). Mahiri and Conner (this issue) use the notions of displacement and scapegoats (Banet and Hayden, 1977; Wells, 1985). In addition to the practical mechanism they quote from Chomsky (1995, p. 34), in psychoanalysis this is the most extreme form of projective identification. Parallel process (Smith and Berg, 1987; Smith, Simmon, and Thames, 1989) is intimated by Hertz-Lazarowitz when she considers the possibility that lessons learned from the conflict on campus can be considered data about the university as a whole, as well as in Israel. Fallis and Opotow (this issue) remind us of Apples' (1996) poignant insight about students' "almost unconscious realization that . . . schooling will not enable them to go much farther than they already are" (p. 99), which provides a powerful glimpse into a student's internal world. Tolman et al. (this issue) organize their inquiry around Rich's (1983) definition of heterosexuality as a universally pervasive institution, with mechanisms that "insure that it functions unconsciously and imperceptibly for most individuals" (Tolman et al., p. 160).

Using clinical language about the unconscious gives us incredible firepower to more authentically construct the complexity within and between individuals and groups. It allows us to account for that which is apparent, and that which operates below the surface. Organizations, too, have an unconscious (Obholzer and Roberts, 1994), with manifest and latent content, conflict and defensive strategies. Daiute et al. (this issue) note this: "When violence prevention programs are placed in contexts where children are presumed to have experienced discrimination conflicts, it should not be surprising that they may need or want to express life experiences that the curriculum actually *represses* [emphasis added]" (p. 98). Fallis and Opotow (this issue) also comment on this, noting that "intransigent conflicts that resist standard solutions are often characterized by misdiagnoses that miss deeper issues such as the basic need for consistency, security, respect, justice, and a sense of personal control" (p. 111). And, above all, it lets us enter the terrain of the imagination, of dreams and images, which are developmentally and politically critical in the identities of youth.

There remains the difficulties of capturing and measuring the inner world in any respectful way: One major danger is that we have all been boys and girls. Transference—clinical, research, and theoretical—appears as a likely problem. First, we have to attempt to make some meaning out of the experiences youth share and the stories they tell. We must wonder about the questions that adults have not asked. While this is always true of the research adventure, our absences make an interesting pattern. Like Tolman's wondering why (all) the research on dating violence hasn't inquired into *why* there is so much violence? There is significant research on gender differences in dating behavior but a marked absence of gendered analysis (for counterexamples see Leadbeater and Way, 1996). This is similar to Fine et al. (this issue) not conceding the possibility of sexual harassment of young women by the police. Or in Phoenix et al. (this issue) wondering about repressed material in adults leading to Black boys being seen as super-masculine. Perhaps these are the kinds of arenas we may not have conscious access to and are not eager (or encouraged) to excavate.

Hertz-Lazarowitz (this issue) looks specifically at meaning making in her study of Palestine and Israeli dynamics at Haifa University. First, she shifts the question away from personal behavior to personal experiences. One of her central interview questions clearly seeks internal meaning: Has someone in authority controlled or acted toward you in an unjust way? In this question, the research puts the question of justice right at the forefront. Her study focuses also on the social meaning, potentially offering a new understanding of the interplay between personal and collective factors.

Solis (this issue) hypothesizes a "dialectical relationship [as] a cycle between the societal abuse *faced* by Mexican immigrants, and the personal acts of violence and abuse *enacted* by Mexican immigrants" (p. 19). From this perspective, violence is a tool youth use to make sense of themselves, other people and institutions. She uses the term "violenced" (Solis, this issue, p. 23) to describe those who have had violence perpetrated upon them as a result of their "illegal" status.

Centrality of Schools?

Schools are the only social institution that can compel young people to be present. For that reason alone, schools are important in any discussion of youth perspectives on violence. In this issue, all of the studies mention schools; six are specifically situated within them. Tragically, schools are increasingly a place where some young people enact violence. We believe, also, that schools are a key site where young people negotiate their understanding in the world and develop their capacity for social engagement and meaning making. Schools have been considered important as an agency of indoctrination, reproduction of social relations, and sites of social violence (Block, 1997). It is an important social institution where the emotional aspects of the youth social system and adult social system interact on a daily basis.

Cross (this issue) provides a complete rereading of Frazier's 1939 work about delinquency in Chicago with a systemic rather than essentialist perspective. While Frazier sought explanations for the behavior in family and community dynamics, Homel (1984) found a more persuasive systemic argument in the schools and their maladaptive attempts to deal with racism and overcrowding. These (systemic) facts undercut the myth that African Americans were crippled in some way by slavery, and yet the (essentialist) myth continues to influence our thinking about Black youth and violence today. Do we still think, as Cross (this issue) asks, that schools are designed " . . . to prevent delinquency through educational engagement" (p. 78)? Or have we given up on that?

School can be a site of violence, and the task of schools is influenced by young people's experiences of violence. Phoenix et al. (this issue) remind us that experiences of school influence how young people see their worlds. Tolman et al. (this issue) note that school is the context in which much of teen dating takes place, between people who are known to one another, and in a context where adults fail to interrupt and may even encourage harassing behaviors. Spencer et al. (this issue) note an important finding in their study: each of the post-traumatic stress disorder (PTSD) symptoms that were predicted by experience with violence was related to focus of attention. They rightly note that feelings of fear, distraction and self-consciousness in response to experiences with violence can interfere with normative learning processes.

This concern about violence in schools is not simply about social interactions, but also occurs in the pedagogy of the school. For example, in explicating the ways that teachers and students struggled together to produce a set of values, Daiute et al. (this issue) remind us that an emphasis on mastery discourages critique or transformation; from this perspective, all questions and challenges emerge as individual failures. Tolman et al. (this issue) discover that school policies that provoke individual discussion about sexual harassment and dating violence, without a critique of the larger systems which produce and perpetuate violence in intimate relationships, leave girls feeling scared and boys feeling unfairly accused.

Mahiri and Conner's (this issue) study findings reflected three broad, highly related themes that clearly contrasted with public discourse on Black youth. In particular, the lives of the youth closely correspond to the circumstances of many of the Black youth that U.S. society has characterized as violent "others" (Fordham, 1996; Payne, 2001; Ward, 2001), with one key difference. Those youth that attended small schools with teachers that were interested in and capable of teaching a unique curriculum unit engaged young people in ways that match their experiences about violence. The impact of school size (Wasley et al., 2000; Fine and Somerville, 1998) was noted also by Fine et al. (this issue). Small schools give the opportunity for innovative curriculum. In the Mahiri and Connor article (this issue) students research and document aspects of their own lives; they interview members of their community and assess positive and negative aspects of their community. Academic work is used to mirror and explore their experience, developing their intellectual ability to think about what actually happens in their world. This schooling experience starts with the lived experience of young people, and does not demand that students create a separate school self. This integrating, unitive approach could be for young people the opposite of Fallis and Opotow's (this issue) "boring" aspects of school. Why is it still news to us that young people bring complex and competing worlds into their classrooms, worlds which require respect and negotiation for the learning task to proceed?

At the Intersection of Social Justice and Development

Unlike the linear and unidimensional "outline" that is much of the public conversation about youth and violence, the young people in these studies emerge in colorful, vivid, and complex terms. They inhabit a world which they must accept as routinely unpredictable and violent by necessity, a world where public policy may make you unsafe, and a world where huge forces like history and war will determine daily interactions with others. And as several researchers discovered, young people describe this simply as *"the way things are."* A world where boys must struggle to act like "real men," and romance requires violence, where girls must balance being desirable, vulnerable, and acceptable. A world where language has no meaning and homophobia is "just" a joke (although boys will go to great lengths to avoid being called "gay"). Not surprisingly, many young people, in several of the studies, "just decide not to care about it" or "to simply ignore it." The numbing burdens of this world become monotonous and debilitating. And too often the responses of adults imply that it is up to the individual young person to take action. Despite our intent, our educational and social policies often *operate* as if young people are our enemy rather than our future.

As a whole, these studies expand our definitions of "violence." Myth making robs and lies and distorts—and is a form of violence against the history and culture of African Americans. Being termed "illegal" is violence against the self and the identity of Mexican immigrant children and families. Microaggressions of disrespect and suspicion (Toussaint, Boyd-Franklin, & Franklin, 2000) are experienced as forms of interpersonal violence. Organizational structures and practices that diminish the sense of self and deny resources are a form of violence. The cumulative impact of these processes on identity development can be devastating. A person or a group can suffer real damage if the world mirrors back to them a confining or demeaning or contemptible picture of themselves. As Solis (this issue) notes, " . . . as long as violence continues to be lived privately and ignored publicly, *and* as long as the means to respond to violence other than with violence remains unfamiliar to [them]" (p. 27), young people will find themselves in a bind. The 10 studies in this issue suggest that interventions with the power to solve the intransigent problems youth face will require youth perspectives leveled "at the intersection of social justice and development" (Daiute and Fine, this issue, p. 12), situated front and center. What does this issue have to say to the school reform, youth development, and violence prevention literatures? It calls into question new interpretations of seemingly straightforward data; it offers methodologies and syntheses. It makes us wonder whether perhaps we should we be interrogating "adulthood" the way we eventually had to interrogate Whiteness? If sampling the internal world of young people is important, then like psychotherapy, it is labor intensive work. It requires relationship and clinical skill, respect and courage.

An Afterthought

In a recent address to the Public Education Network national convention, Nobel laureate Toni Morrison (2002) used her own narrative as a student to inspire and provoke her audience to think about education in a post–9/11 world. Her earliest desire for academic achievement was fueled, she said, by a "terror" or desire that she wouldn't be competent in an adult world. This is the world that no longer exists for young people. In the absence of adult engagement with youth voices and experiences, popular culture (Lasn, 2000; Wolff, 1999) sells a version of adult life that always feels in reach. There is less and less that schools or real adults have to teach that TV and movies don't provide a more powerful and immediate "curriculum." That terror she felt has now been assuaged by a plastic sense of order and certainty; no problem exists that is not solved by the end of the episode (with suitable commercial breaks) or turned into a meme of stimulation.

Cross (this issue) notes that it is unclear how Frazier (1939/1948) missed the role of schools overcrowding and double-shift schools in understanding youth problems in Chicago. Are researchers also overlooking the impact of popular culture now? Will we look back and wonder about the unrestrained impact of violence as entertainment on issues of identity and violence; depictions of this violence are easily found on television, in video games, and in films. Interesting that it may elude us too if we do not recognize it as a force (Daspit and Weaver, 1999; Minow and LeMay, 1995). If we fail to consider it as a potential variable— the way Frazier may never have thought about the structure of the day—then we will miss the potential impact of this multibillion-dollar, saturating industry (Daspit, 1999). The challenge is that popular culture lives in our imaginations, in our unconscious, away from our immediate awareness and public selves. The major power of advertising is its ability to convince us that we are not influenced by it (Kilbourne, 1999).

Cross (this issue) imagines the comments from the 1940s: "yes, now that you point it out to me, double-shifting probably does not help matters, but there must be some cultural or genetic reasons why so many Black teens keep getting into trouble" (p. 79). We ruminate in the same way about the steady diet of stimulating images fed to all of us, with young people perhaps more vulnerable than others; we know that it affects brain chemistry; we sense that it is changing the ways that we relate to ourselves and each other, we know that our consuming behaviors are sustainable only at the costs of lives around the globe, *and* then *we look away*. Like the adults that Cross describes, we assume that it must be about something else: bad genes, the education system, the mental health system, racism, etc. And while all of these contribute to our understanding of youth violence, there is a strange silence in this issue and in general about what de Zengotita (2002) calls "The Numbing of The American Mind" and the particular impact that has on children and youth. We, too, struggle with the addictive properties of popular culture; however, we would rather project all of our concern on young people.

Hertz-Lazarowitz reminds us of McLaren and Giroux's (1994) reflection: "education has to be viewed as a political matter related to the power structure of the society" (p. 64). Maybe schools are less potent as critical sites for identity development, and popular culture reigns. Mahiri and Connor (this issue) allude to this when they suggest that "elements of hip-hop culture and rap music constituted a kind of 'pop culture pedagogy' that extended, offered alternatives to, or challenged the pedagogy of schools" (p. 124).

However, I would go further. The images and values of popular culture have colonized the imagination, subtly defining what is important, the ways in which we interact and the meanings we construct. Certain images, especially those that link sexuality and violence (the critical link of the last two articles in this issue) take up a place in our imaginations, whether we consciously "know" or acknowledge it. The preponderance of violence as entertainment does at least three things: First, the very medium of television, movies, video games, and the Internet pulls us into an external focus and risks making us passive and "receptive" in the most intimate areas of our own lives. This contributes to the sense reported by many young people that "this is just the way things are," and "you get used to it . . . ." This passivity develops separate from the "content" of specific films or music. This is a meta-effect, provoked by intensity and saturation. Secondly, popular culture teaches an amazingly consistent and "standardized" curriculum of consumerist and materialist values. In a world of harsh policy battles about what young people should be taught in schools, there is a seemingly clear consensus in the curriculum of popular culture that individualism, efficiency, and materialism are the keys to a happy life. And that violence is a common, legitimate, and sometimes glamorous way of handling conflict and difference. And finally, popular culture holds identity development processes hostage to a false reality, away from the human, interactive, social field. This may be why the focus in so many of these studies on actual experience—shared between adults and young people—proved to be so riveting. Several studies note that relationships over time with youth participants led to deeper levels of comfort with process and reflection on their involvement in the study. This proves especially important in Solis's (this issue) case study of her work with one student over time.

While there is much additional research to chart this new terrain, it seems likely that popular culture has *some* impact on issues of youth and violence and it has *some* impact on how adults view and engage with issues of youth and violence. For instance, in my most recent work with educators, it has become clear that adults are often quite clear about the implications of consumerist values on the young people with whom they work. They are usually quite enthusiastic about the need for critical media training and coursework about advertising and marketing. Although they say that young people are rarely initially engaged by these ideas, believing themselves to be about this kind of influence—while they wear the clothes, buy the music, and incorporate the values of the culture that surrounds them. However, these educators are routinely less interested in exploring their own reaction to popular culture and the ways in which issues of consumption, externalization, and ambition affect them on a daily basis.

Studying this new terrain will be fraught with methodological, psychological and political difficulties. One of the greatest challenges may be the requirement that adults, researchers, and educators examine our own values about popular culture, examine our own values about "entertainment," and not simply lump it into some larger vague category called "the media." The simple fact that a multi-billion dollar industry exists and thrives on images of violence seemingly unfettered may communicate to young people what we really believe.

References

Apple, M. (1996). *Cultural politics and education*. New York: Teachers College Press.

Bailey, S. (1992–93). Gender equity: The unexamined basic of school reform. *Stanford Law & Policy Review, 4*, Winter.

Banet, A. G., Jr., & Hayden, C. (1977). The Tavistock primer. In J. E. Jones, & J. W. Pfeiffer (Eds.), *The 1977 handbook for group facilitators* (pp. 155–167). La Jolla, CA: University Associates.

Block, A. (1997). *I'm only bleeding: Education as the practice of social violence against children*. New York: Peter Lang.

Chomsky, N. (1995). A dialogue with Noam Chomsky. *Harvard Educational Review, 65*(2).

Daspit, T. (1999). Rap pedagogies: "Bring(ing) the noise of knowledge born on the microphone" to radical education. In T. Daspit & J. A. Weaver (Eds.), *Popular culture and critical pedagogy. Reading, constructing, connecting* (pp. 163–181). New York: Garland Publishing.

Daspit, T., & Weaver, J. A. (Eds.). (1999). *Popular culture and critical pedagogy. Reading, constructing, connecting*. New York: Garland Publishing.

de Zengotita, T. (2002). Numbing of the American mind. *Harper's Magazine, 304* (1823), 33–41.

Fine, M. (1991). *Framing dropouts: Notes on the politics of an urban public high school*. Albany, NY: State University of New York Press.

Fine, M., & Somerville, J. I. (Eds.). (1998). *Small schools, big imaginations: Creative look at urban public schools*. Chicago: Cross City Campaign for Urban School Reform.

Fordham, S. (1996). Blacked out. *Dilemmas of race, identity, and success at Capital High*. Chicago: University of Chicago Press.

Frazier, E. F. (1939). *The Negro family in the United States*. Chicago: University of Chicago Press; revised edition 1948. New York: Dryden Press.

Giles, H. C. (2001). Transforming the deficit narrative: Race, class and social capital in parent-school relations. In C. Korn & A. Bursztyn (Eds.), *Case studies in cultural transition: Re-thinking multi-cultural education*. Wesport, CT: Greenwood Press.

Harre, R. (1979). *Social being*. London: Blackwell.

Homel, M. W. (1984). *Down from equality: Black Chicagoans and the public schools, 1920–1940.* Champaign-Urbana, IL: University of Illinois Press.

Jaques, E. (1955). Social systems as a defense against persecutory and depression anxiety. In M. Klein, P. Heimann, & R. E. Money-Kyrle (Eds.), *New directions in psychoanalysis* (pp. 277–299). London: Tavistock.

Kilbourne, J. (1999). *Can't buy my love: How advertising changes the way we think and feel.* New York: Simon & Schuster.

Kuhn, T. (1962). *Structure of scientific revolutions.* Chicago: University of Chicago Press.

Lasn, K. (2000). *Culture jam: How to reverse America's suicidal consumer binge—And why we must.* New York: Quill.

Leadbeater, B. J. R., & Way, N. (Eds.) (1996). *Urban girls: Resisting stereotypes, creating identities.* New York: New York University Press.

Lewin, K. (1951). *Field theory in social science: Selected papers* (D. Cartwright, Ed.). New York: Harper.

McLaren, P., & Giroux, H. A. (1994). *Between borders: Pedagogy and the politics of cultural studies.* New York: Routledge.

Menzies, I. E. P. (1975). A case-study in the functioning of social systems as a defense against anxiety. In A. D. Colman & W. H. Bexton (Eds.), *Group relations reader I.* Washington, DC: A.K. Rice Institute.

Minow, N. N., & LeMay, C. L. (1995). *Abandoned in the wasteland: Children, television, and the first amendment.* New York: Hill & Wang.

Morrison, T. (2002). *Freeing the imagination of America.* Keynote address, PEN Annual Conference. Assessment and Accountability: The Great Equity Debate 11/11/02–11/13/02.

Obholzer, A., & Roberts, V. Z. (Eds.). (1994). *The unconscious at work: Individual and organizational stress in the human services.* London, New York: Routledge.

Payne, Y. A. (2001). Black men and street life as a site of resiliency: A counter story for Black scholars. *International Journal of Critical Psychology* (4), 109–122.

Powell, L. C. (1994). Interpreting social defenses: Family groups in an urban setting. In M. Fine (Ed.), *Chartering urban school reform: Reflections on public high schools in the midst of change.* New York: Teachers College Press.

Rich, A. (1983). Compulsory heterosexuality & lesbian existence. In A. Snitow, C. Stansell, & S. Thompson (Eds.), *Power of desire: The politics of sexuality* (pp. 177–205). New York: Monthly Review Press.

Rioch, M. J. (1975). "All we like sheep—" [Isaiah 53:6]: Followers and leaders. In A. D. Colman & W. H. Bexton (Eds.), *Group relations reader I.* Washington, DC: A. K. Rice Institute.

Shapiro, E. R., & Carr, A. W. (1991). *Lost in familiar places: Creating new connections between the individual and society.* New Haven, CT: Yale University Press.

Senge, P. M. (1990). *The fifth discipline: The art and practice of the learning organization.* New York: Doubleday.

Smith, K. K., & Berg, D. N. (1987). *Paradoxes of group life: Understanding conflict, paralysis, and movement in group dynamics.* San Francisco: Jossey Bass.

Smith, K. K., Simmons, V. M., & Thames, T. B. (1989). "Fix the women": An intervention into an organizational conflict based on parallel process thinking. *The Journal of Applied Behavioral Science, 25*(1), 11–29.

Style, E., & Powell, L. C. (1995). In our own hands: A diversity primer. *Transformations,* (2), 65–84.

Toussaint, P., Boyd-Franklin, N., & Franklin, A. J. (2000). *Boys into men: Raising our African American teenage sons.* New York: Dutton/Penguin Books.

Walkerdine, V. (2002). *Challenging subjects.* London: Palgrave Publishers.

Ward, J. (2001). Raising resisters. In M. Fine & L. Weis (Eds.), *Constructions sites.* New York: Teachers College Press.

Wasley, P., et al. (2000). *Executive summary: Small schools: Great strides: A study of new small schools in Chicago.* New York: Bank Street College.

Wellesley College, C. f. R. o. W. (1992). *How schools shortchange girls: A study of major findings on girls in education.* AAUW Educational Foundation.

Wells, L. (1985). The group-as-a-whole perspective and its theoretical roots. In A. D. Colman & M. H. Geller (Eds.), *Group relations reader 2*. Sausalito, CA: GREX.
Wolff, M. J. (1999). *The entertainment economy: How media forces are transforming our lives*. New York: Crown Publishing Group.

LINDA C. POWELL is a Clinical Psychologist and an internationally-known group relations consultant, in the tradition of the Tavistock Institute of Human Relations in London, England. Currently, she is Visiting Professor at the Graduate Center of the City University of New York as well as Affiliated Faculty at the Leadership Institute, University of San Diego. Using an interdisciplinary set of skills as Educator, Organizational Consultant, and Psychotherapist, Dr. Powell has been working with groups and individuals on issues of power and change for almost thirty years. In addition to her corporate consultation and coaching efforts, she works in education reforms, most recently with the nationally-noted research report on the impact of Chicago small-schools movement, "Small Schools, Great Strides." Dr. Powell has authored several articles and book chapters on leadership and urban school reform, most recently, "Savage inequalities indeed: Irrationality and urban school reform" with Maggie Barber and "From charity to justice: Toward a theology of urban school reform." She is the co-editor of *Off-White: Reading on race, power and society* (Routledge Press). She is currently working on a book-length exploration of the dilemmas of social identity, leadership, and organizational change and is the President of Resources for Change, Inc., a consulting firm specializing in organizational transformation.

Journal of Social Issues, Vol. 59, No. 1, 2003, pp. 213–216

The Timeliness of Time for Blacks and Whites: An Introduction of Professor James M. Jones, Winner of SPSSI's 2001 Lewin Award

Norman Miller*

University of Southern California

Professor James M. Jones was the winner of SPSSI's 2001 Lewin Award. In conjunction with his receipt of this coveted honor, he presented a talk at the August annual meeting of the American Psychological Association meeting of 2001 in San Francisco titled "TRIOS: A Psychological Theory of the African Legacy in American Culture." It was based on the article that accompanies this introduction of him.

On the one hand, Professor Jones' research interests center on the effects of culture, and racism on Black personality. In studying how culturally determined power structures interact with principles of ethnocentrism to affect Black personality, he examines the causal role of situational factors. At the same time, another prong of his research activity is concerned with how fundamental differences in personality affect goals and action. Specifically, he examines the effects of an individual's temporal orientation—whether focused toward the past, the present, or the future. How, for instance, does variation in an individual's temporal orientation affect achievement motivation and expressive style? Here, Professor Jones' work specifically examines the causal impact of personality structures on behavior.

Few contemporary social psychologists as readily fit a template characterizing major themes of Kurt Lewin's intellectual activities as does Professor James M. Jones. In Lewin's field theory, no behavioral action is caused simply by a

---

*Correspondence concerning this article should be addressed to Norman Miller, Department of Psychology, University of Southern California, Los Angeles, CA 90089-1061 [e-mail: nmiller@rcf.usc.edu].

person. Nor is it ever solely determined by features of the situation in which that person is embedded. Instead, Lewin saw all behavioral action as being a consequence of the interaction between these two causal sources—as the resultant effect of these two bi-directional causal processes each simultaneously affecting the other.

Another strong theme in Lewin's work was his commitment to action research. Much of his research, while grounded in theoretically derived ideas, sought to solve practical social problems. It focused on such topics as leadership training, group productivity, and changing attitudes towards non-preferred foods. Throughout his life, however, and during the last years in particular, he was deeply concerned with prejudice and the improvement of intergroup relations. His experiences as a Jew during his early life in Berlin and his loss of family in concentration camps undoubtedly fueled these latter interests. They were reflected in his role in establishing the Commission on Community Interrelations as a research arm of the American Jewish Congress in New York and in his writings as well (e.g. Lewin, 1948, "Resolving Social Conflicts," and his discussion of self-hatred among the Jews).

As a recipient of the Lewin award, it is the meta-theoretical implications of simultaneously engaging in his two major research programs that make Professor Jones' research of special interest. By studying both (a) how culturally determined power structures interact with principles of ethnocentrism to affect Black personality, and (b) how fundamental differences in personality affect goals and action, he exhibits an acceptance of Lewin's theoretically postulated necessity of understanding the interactive effects between the situation and the person in order to predict behavior. That is, when considered together, these two research programs emphasize and exemplify the simultaneous bi-directional causal effects reflected in the interaction between person and situation that are at the core of Lewin's field theory of human behavior.

In addition, however, Professor Jones' pursuit of these particular research interests maps onto Lewin's own substantive intellectual concerns. For instance, Professor Jones' now classic 1972 text, '*Prejudice and Racism*', recently revised in a second edition (1997), exemplifies this fit with respect to intergroup relations. It has received not only glowing reviews, but evidences the sophistication that interest, commitment, and creative scholarship can bring to the analysis of the source of what many argue is our nation's greatest and continuing historical shame. Moreover, like Lewin, who thought seriously, also, about the role of time in social psychological explanation, Professor Jones is one of the relatively few contemporary psychologists whose research explicitly centers on an examination of temporal effects.

A second aspect of Professor Jones' career meshes nicely with the second thrust of Kurt Lewin's interests—his concern with applied issues that concern important arenas for public policy implementation. Here, his contributions extend well beyond what might be inferred from the dry descriptive record of his service that is presented below. For instance, for over two decades, almost as an institution unto himself, Dr. Jones has administered the APA Minority Fellowship program. This program has supported over 975 fellows in their pursuit of their doctoral degrees in psychology. Of special relevance to public policy, however, are the two issues of the American Psychologist that he edited—one on HIV/AIDS in 1987 and one on homelessness in 1992. Both of these empirical and policy-oriented collections exemplify his important leadership at the forefront of psychology's involvement with major social issues.

Professor Jones received his B.A. in psychology from Oberlin College in 1963; an M.A. from Temple University in 1967; and in 1970, his Ph.D. in Social Psychology at Yale University, where he had worked with Bob Abelson. He taught at Harvard University for six years and is currently a Professor of Psychology at the University of Delaware. Over the years he has authored three books, some 30 book chapters, about two dozen empirical articles, and 10 book reviews and encyclopedia articles. In addition, he has given almost 100 talks at national and international conventions and at major universities.

Among various honors he has received, Professor Jones was a John Simon Guggenheim Fellow, 1973–74 and was the recipient of a Lifetime Achievement Award, Division 45, American Psychological Association, August 1999. In addition, he has served as a member of the NIMH Small Grants Review Committee, 1973–77; the Fulbright Hays Screening Committee on Psychology, Council for International Exchange of Scholars, 1976–80, Chair 1977–79; the NIMH Behavioral Science Research Review Committee, 1984–88; the National Academy of Sciences, Committee on Program Evaluation, 1980; the Publications Committee of the Society for Personality and Social Psychology as a member (1987–1990) and as Chair (1989–90); the Executive Committee (1991–1994, chair 1993–1994) and Secretary/Treasurer (1992–93) of the Society of Experimental Social Psychology; the National Institute of Mental Health Task Force on Social and Behavioral Science Research, 1993; the National Science Foundation, Task Force on The Human Capital Initiative, 1994; and the President's Working Group on Psychology and Law, American Psychological Association, 1999–2000. From 1983–1990 he served as Consulting Editor, *Journal of Personality and Social Psychology*, and for the past decade he has been a member of the editorial boards of four other journals.

The Kurt Lewin Memorial Award is presented annually to honor "outstanding contributions to the development and integration of psychological research and social action." As the 2001-year recipient of the award, James M. Jones has fulfilled this aspiration with an unusual aptness, enthusiasm, and success. This year's selection committee consisted of Norman Miller, University of Southern California; Daphne B. Bugental, University of California at Santa Barbara; and James S. Jackson, University of Michigan.

NORMAN MILLER is a prior winner of the Lewin Award. He has also been a Guggenheim Fellow, a Fulbright Research Fellow, a James McKeen Cattell Fellow, and a Haynes Foundation Fellow. His research centers on intergroup relations, aggression, and social projection.

Journal of Social Issues, Vol. 59, No. 1, 2003, pp. 217–242

TRIOS: A Psychological Theory of the African Legacy in American Culture

James M. Jones[*]
University of Delaware

TRIOS is comprised of attitudes, beliefs and values about time, rhythm, improvisation, orality and spirituality. It is proposed that TRIOS represents the cultural foundation of an African legacy for African Americans and provides a means of coping with slavery and various forms of racism over time. TRIOS is a model for the dual processes of self-protective and self-enhancing motivations for targets who must live in a universal context of racism. TRIOS is described as a context-dependent theory of being-in-the-world, as opposed to doing-in-the-world. Evidence for the origins of TRIOS elements in African and Caribbean culture is presented. A scale to measure TRIOS is described and evidence for racial/ethnic differences shows that African Americans score higher than other racial/ethnic groups. The implications of TRIOS for psychological well-being of African Americans and a wide array of future research questions are discussed.

[*]Correspondence concerning this article should be addressed to James M. Jones, Department of Psychology, University of Delaware, Newark, DE 19716 [e-mail: jmjones@udel.edu]. This paper is based on an invited address as recipient of the Society for the Psychological Study of Social Issues Kurt Lewin Award, August 25, 2001, San Francisco, CA. Thanks to Irene Frieze, Sam Gaertner, Jennifer Eberhardt, Olaive Jones, and Eun Rhee for helpful comments on earlier drafts of this article, and to Emily Mull who helped in early stages of data coding and analysis.

It is a humbling and profound honor to receive the Kurt Lewin Memorial Award. Thank you Norman Miller and other members of the selection committee, and SPSSI for continuing the Lewinian legacy, and embodying the essence of the positive possibilities of a humane society. In recent years, the haiku has become my ally to express profound feelings or ideas. By way of thanks I offer this:

Lewin's impact huge
His theories practical
The Honor is mine.

Lewin is my intellectual great grandfather (Lewin begat Festinger who begat Kiesler who begat Jones), I have been shaped and molded in many ways by his ideas. An émigré from the Holocaust in Nazi Germany, he understood the inhumanity of racism and the magnification of its pernicious effects in the context of authoritarian dominance. As a proponent of field theory, he understood the significance of context and the psychological force of multiply determined perceptions and actions. For Lewin the field was not simply a description of relevant aspects of the environment, but the dynamic energy that moved the person through it with direction, purpose and intention. The field is culture and personality and interpersonal and intergroup relationships extending across time from the past into the future. It is experiences and imaginings, in one's own life or that of others with whom one is connected. The field exists in a person's head at a given moment in time. The vector of these cognitive structures into the force that propels people to move or locomote is expressed by the equation $B = F(S_t)$, where S is the situation at the moment t and is comprised of the Person (P) and his or her Psychological Environment (E) at time t. This leads to the well known formula $B = f(P, E)$. To simplify, "context matters," all of it. That it matters is vitally important to our contemporary understanding of human behavior. How it matters is the focus of our most significant and meaningful theories and their practical consequences.

In this paper, I will explore my ideas about context in the Lewinian tradition. I propose a theory of behavior in a field that includes pre-Diaspora African cultural foundations, their evolution, adaptation and transformation in the Diaspora among African descended peoples, and their infusion into the general psychological fabric of human tendency and possibility over time. Personal lifespace conjoins the cultural lifespace to tie a Gordian knot that cultural psychologists express thus: "culture and psyche make each other up" (Shweder and Sullivan, 1992).

I'll begin by recapping my ideas about prejudice and racism, emphasizing cultural racism, as a critical component of this theory. Next, I will introduce TRIOS and outline a set of principles about African culture and its continuing influence on the cultural psychology of African Americans. To preview, TRIOS is an acronym for the psychological elements of a cultural system and consists of time, rhythm, improvisation, orality, and spirituality.

TIME: personal perspectives on the past, present and future
RHYTHM: patterns of behavior in time, flow, entrainment, movement
IMPROVISATION: goal directed creative problem solving under time pressure; a distinctive style
ORALITY: preferences for oral face-to-face communication, and personal expression, and the meaningful role of spoken words in human affairs
SPIRITUALITY: belief in the value of a higher power and unknown forces that influence all living things and one's life in particular

Next I will describe TRIOS, the instantiation of this cultural legacy, in contemporary psychological terms. I will review recent findings that attach empirical possibilities to this TRIOS vision, and suggest new ways to think about contemporary issues in social relations. And I will conclude by suggesting theoretical and empirical possibilities that may be fruitful to pursue in the future.

Cultural Racism: An Origination Story

Racism is a crime against humans and against humanity. Social psychological analysis has focused on prejudice—but racism is different. I have suggested a three-part model of racism by which individual, institutional, and cultural levels combine to create and reflect social structures and influence individual cognitive structures (cf. Jones, 1997, Figure 17.1). Racism presupposes the superiority of one's own racial group over others; it rationalizes privilege based on the superiority presumption, and provides a rationale that makes privileged dominance both rational and normative (cf. Jones, 1997; Sidanius and Pratto, 1999). These tendencies operate at the individual level and function much like race prejudice. These tendencies operate also at aggregate organizational levels by which institutional policy, practice, organization, and outcomes are manifestly linked to racial disparities. This edifice of racism suffuses our culture in prevailing ideologies and worldviews, including values, beliefs, symbols and myths, language, aesthetics, and so on. These levels of analysis have both top down and bottom up influences on how we think about and respond to race.

Further, the need to formulate identifiable connections between culture and individual levels of psychological processes requires that we recognize the commonalities and differences in racial socialization of people from privileged and stigmatized groups. Traditional psychological research on racism has focused on the effects of race on members of privileged groups. TRIOS focuses more on the psychological processes that characterize stigmatized groups, in this case, African Americans. While we represent these macro-level elements in our theories, specific theoretical propositions occur at the level of the individual, as do, of course all of our measurements. If culture and psyche make each other up, we need to formally represent culture in our theoretical formulations. TRIOS is an attempt to do that.

The Universal Context of Racism

Continuing to employ Lewinian ideas, I believe that racism's implications and consequences are asymmetrical with respect to targets and others. Targets are people who live daily with the possibility of threat, bias, denigration, denial, and truncated opportunity. Individual and collective histories of targets are psychologically available at any given moment, and, thus, are part of the situation that influences behavior. This leads me to two assumptions:

First, *racism is an accessible, explanatory construct with motivational consequences.* Lewin offers the *Principle of Contemporaniety*—"... any behavior or any other change in a psychological field depends only upon the psychological field *at that time*" (Lewin, 1943, p. 201). This principle means that a person's psychological *past* and his or her psychological *future*, and his or her construal of the immediately *present* context, is contemporaneously accessible and capable of dynamic interplay. I am proposing that racism is a psychological reality at any given time for targets and it consists of the targets' personal, as well as collective, racial pasts and futures, and their construal of the racial nature of their immediate experience. There are two types of motivational consequences of the universal context of racism: (a) *self-protective motivations*, by which one is oriented to detecting the occurrence of, protecting oneself from, the avoidance of anticipated, and conquering if confronted with, racism. Needless to say this takes a lot of energy. (b) *self-enhancing motivations* by which one is oriented to sustaining, defending, and enhancing one's self-worth and humanity. I argue that both of these motivational tendencies are triggered by the universal context of racism, but the self-protective, more than the self-enhancing motives, have been the subject of theory and research on race. TRIOS is a theory that combines both in the service of promoting psychological well-being among African Americans.

In essence, this is a dual-process model of adaptation and psychological health. It shares certain features with an ego-resiliency approach (cf. Block and Kremen, 1996). When the threatening qualities of a context are perceptually, cognitively or emotionally salient, self-protective motives and mechanisms are aroused (e.g., stereotype threat, Steele, 1997). In the ego-resiliency model, self-enhancing motives are released when the context is perceived to be secure. However, I argue that, in addition, self-enhancing motives may be released: (a) as a way to combat the negative elements of a threatening environment (eat, drink, and be merry for tomorrow you may die), or (b) as a way to convert a threatening environment to a non-threatening context (I can't be hurt if I stay true to my inner core, principles, or being). This dual-process model, then, provides an understanding of how a stigmatized, dehumanized and targeted context can elicit adaptive mechanisms that are both self-protective and self-enhancing. I am, here, referring to individual level processes by which a person feels threat as an individual, but it could be based on his or her membership in a stigmatized group. Self-protective and self-enhancing processes may occur at either the individual level (an action a person might take), or in concert with others in the stigmatized group (collective action).

Another feature of this model is that while self-protective process may more likely be individually based (the person's construal of the psychological moment in time stimulates an adaptive response), the self-enhancing mechanisms are aided by a psychological community of others whose positive responses affirm self-worth. This dual-process model may help explain the strong tendency toward individualism among African Americans (cf. Oyserman, Coon, and Kimmelmeier, 2002), but suggest also that traditional notions of collectivism (e.g., Triandis, 1994) may need to be modified to capture the psychological dynamics of self-enhancement through collectivism suggested here (cf. Jones, 1999). Further, this dual-model is consistent with a distinction between stereotype *threat* (evoking self-protective mechanisms), and stereotype *obligation* (evoking collective affirmation mechanisms; cf. Marks, 2002).

Second, *psychological tensions result from individual versus group level dynamics.* Lewin defines *Psychological Conflict* as the " . . . *overlapping of at least two force fields* . . . in such a way that equally strong and opposite forces overlap at certain points (Lewin, 1944, p. 197). I propose three sets of conflicted force fields: (a) Personal identity versus reference group orientation captures the relative importance of personal uniqueness versus group belonging needs at a moment in time (Brewer, 1991); (b) Racial identity versus superordinate identity reflects the relative importance of in-group distinctiveness versus superordinate group identity. For example, Marvin Kalb queried Jesse Jackson on *Meet the Press* in 1984, asking him whether he was "a Black man who happened to be an American running for the presidency or the reverse, an American who happened to be a Black man running for the presidency." Mr. Jackson resisted this imposition of psychological conflict by claiming their compatibility—". . . my interests are national interests"; and (c) Instrumentality versus expressivity pits the desire for self-expression against the perceived self-constraint that may be required for mainstream success.

Belonging to a marginalized minority group creates the potential for conflicts and tensions in each of these domains. How targets resolve these psychological tensions or conflicts substantially influences their range of behavioral and attitudinal options in a universal racism context.

Lewin made the following observation in 1946:

> . . . One of the most severe obstacles in the way of improvement seems to be the notorious lack of confidence and self-esteem of most minority groups. Minority groups tend to accept the implicit judgment of those who have status even where the judgment is directed against themselves. There are many forces which tend to develop in the children, adolescents, and adults of minorities deep-seated antagonisms to their own group . . . The discrimination which these individuals experience is not directed against them as individuals, but as group members, and only by raising their self-esteem as group members to the normal level can a remedy be produced. (Lewin, 1946, p. 151)

Lewin presupposes that targets in general suffer devalued collective self-esteem (cf. Luhtanen and Crocker, 1992). However, research on racial identity suggests that racial identity for Blacks is based in part on a high regard for Blacks as their reference group (Cross, 1991; Sellers, Rowley, Chavous, Shelton, & Smith, 1997). At the individual level, Crocker and Wolfe (2001) found no support for diminished self-esteem of Blacks. If anything, Black self-esteem is demonstrably higher than other ethnic/racial groups including Whites. One mechanism by which Black self-esteem can be maintained is by decoupling self-worth from outcomes in domains perceived to offer low probabilities of self-affirmation. Crocker and Wolfe (2001) argue that contingencies of self-worth (CSW) may be selectively chosen to reflect self-protective or self-enhancing needs. Osborne (1995) used a protective disidentification analysis to explain the observation that the correlation between self-esteem and grade point average declined substantially for Black males between 8th (.22) and 10th (.08) grades, but not for White males (.25 and .26, respectively). What matters, I believe, is the perceptual context in which one's experience is set, and the motivational systems that provide meaning and understanding to it. The psychological dynamics and normative cultural influences will affect a host of interpretations of phenomena related to psychological well-being.

Lewin proposed that minorities developed deep-seated antagonisms toward their own group, and that their self-esteem suffered by virtue of their group membership. The Osborne data suggest that self-esteem may actually be strengthened by embracing one's own group and "dis-identifying" with the broader social context in which adverse outcomes are widely expected. Rather than being a source of antagonism, the in-group can be a source of self-esteem maintenance and enhancement. This possibility requires a more complex cultural theory of African Americans. It is certainly true that minority groups are aware of the implicit judgments of high status groups and do take them into account. However, it does not necessarily follow that *awareness* of those judgments leads, as Lewin suggests, to deep-seated antagonisms to their own group. I propose that TRIOS provides a way of conceptualizing a basis for positive regard at both individual and collective levels. Further, TRIOS proposes a worldview that organizes the meaning of behavior, and charts strategies for navigating the universal context of racism toward positive psychological well-being. Let me now turn to assumptions underlying these theoretical possibilities.

TRIOS: A Theory of Culture and Psyche

There are many different ways to think about culture. I borrow from the Kroeber and Kluckhohn (1952) definition that culture consists of: (a) patterned ways of thinking, feeling, and reacting that are transmitted by and through symbols; (b) the core of traditional ideas and the values attached to them; and (c) products of action and conditioning elements of future actions. By these criteria, culture is: *psychological*—patterns of thinking, feeling, behaving, and valuing; *symbolic*—representations of psychological meaningful patterns; *historical*—cultural elements are selectively derived and transmitted over time; and *dynamic*—cultural elements both shape meaning and are transformed by events and actions.

I argue that contemporary African American culture is continuous with its African origins. The evolution of contemporary African American culture follows a dual-process model of *reactionary* and *evolutionary* mechanisms (cf. Jones, 1988). Reactionary mechanisms consist of adaptation-coping sequences that emerge over time to address the ecological challenges members of the cultural group face. These challenges require a variety of psychological and social means of coping with two fundamental aspects of an oppressed status—(a) loss of freedom, and (b) dehumanization. Evolutionary mechanisms consist of those expressions of psyche that reflect the core cultural ethos of a people. I propose that TRIOS can be used instrumentally as a means of recovering certain forms of physical and psychological freedom, and that TRIOS can frame the foundation of a humanized existence in a hostile environment. I also suggest that TRIOS reflects the core African cultural ethos.

Slavery is defined by the loss of individual freedoms and liberties for those who are its victims (for an excellent general overview of slavery and its influences see Franklin and Moss, 1994, chapters 3–8). The abject loss of freedom resulting from enslavement generated a primary psycho-cultural motivational system designed to gain control over one's body and over one's life. As a result, claiming psychological freedom in any and every form possible can be seen as a consistent pattern of psychological adaptation and a cardinal goal of social psychological development. Although slavery was officially abolished in the United States in 1865, the truncated rights and informal systems of constraint remained in effect for years after (cf. Vann Woodward, 1951).

Physical dehumanization was related to cultural and psychological dehumanization. African civilization was judged to be primitive and its inhabitants barely human. Over more than 400 years, persons of African descent in America have been dehumanized and marginalized. It is not surprising that self-esteem, self-worth, and individual and collective identity have been issues at the forefront of our psychological analysis of African Americans. Taken together, we can reasonably expect that the ongoing quest for freedom and dignity is not just a civil rights agenda, but psychological motivation that organizes and energizes the dual-process mechanisms of self-protection and self-enhancement.

This dynamic process has unfolded over centuries with psychological consequence. The foundation for psychological mechanisms and adaptation capacities followed from the cultural conditioning that preceded the arrival of Africans in America. Faced with a new and challenging situation, Africans in America utilized those cultural patterns they knew to cope with and adapt to these new dangerous and threatening contexts. It is these prior culturally conditioned attributes and capacities that make up the evolutionary mechanisms. As a result, the reactionary

mechanisms were not invented out of whole cloth on the spot of the first conflict on a slave ship or at Jamestown plantation in 1619. Rather, they constitute
the application of the evolutionary tendencies (here I am suggesting they can be
summarized by TRIOS) to survival and adaptation.

We should note that this dual-process model is the cultural equivalent of the
dual-process model presented earlier as an individual-level mechanism. That is,
the self-protective mechanisms correspond to reactionary mechanisms, and the
self-enhancing mechanisms correspond to the evolutionary mechanisms. Whether
describing a person coping with a potentially threatening environment or a cultural group who are stigmatized and targeted for dehumanization and systematic
oppression and constraint, these two classes of responses and human needs operate.

This dual-process model also parallels DuBois' (1903) observation about
"double-consciousness" at the turn of the last century:

> ... It is a peculiar sensation this double-consciousness, this sense of always looking at one's
> self through the eyes of others, of measuring one's soul by the tape of a world that looks
> on in amused contempt and pity. One ever feels his twoness,—an American, A Negro; two
> warring ideals on one dark body, whose dogged strength alone keeps it from being torn
> asunder. . . . (pp. 214–15)

Over time, the dynamics of these processes expand from simple physical and psychological *survival*, to physical and psychological *well-being*. Progress in rights
and opportunities, however much qualified, opens up new avenues of possibility
and expands the range of goals to which the reactionary and evolutionary mechanisms may be directed. As progress in individual rights and statutory protections
has progressed, the contexts for constraint and dehumanization become more subtle. The psychological mechanisms that mediate appropriate adaptation to these
perhaps more ambiguous contexts are importantly transformed over time by the
subtle necessities of coping with threats that are more veiled but not necessarily
less pernicious.

Through this dynamic interaction, the conditioning or evolutionary mechanisms are modified and transformed by the reactionary adaptation-coping sequences. We may project a dynamic process of continuity and change that connects contemporary African American psychological culture to its historical roots.
I propose that TRIOS comprises one version of those psychologically meaningful
historically derived mechanisms. I further argue that TRIOS provided the reper-
toire of skills, perspectives, beliefs, and values that informed the initial means of
adapting to and coping with the horrific experiences of slavery. Overtime, TRIOS
elements were modified by the exigencies of ecological challenges, and underwent
transformations that established their relevance and utility as modes of adaptation
for survival in the new world.

In order to make this set of assumptions practical, one needs to (a) specify
the cultural elements of origin, (b) describe the ecological challenges, (c) trace
the reactivity processes and their influence on these original cultural elements,

and (d) describe the current set of core cultural elements and how they function in a contemporary context. For the purposes of this paper, I will *stipulate* that TRIOS can define those psychologically meaningful origins, and that these TRIOS elements mediated reactivity to the ecological challenges faced by Africans in the 17th and 18th century Diaspora. Over time, the TRIOS elements define both the evolution of African cultural origins in the Diaspora as well as their dynamic change as a result of reactionary processes.

Origins of TRIOS

TRIOS emerged as a way of organizing several different observations I made about African American culture. It began with the observation that racism was at its core a problem of culture (Jones, 1972, 1997). Research on sports activities (Jones & Hochner, 1973) led to the differential assessment of the self-paced versus reactive hypothesis (Worthy and Markle, 1970) which proposed that Blacks would be better at reactive sports activities (hitting in baseball, shooting field goals in basketball), while Whites would be superior at self-paced activities (free throw shooting in basketball, pitching in baseball, golf, bowling). Our data showed that Blacks were superior at all baseball activities (although they were underrepresented among pitchers, suggesting not so much ability, but a racially biased selection criterion). There was no racial difference in field goal accuracy, but Whites were reliably more accurate at free throws. Given the dominance of Blacks in basketball, I reasoned that it could not be a matter of ability, but the cultural context in which basketball skills develop. I argued that the improvisation characterized in part by individual style could explain this difference. Free throws lacked currency in this improvised world of stylistic expression, and this *psychological* element could explain the statistical difference in performance.

To this notion of improvisation was added concepts of time, rhythm, spirituality, and orality derived from spending a year in Trinidad. The idea that "any time is Trinidad time" led to the understanding that a present-time orientation is not simply a failure of valuing time and the future (which has been called temponomics; cf. McGrath & Kelly, 1986), but a way of exercising personal freedom and control. It fed into both rhythm and orality, as patterns of behavior were free and hence often irregular or syncopated. Orality, defines the primacy of the spoken or sung word, and the ability of speech to forge bonds between and among people. Calypso music told the stories of the Trinidad people from year to year, and the celebration of Carnival put these stories in a musical context, expressing themselves in humor, joy, and vibrant rhythms of color and movement. The Calypsonian emerged as the modern day griot, telling the tales of life in Trinidad and Tobago in rhythm and song. Finally, Shango captured the intersection of religion and spirituality and contributed to the final TRIOS element.

African Associations With TRIOS

From these inductive process of observation and association, I summarize selective evidence that these relatively contemporary observations are linked to more
substantial and compelling cultural data that are consistent with the origination of
these TRIOS concepts in an African cultural context. I have borrowed from the
writings of more or less contemporary scholars who are historians, anthropolo-
gists, philosophers, and linguists (e.g., Mbiti, 1970; Jahn, 1961; Senghor, 1956;
Sobel, 1987).

Time. Time is typically parted into past, present, and future. Cultures around
the world have come to value different aspects of these time zones and characteristic
cultural and personality differences have emerged. For Africans, time was slow
moving and practical, *deriving from* tasks and behaviors *not prescribing them.*
This view distinguishes event time from clock time (Levine, 1997). Mbiti (1970)
suggests that in Swahili no word for the future exists, only for the past (Zamani)
and present (Sasa). Thus I believe that a present-past time orientation may be
central to early African cultural systems.

Rhythm. Chernoff (1979) comments that:

> ... one of the most notable features of African cultures is that many activities—paddling
> a canoe, chopping a tree, pounding grain, or simply moving—seem set in a rhythmic
> framework ... the African dancer may pick up and respond to the rhythms of one or more
> drums, the dancer, like the drummer, adds another rhythm, one that is not there. He tunes
> his ear to hidden rhythms and he dances to gaps in the music. (pp. 143–144)

Rhythm is recurring patterns of behavior set in time and gives shape, energy,
and meaning to psychological experience. It is complex and is a means of attaching
psychological structure to the external world. It is also an internal response to the
rhythmic patterns of the external world. Entrainment captures this process and
links a person to his or her environment in a dynamic way.

Improvisation. Like rhythm, improvisation is a way of connecting the internal
and the external worlds. Improvisation is a means of control and a way to structure
interactions among people. With respect to music, Chernoff (1979) notes that:

> Improvisation is not so much in the genesis of new rhythms as in the organization and form
> given to the already existing rhythms, and a musician's style of organizing his playing will
> indicate the way he approaches from his own mind the responsibility of his role toward
> making the occasion a success (p. 82).

Improvisation then serves both a social integrative function as well as a personally
expressive one. Improvisation is an organizational principle that is goal-oriented
and expressive. Improvisation enables creative solutions to problems that arise in

a given situation. Moreover, the expression of one's soul and spirit is an improvisational action.

Orality. This is a broad concept, which in an oral tradition, includes storytelling, naming, singing, drumming, and the important lessons of socialization and cultural transmission. The Word (Nommo) is the life-force, and as Jahn (1961) suggests, " . . . all activities of men and all movement in nature rest on the word . . . a newborn child becomes human only when his father gives him name and pronounces it." This tradition was shown to dramatic effect when Kunta Kinte was named in a ceremony in the 1977 television miniseries, *Roots* (Haley, 1976). The important meanings and values of African culture are spoken or sung, not written down. The organizing principles and values of culture are handed down through stories and parables. The oral tradition connects the present to the past. Orality gives meaning to life and binds people together in common understandings and humanity. The griot in the African cultural tradition is a professional storyteller. The life of a people is told in stories that chronicle major events, parables or truths to live by, and important values and life lessons that serve as guides for living.

Spirituality. This may be the most central aspect of African origins. According to Jahn (1961) all things can be assigned to one of four categories: *Muntu*—god, spirits, and human beings; *Kintu*—all forces which do not act on their own but under the control of Muntu; *Hantu*—time and space; *Kuntu*—modalities such as beauty, laughter. The importance of this taxonomy is that all categories are *forces*, which lead them to have effectance in the world. The universal force comes from the stem *-ntu*. Spirituality in this conception is the idea that forces beyond human beings act with effect in the world of human beings. In a field force sense, causality is multiply determined, and not all causes are material or knowable. TRIOS, then, is a worldview that directs culture as well as reflects it. The psychological correlates of this cultural conception diverge from one constructed on the principles of a European-derived materialistic individualism. TRIOS is the nexus from which we trace the dynamics of African-European cultural contact in America.

Ecological Challenges in the New World

The ecological challenges of slavery engaged the patterns of TRIOS in adapting-coping sequences. In this oppressive environment, the opportunities for expression, social organization, and control demanded each of the TRIOS elements. Creole or pidgin languages emerged to enable oral communication among people who may have spoken somewhat different languages or dialects (cf. Morgan, 1998). Improvisation was a means of creating linguistic meanings that were privileged among the native speakers and, thus, shielded the speaker from adverse consequences when speech was heard by a person hostile to his well-being. Expression of the human spirit was made possible through music, song, and dance. Social organization was necessarily improvised as were strategies for control of self-protective, collective actions. The cultural patterns became practical means of coping, adapting, and surviving. Thus, humanity was preserved through employing known and deep cultural principles and practices.

TRIOS: Psychological Principles and Hypothetical Possibilities

As a cultural worldview, each TRIOS dimension reflects human capacity developed from the fabric of experience, necessity, belief, and evolutionary success. Psychological concepts derive from a particular cultural history and the problems and issues it defines. Mainstream psychology is inspired by European-American cultural concerns and worldviews that celebrate individual initiative and success. TRIOS offers an alternative origination of basic psychological ideas, situated in the context of African psychological culture and its elaboration in the African Diaspora. In this context, psychology is inspired by African American cultural concerns and worldviews that emphasize the human life force and the universal spirit that sustains the individual.

TRIOS rests on three related organizing principles: (a) TRIOS concepts are driven by and responsive to context; (b) contexts are immediate and contain relevant information that shape what things mean, and validates or confirms one's self-conception; (c) individual elements of TRIOS are distinctive as well as synergistic in combination. As a result, TRIOS as a whole should be taken as a worldview, instantiated over time, and expressed by individuals who have been enculturated to it. Let's examine each of these principles in turn.

TRIOS and Context

TRIOS presumes that a large percentage of meaningful events occur within a context. Context describes a moment in time, but contains cognitive, emotional, and attitudinal representations of people, places, things, and events that are not only psychologically or physically extant in the immediate context, but may exist outside of that moment. This approach reflects Lewin's idea of the situation as it can be objectively portrayed and as it is construed by a person at a particular moment in time. From the outside looking in, we speculate on a person's construal of the situation and its impact on behavior.

Another way of looking at context is as an object of regard with goal-relevant properties. Goals that can be achieved in a context include self-presentation, social influence, hedonic intentions, desires, and social control. Each of these context-driven goals can be achieved through the elements of TRIOS. Further, these goals can be linked also to motivations triggered by historically-derived responses to loss of freedom and dehumanization.

Encounters in the moment derive meaning from the relevance of ongoing behaviors and their interpretation. Simply put, context is dynamic. For example, from a contextual viewpoint language is not dependent on semantic meaning so much as its paralinguistic features, inflections, body language, facial cues, and so on. Conventional meanings of words are replaced by colloquial or neologistic meanings that privilege the speaker over the audience. In Trinidad, "mamaguy" describes verbal utterances whose meaning is opposite to its semantic content. "Your hair looks very nice today," means just the opposite when a person is "mamaguying" you. More commonly, we are culturally aware, now, that "bad" can mean "good," as can "stupid" or "dope." Understanding is not just cognitive ("I understand") or perceptual ("I see what you're saying," or "I hear you"), but emotional ("I feel you"). By strategic use of inflection, a simple affirmation ("uh-huh" with a rising inflection and head nod) can become a negation ("uh-huh" with a falling inflection and head shake). Alternative linguistic conventions in this contextual arsenal include the diminutive alternative (home equals "crib"), the graphically illustrated action (to leave is to "bounce," to show appreciation is to "love," to be an exemplar of the group or geographical area is to "represent").

Language provides a compelling argument for power "in" the situation. In each of these cases, the language captures the interpersonal, intragroup, and the intrapsychic meaning of things, and links the speaker and the audience in a union fortified against the outsider who, absent cultural understanding, is marginalized and stripped of power to harm. What an utterance means or an actor intends is defined by the parameters in the context itself. The anthropologist E. T. Hall (1983) made a similar point in his distinction between *context-rich* and *context-poor* communications. Context-rich communications are semantically sparse and thus their meaning is derived by locating the utterances in a rich web of cultural nuance and meaning. Context-poor communications, on the other hand, are of necessity semantically dense and rely on the literal meaning of words which are both explicit and durable over time and place.

The community of perceivers who know the culture-symbols get it, and outsiders don't. Thus one gains a measure of control when meaning is context-dependent. Conversely, imposed meanings that are instantiated and defined in a hostile culture impose external controls and reduce one's flexibility at self-definition. It is reasonable, then, to perceive this reliance on context as a means of gaining personal control in the situation and ultimately, control of one's self-worth.

The resurgence of culture in psychology (Fiske, Kitayama, Markus, & Nisbett, 1998; Markus and Kitayama, 1991) has focused attention on the context as a variable in human behavior. One aspect of culture-as-context is the way in which the self is implicated in the construal of the meanings of things. The broadest distinction of self-relevant variables is independence from or interdependence with others (Markus and Kitayama, 1991). A similar distinction is made by Individualism and Collectivism (cf. Triandis, 1994). The TRIOS analysis, though, conceives the collective and individualistic self-construals as complementary, not oppositional.

Collectivism can be expressed at the level of the individual (Jones, 1999). Psychologically, meaning is defined in this context, at this time. What a person means is determined by parameters of the immediate context itself. Further, who I am is also defined in that context. My creative improvisational performance, if accepted by the audience, defines the qualities of character I possess and lay claim to. My audience is crucial to who I am, as a result. My authentic self is not imposed on me, but defined by my actions, my speech, and my dress. It makes a self-defining statement of who I am. As we will see, the vital elements of TRIOS are jointly impacted in this contextual analysis.

What is important here is that the collective may affirm the individual, but also that through the expression of culturally sanctioned individualistic aspects of TRIOS, an individual may simultaneously affirm the collective (cf. Jones, 1999). Rather than choosing between an individualistic or collectivistic orientation, TRIOS joins them. A recent meta-analysis of individualism and collectivism has shown that African Americans are more individualistic than Whites, and are not more collectivistic (Oyserman et al., 2002). African Americans are more individualistic than Whites with respect to directness of communication with others, privacy of self-thoughts, and competition with others. Two other distinguishing features of African American individualism are that when individualism is defined by self-knowledge, African Americans are *not* more individualistic, but when defined by their personal uniqueness, they are *more* individualistic.

With respect to collectivism, although African Americans are less collective than Whites overall, they are more collective when it *excludes* seeking advice from others, moderating one's behavior to fit the context, or accepting authority. Blacks are not more collective than Whites when collectivism is defined by group harmony, a preference for group-based work, or inclusion in groups. In sum, the TRIOS perspective emphasizes strong individualistic and collective orientations to adaptation, coping and well-being, and the data on individualism-collectivism seem to support this general tendency. However, the story may be more complex than that.

Centuries of oppression, dehumanization, and discrimination require African Americans to seek and secure relatively independent sources of self-worth. Further, the community of others who can validate an African American's self-worth must be carefully chosen in a generally hostile context. It is possible that being individualistic means something different for a person in an oppressed context than it does for a person who is in a relatively secure context. Individualism in the service of survival and establishing self-worth may be of a different quality than individualism that serves personal achievement and enculturated self-representations. Further, collectivism may have less to do with duty and obligation—which can impose significant restrictions on individual freedoms—than with establishing a self-protective community (meta-culture) whose symbolic representations and privileged understandings help to establish support for individualistic expression and well-being. Collectivism, like individualism, serves survival and self-worth needs and goals for individuals. The ability of members of a group to validate one's self-worth is not specifically reflected in the collectivism concept, and duty to others in one's group is not the same thing.

TRIOS as Worldview

TRIOS is well suited to a context-driven worldview because each of its dimensions either reflects or provides a means of controlling aspects of a given context. We often consider goals, expectations, plans, and intentions in an extended time frame. That is, the basic motives in psychology seem to rest on connecting the present to a distant future that is typically desirable and presumed to be attainable (McGrath & Kelly, 1986; Zaleski, 1994; Zimbardo & Boyd, 1999). Specific motives consist of figuring out where we want to be in the future, and establishing means-end sequences that help us reach our goals (Jones, Banicky, Lasane, & Pomare, 2003).

As a cultural syndrome, TRIOS reflects the psychological realism of being-in-the-world. Being-in-the-world is not only a present-time focus, but it is also a spiritual focus where living status (being) is shared with others in the broad lexicon of spirituality related to Muntu (Jahn, 1961). It is improvisational because one is successful by virtue of continued life (being), not by life's products (doing). It is oral because it is only now that we meet face to face and define and redefine, express and reveal our essential nature. The language of being-in-the-world is immediacy (the durative "be" in linguistics, "I be going . . . "; cf. Smitherman, 1977). Being-in-the-world, then, is defined as a focus on the fundamental challenges of living and the acceptance of a place in a universe in which all things matter. More practically, being-in-the-world is a self-system that does not take the future for granted, and lets go of the past.

What might one expect from such a theory? Well, one thing is that TRIOS elements may formulate themselves in a coherent way that is structurally integrated. Second, African Americans who are relatively more TRIOSic should have a higher level of psychological well-being. Third, to the extent that other groups may also experience dehumanization, restricted freedom, and marginalization, they may also be inclined toward TRIOSic qualities.

Now let us turn to some initial attempts to organize these ideas into empirically measurable and conceptually testable hypotheses.

The Structure of TRIOS

Since the first publication of the TRIOS concept (Jones, 1979), I have described the basic five dimensions and talked about their possibilities as reflections of psychological processes for African Americans. I will now describe some of the preliminary evidence for the psychological coherence of TRIOS.

The conceptual premise is that TRIOS represents a worldview that has psychological correlates in the attitudes, cognitions, values, and behaviors of African

Americans, and that the structure of this worldview moderates or mediates important behavioral outcomes. It is hypothesized that persons of African descent will endorse the TRIOS dimensions, and that the dimensions will mediate psychological well-being to a greater degree than for members of other ethnic/racial groups. The following sections discuss preliminary evidence for the structure of TRIOS and ethnic/racial differences in their endorsement.

Measuring TRIOS

Thurstone's (1928) declaration that "Attitudes Can Be Measured" became for me an interrogative, *"Can* TRIOS be measured?" First, students from my graduate seminar on the Cultural Psychology of African Americans and I wrote 100 questionnaire items constructed to tap the five TRIOS dimensions. Table 1 describes the underlying characteristic of each TRIOS dimension and a sample item assessing it. Using a 7-point Likert scale for responses with a range of −3 "not at

Table 1. TRIOS Domains and Assessment

Dimension Name	Description	Sample Item
Time	*Focuses attention on the present; immediacy of goals or behavior.	I try to live one day at a time.
	*Setting goals and planning for the future.	I make extensive plans for the future.
	*Emotion laden thoughts about the past.	I think about the past a lot.
Rhythm	*An internal rhythmic process with external dynamic properties—flow, entrainment.	I always try to get in synch with surroundings.
	*Importance of and preference for physical expression.	Music and dance are important forms of personal expression.
Improvisation	*Creative problem solving in conflicted contexts.	When something disrupts my goals, I often figure out how to achieve them anyway.
	*Personally characteristic expressiveness or style.	I have a personal style that is all my own.
Orality	*Preference for verbal exchange that is face-to-face.	I always try to deal with people straight up and face to face.
	*Words, speech, and humor are fundamental modes of personal expression.	I often feel that my experiences are not "real" until I tell someone about them.
	*Means of creating and maintaining social bonds.	In my social group, laughter often holds us together.
	*Means of communicating cultural values, knowledge and expectations.	The most important things I know come more from stories I have heard than things I have read.
Spirituality	*Belief in a higher power or force.	Belief in God or a greater power, helps me deal with the circumstances of my life.
	*Control and responsibility is shared with this force.	There are forces that influence my life that I cannot explain.

all true of me" to +3 "very true of me," with the "0" point labeled "not-relevant to me," we obtained responses from 200 people including students in classes at the University of Delaware, Howard University, friends, relatives, and neighbors. We created non-empirically-derived subscales based on the TRIOS dimensions the items were written to assess, and computed item-subscale correlations. We eliminated those items with a poor correlation, along with those that we judged to be poorly worded or confusing. This left us with 60 items, which we augmented with additional items to assess aspects of the TRIOS concept that were missing in the original item set.

Specifically, we added several items related to the interpersonal and social nature of Orality that included (a) in-group cohesion through humor, (b) the high context nature of Orality which implies that nonverbal cues matter more than literal utterances, and (c) the significance of psychological comfort in a social context as a condition for success. We further added two items from the Singelis (1994) scale assessing cultural differences in construal of the self (one tapping interdependence and one independence). Finally, we added several items designed to tap the past orientation, since the original set only addressed present and future orientations.

We then administered this expanded set of 77 items to a larger sample from several sources including a private university in California, a city college in Los Angeles, a private predominately Black university on the East Coast, a public university on the East Coast, Delaware, a predominantly Black high school in Philadelphia, a public university in South Florida, and others notable by their convenience. The final sample consisted of 1415 respondents of whom two thirds were women and one third men, a little over 40% were White, 21% were Black, 19% were Latin, 11% were Asian, and 9% were of mixed race or did not provide racial information. The age range was 14 to 62, with the average age for each group between 20 and 21 years.

The Structures of TRIOS

We conducted an exploratory principal components factor analysis (EFA) on the entire sample of respondents for the 77 items, setting an eigenvalue cutoff at 2.0. This produced six factors. We then removed all items whose commonalities were less than .30 and re-ran the EFA, setting a five-factor criterion, and using an oblimin rotation. The five factors that emerged accounted for 43 percent of the common variance. Table 2 summarizes the factor structures and items that loaded above .40 on each.

I will summarize the factor structure in order of the TRIOS model rather than the order in which the factors were extracted. The factor structure reproduces the TRIOS dimensions rather well.

Time in the TRIOS model is represented broadly as a present-time orientation—living-in-the-now. Time emerged as the fourth factor extracted and is characterized as present orientation. Its character appears to be as much

Table 2. Five-Factor Structure of TRIOS

	Factor Loading
F1–Spirituality–alpha = .88	
Belief in God or a greater power helps me deal with the circumstances of my life.	.87
Belief in a higher power is important to me.	.85
Sometimes, you just have to put your life in the hands of a higher power.	.82
There is a higher force (other than myself) that directs my path in life.	.77
I pray or consult with a person who shares my spiritual beliefs before I make a major life decision.	.75
In most every aspect of my life, I am strengthened by my spiritual beliefs.	.71
I believe that the world is full of powerful and unknowable forces.	.58
There are reasons beyond our understanding for everything that happens.	.56
There are forces that influence my life that I cannot explain.	.43
F2–Improvisation–alpha = .72	
When a situation arises, I usually know 2–3 different ways to handle it.	.68
When things do not go as planned, it is easy for me to devise another plan right on the spot.	.67
I can figure my way out of almost any situation.	.67
When something disrupts my goals, I often figure out how to achieve them anyway.	.64
I always try to deal with people straight up and face-to-face.	.60
I have a personal style that is all my own.	.48
F3–Orality in Social Context–alpha = .69	
It is important to be yourself at all times.	.67
It is important for me to be comfortable in a situation in order to be successful.	.63
In my social group, laughter often holds us together.	.61
Humor is key to my relationships with my friends.	.60
It is important for me to maintain harmony in my group.	.60
My personal identity is very important to me.	.55
F4–Present Orientation–alpha = .61	
Preparing for what might happen in the future is often a waste of time.	.63
It's better to live the present moment to the fullest than to plan for the future.	.60
When I try to envision the future, I draw a blank.	.58
It is important for me to plan ahead and have goals that organize my life.®	−.52
I have made extensive plans for the future.®	−.48
F5–aRhythmia–alpha = .35	
I often feel anxiety when I am late for a scheduled event.	.53
If I feel someone is attacking me, I sometimes struggle not knowing what to do.	.50
I often feel that my experiences are not "real" until I tell someone about them.	.47

Note: Based on sample *N* of 1415, Principle Components Analysis, Oblimin Rotation. ® indicates that an item is reverse scored.

anti-future as it is present focus. Two items pit a present focus opposite a future one, and a positive response chooses the present over the future. A third item renders the future invisible. And the final two items reject planning for the future as an important life process. This leaves us with a self-contained present notable by the absence of thoughts about the future. It is important to note that this version of present orientation is neither hedonistic or pleasure seeking, nor a fatalistic view of an uncontrollable future as other scales have found (cf. Zimbardo & Boyd, 1999).

It is simply an expression of living-in-the-now uninfluenced by future possibilities, and a *preference* for this approach to life. The reliability of the six-item time (present orientation) subscale is acceptable at .61.

Rhythm does not emerge clearly as a factor in this TRIOS structure. It was the fifth factor extracted, and had an eigenvalue of 1.98. The three items that form this factor were written to tap, in order, improvisation, time and orality. Although they do not reflect the original ideas of rhythm, they do seem to reflect an asynchrony in relationships between a person and his or her surroundings. I have tentatively labeled this factor "*aRhythmia.*" The inability to mesh with one's circumstances or to handle aggressive actions or even to understand the meaning of things without further consultation suggests a negative reaction to one's environment. This may capture a blocked sense of flow between the person and his or her environment. This would be a negative instance of rhythm as conceived in the TRIOS model, and a high scorer on this factor would be considered "a-TRIOSic." The low reliability of these three items (alpha = .35) may be due to the small number of items that comprise it. Rhythm is a hard concept to capture in a paper and pencil measure. This dimension needs more work as it could be that we have unreliably selected items to assess it. I should note that one of the best rhythm items, "Music and dance are important forms of personal expression," emerges as a significant element in the first factor extracted for both African Americans and Hispanics in group-based EFAs. It could be that rhythm is more distinctively different across groups and that is why it works so weakly in the composite factor structure. Research to sort this out is ongoing.

Improvisation is a reflection of the belief that one can successfully overcome unforeseen obstacles, that one can achieve in spite of external barriers to success, and that one's manner of accomplishing this is heavily based on personal qualities that are self-defining. Improvisation is an individualistic orientation that can engender optimism about the future. It is also clearly set in the present and thus fits the more general idea that TRIOS is a context-driven concept. Improvisation was the second factor extracted, and the six items fit the TRIOS model quite well and form a reliable subscale (alpha = .72). Improvisation is captured by creative and effective problem solving in a challenging context. Uncertainty of expectations is countered by the belief that one will handle whatever arises. In this belief resides a feeling of control. This form of control is different from the kind based on control of events external to the self. Improvisation holds the self capable of controlling outcomes even when the circumstances are unpredictable, controlled by others, or perhaps even relatively likely to produce adverse outcomes. Belief in one's ability to handle whatever comes along is a comforting feeling and provides the person with a sense of optimism about the future. The addition of personal style to improvisation reflects the individuality of improvisation and its self-defining quality. Further, handling issues "face-to-face" implies the directness of the improvisational approach. Like the other dimensions, improvisation is context dependent, and conveys both the self-protective motives through problem solving, and the self-enhancement motives through personal style and expression.

Orality was conceived principally as the oral expression of meaning through words and song in a social context. Orality conveys meanings handed down over time through stories, but also establishes social bonds through the privileged meanings, styles of speech, and preferences for in-group relations. Orality presupposes a high context social environment (cf. Hall, 1983). The complex nature of orality suggests that it might be captured by two or three different factors. The one that emerged as the third factor is labeled orality in social context (OSC). This six-item subscale attained acceptable reliability (alpha = .69). OSC is characterized by a generalized sensitivity to interpersonal relationships in a social context. Relations with friends and in-group harmony reflect the use of orality to maintain social boundaries and promote in-group cohesion. The self as socially constructed also is reflected by the need for a personal social identity defined by personal properties and invariance across settings. Further, feeling comfort in the social context may be a precondition for psychological well-being. The implication of being in a comfortable social setting, tied to others through humor and social sharing, while maintaining positive personal identity support the idea that personal distinctiveness and group belonging are highly related (cf. Brewer, 1991). It also makes plausible the connections between individualism and collectivism as suggested earlier in this paper and elsewhere (Jones, 1999). Interestingly, the independent item ("be yourself at all times") and the interdependent item ("valuing harmony in my group") from Singelis (1994, p. 585) *both* loaded on this factor, again suggesting that this factor may tap both individually oriented and more collectively oriented sentiments. OSC suggests also that social context can be both a source of self-protective motives (cf. Tatum, 1999: *Why are all the Black kids sitting together in the cafeteria?*), as well as a means of self- and collective expression and self-enhancement. Sitting together in one's group may convert an uncertain and uncomfortable environment into one that is more secure. The resulting psychological comfort then enables one to perform successfully.

Spirituality is defined by a belief in a higher power as a functional element of one's daily life. It is not synonymous with religiosity, but would probably be modestly correlated with it. It is further defined by the belief that there are forces in the world that influence one's outcomes that one neither knows nor can explain or understand. This view of spirituality is consistent with the conceptualization of spirituality in the TRIOS model. Eight items comprise the spirituality subscale, which was the first factor extracted, and had the highest reliability coefficient (alpha = .88). There are two aspects to this spirituality subscale. First is the everyday functionality of spirituality. Six of the items capture the idea that spiritual beliefs and priorities help one cope with everyday life. An additional three items portray spirituality as the powerful and unknown forces that intervene to determine life events. It is often suggested that spirituality is related to an external locus of control, and is a substitute for the feeling of control implied by an internal self-focused locus. These spirituality items acknowledge that one may not be in control of everything that happens, but does not imply a passive, pawn-like relationship to one's circumstances. Rather, spirituality can serve an important function in taking control of one's life on a daily basis. Like improvisation, spirituality provides a sense of confidence that living and doing one's best is what one has a responsibility to do. This may be a very healthy attitude for a person who in fact faces a challenging circumstance that contains many obstacles that are unscripted and must be managed.

Taken as a whole, then, these measures of TRIOS fit the overall concept of TRIOS as a context-driven focus on being-in-the-world, and a five-dimensional structure reasonably well. Spirituality, improvisation and time (present-orientation) are quite faithful and reliable representations of the TRIOS model. Orality is well organized and reasonably reliable as well, but there are important aspects of orality that this single factor does not represent. Rhythm is clearly the weakest dimension and on the basis of the reliability coefficients, needs to be evaluated carefully and perhaps more items need to be chosen.

One recurring question concerns whether the five TRIOS dimensions function as separate factors, or can be combined into a single TRIOS index. To explore this question we conducted an EFA on the five-factors described above, and a two factor solution emerged in which spirituality, improvisation, orality in social context and present orientation constitute the first factor (26% variance) and aRhythmia and a negative loading of improvisation constitute the second factor (25% variance). We calculated the reliability index of all 29 items (reverse scoring the three aRhythmia items, and two present orientation items as noted) and obtained an alpha of .69. This suggests that the items comprising the five factors can be combined as a single TRIOS index. We combined these 29 items into a composite index of TRIOS and labeled it TRIOS-C. However, since the individual factors were also reliable (with the exception of aRhythmia), a preliminary conclusion is that a hierarchical model can describe the TRIOS structure. That is, TRIOS-C scores may be used as an estimate of an individual's overall level of TRIOSity. In addition, their individual subfactor scores could be used independently as predictors of attitudes and behaviors more relevant to specific dimensions. For example, present orientation is often linked to a variety of negative behaviors like unhealthy risk-taking and poor academic performance. But when present orientation is part of the TRIOS-C structure, it is tempered and buffered by the other TRIOS dimensions which may be related to more positive outcomes. The higher order TRIOS-C and the second order present orientation would thus make differential predictions about behavioral outcomes. Determining the validity and utility of these hierarchical relationships between TRIOS-C and the subscales remains for future research.

Table 3. Mean TRIOS Scores by Race and Gender Total Sample Factor

	Spirituality	Improvisation	Orality in Social Context	Present Orientation	aRhythmia	TRIOS-C*
Race/Ethnicity						
White ($N = 603$)	.41$_a$	1.36$_a$	2.18$_a$	.05$_a$	0.45$_a$	.72$_a$
Black ($N = 293$)	1.52$_b$	1.44$_a$	2.37$_b$	.29$_c$	0.17$_b$	1.09$_b$
Hispanic ($N = 295$)	1.06$_c$	1.49$_{a,b}$	2.03$_c$	.24$_b$	0.33$_{a,b,c}$	.90$_c$
Asian American ($N = 150$)	.87$_c$	1.23$_{a,c}$	2.17$_{a,c}$	.08$_a$	0.61$_{a,c}$	.75$_a$
Gender						
Males ($N = 408$)	.70	1.49	2.15	0.17	0.12	.88
Females ($N = 804$)	1.00	1.36	2.22	0.15	0.49	.85
Significance						
Race/Ethnicity	.000	.05	.000	.000	.023	.000
Sex	.000	.06	.018	.022	.000	ns
Race/Ethnicity × Sex	ns	ns	ns	.06	ns	ns
Cronbach Alpha	.88	.72	.69	.61	.35	.70

Note. Values within columns with different subscripts are significantly different from each other based on Tukey post hoc HSD statistic. *TRIOS-C is the average of scores on Spirituality, Improvisation, Orality in Social Context and Present Orientation minus scores on aRhythmia.

Ethnic/Racial Differences in TRIOS

Mean scores for each empirically derived TRIOS factor including TRIOS-C served as dependent variables in a 4 (race) by 2 (sex) multivariate analysis of variance (MANOVA). Tukey Honestly Significant Differences (HSD) statistics were computed for post hoc comparisons of racial/ethnic differences. Table 3 presents the mean factor scores for Whites, African Americans, Hispanics and Asian Americans for each of the five factors and TRIOS-C.

There were significant race main effects on each of the five dimensions, and significant sex main effects on all but improvisation. There were no reliable race by sex interactions on any of the dimensions. To summarize, African Americans scored significantly higher than all other groups on TRIOS-C. In addition, they scored significantly higher than or as high as any of the other racial/ethnic groups on all of the TRIOS dimensions. Hispanics scored higher than Whites and Asian Americans on TRIOS-C, and Asians and Whites did not differ. Hispanics also scored higher than Whites on spirituality, and present orientation. These results support the idea that dimensions of TRIOS have greater representation among persons of African descent as reflected in scores on the TRIOS scale.

Sex Differences in TRIOS

There were no differences between men and women on TRIOS-C. However, there were significant sex differences on several of the TRIOS dimensions, which further attests to the utility of a hierarchical view of TRIOS. Since we made no predictions about sex differences, and since none were found on TRIOS-C, we will not discuss these further.

Another way to explore racial ethnic differences in TRIOSic structure is to conduct separate EFAs for each group. Space limits do not permit a detailed discussion of these results, but suffice it to say that there were several differences in items that loaded on individual factors, as well as the order in which factors were extracted. For example, the EFA for Whites revealed a fourth factor labeled time, but it consisted of a *future* orientation. For Blacks, the present orientation did not emerge as a separate factor, but combined with orality to create what we labeled orality-in-the-now. Each separate factor structure suggested differences that could be interpreted to reflect subtle differences in cultural orientation. Whereas the differences in factor scores based on the total sample are nomothetic differences based on a common metric, the different factor structures may be more idiographically representative of cultural differences. Much more work needs to be done, but strong evidence is presented that the TRIOS measure captures ways in which ethnic/racial groups differ from each other on a common set of TRIOS dimensions. Preliminary factor analysis of each group suggests further that the items that comprise the TRIOS dimensions may array themselves somewhat differently for different racial/ethnic groups. The idea that they may differ from each other in how those dimensions are organized within ethnic/racial cultural contexts is worth exploring.

Conclusion

TRIOS is conceptualized as a worldview reflecting a cultural ethos of African origins, and expressed by individual motivations for self-protection and self-enhancement in a universal context of racism. It is proposed that TRIOS is psychologically adaptive because it represents self-relevant beliefs and values that foster ego-resilience and optimism. TRIOS is an effective approach to living because it presupposes individual capacity, skill and successful functioning in challenging circumstances. A TRIOSic worldview is also supported by the value of others and the assistance that a spiritual life can provide.

It would follow from the outline of origins and character of TRIOS that African Americans should embrace its elements to a greater degree than other ethnic/racial groups, particularly Whites. Further, it could be argued that a high level of TRIOS-ity would mediate psychological well-being in challenging psychosocial contexts. The empirically derived psychometric structure supports the underlying assumptions about its organization and coherence. The comparative analyses show that African Americans could be described as more TRIOSic than other racial/ethnic groups. This is a promising extension of the descriptive hypothesis about the TRIOS concept to an empirically validated measure of it.

A number of theoretical and empirical questions suggest themselves. Is TRIOS a personality or a cultural construct or both? The fact that the items are neither racially nor culturally specific, yet we obtain significant race and ethnic differences, suggests TRIOS taps into values and beliefs that vary by cultural group; hence it is a cultural construct. However, the factor analytic method itself implies a personality basis to the scale. It is most likely that the answer is both, and determining how the personality and cultural aspects operate will be an important future project. A related question is does TRIOS mediate or moderate psychological well-being similarly for different racial/ethnic groups? One might hypothesize that a high TRIOS score would be more significant for African Americans, or for persons who live in challenging circumstances.

One might also ask if TRIOS is represented by specific psychological mechanisms or cognitive structures and if so what are they? For example, in some preliminary research we find that high scores on TRIOS-C are related to the values (cf. Schwartz, 1992) of achievement, self-direction, stimulation, benevolence, and universalism, and are related to self-worth contingent on virtuous living (cf. Crocker and Wolfe, 2001). By contrast, spirituality is related to self-worth contingent on God's love (cf. Crocker and Wolfe, 2001) and improvisation is related to ego-resilience (cf. Block and Kremen, 1996). This sort of validity research will help direct us to domains in which we might expect TRIOS level to matter, and allow us to contrast the first-order TRIOS-C with the second order individual TRIOS dimensions.

Finally, since the items are not about race, but produce significant racial differences, it is possible that a person's TRIOS level might serve as a non-reactive index of his or her level of prejudice. The reason for this association would be that the TRIOSic worldview is generally non-evaluative and non-judgmental, and non-comparative. People who have such a worldview should be less likely to hold beliefs associated with conventional prejudice, and to embrace views more similar to African Americans. These and other questions are the focus of our current research.

References

Block, J., & Kremen. (1996). IQ and resilience: Conceptual and empirical connections and separateness. *Journal of Personality and Social Psychology, 70*(2), 349–361.

Brewer, M. B. (1991). The social self: On being the same and different at the same time. *Personality and Social Psychology Bulletin, 17*, 475–482.

Chernoff, J. M. (1979). *African rhythm and African sensibility: Aesthetics and social action in African musical idioms*. Chicago: University of Chicago Press.

Crocker, J., & Wolfe, C. T. (2001). Contingencies of self worth. *Psychological Review, 108*(3), 593–623.

Cross, W. E. (1991). *Shades of Black: Diversity in African American identity*. Philadelphia: Temple University Press.

DuBois, W. E. B. (1903). *The souls of Black folk*. Chicago: A. C. McClurg and Company.

Fiske, A., Kitayama, S., Markus, H. R., & Nisbett, R. E. (1998). The cultural matrix of social psychology. In D. T. Gilbert, S. T. Fiske, & G. Lindzey (Eds.), *Handbook of social psychology* (vol. 4, pp. 915–981) New York: McGraw-Hill.

Franklin, J. H., & Moss, A. A. (1994). *From slavery to freedom: A history of African Americans* (7th ed). New York: McGraw-Hill.

Haley, A. (1976). *Roots: The saga of an American family.* New York: Doubleday.

Hall, E. T. (1983). *The dance of life: The other dimension of time.* Garden City, NY: Anchor Press/ Doubleday.

Jahn, J. (1961). *Muntu: An outline of the new African culture.* New York: Grove Press.

Jones, J. M. (1972). *Prejudice and racism.* Reading, MA: Addison Wesley.

Jones, J. M. (1979). Conceptual and strategic issues in the relationship of Black psychology to American social science. In A. W. Boykin, A. J. Franklin, & J. F. Yates (Eds.), *Research directions of Black psychologists* (pp. 390–432). New York: Russell Sage Foundation.

Jones, J. M. (1988). Racism in Black and White: A bicultural model of reaction and evolution. In P. A. Katz & D. A. Taylor (Eds.), *Eliminating racism: Profiles in controversy* (pp. 117–158). New York: Plenum Press.

Jones, J. M. (1997). *Prejudice and racism* (2nd ed.). New York: McGraw-Hill Publishers.

Jones, J. M. (1999). Cultural racism: The intersection of race and culture in intergroup conflict. In D. A. Prentice & D. T. Miller (Eds.), *Cultural divides: Understanding and overcoming group conflict* (pp. 465–490). New York: Russell Sage Foundation.

Jones, J. M., Banicky, L. A., Lasane, T. P., & Pomare, M. (2003). *A temporal orientation scale: Focusing attention on the past, present, and future.* Unpublished manuscript, University of Delaware.

Jones, J. M., & Hochner, A. R. (1973). Racial differences in sports activities: A look at the self-paced versus reactive hypothesis. *Journal of Personality and Social Psychology, 27*(1), 86–95.

Kalb, M. (1984, February 13). Interview with the Reverend Jesse L. Jackson. *Meet the Press.* NBC Television.

Kroeber, A. L., & Kluckhohn, C. (1952). *Culture: A critical review of concepts and definitions.* New York: Random House.

Levine, R. E. (1997). *A geography of time.* New York: Basic Books.

Lewin, K. (1943). Defining the "field at a given time." *Psychological Review, 50,* 292–310. Reprinted in D. Cartwright (1997) (Ed.), *Field theory in social science: Selected theoretical papers* (pp. 200–211). Washington, DC: American Psychological Association.

Lewin, K. (1944). Constructs in psychology and psychological ecology. *University of Iowa Studies in Child Welfare, 20,* 1–29. Reprinted in D. Cartwright (1997) (Ed.), *Field theory in social science: Selected theoretical papers* (pp. 191–199). Washington, DC: American Psychological Association.

Lewin, K. (1946). Action research and minority problems. *Journal of Social Issues, 2,* 34–46. Reprinted in G. W. Lewin (1997) (Ed.), *Resolving social conflicts: Selected papers on group dynamics* (pp. 143–152). Washington, DC: American Psychological Association.

Markus, H. R., & Kitayama, S. (1991). Culture and the self: Implications for cognition, emotion, and motivation. *Psychological Review, 98,* 224–253.

Mbiti, J. S. (1970). *African religions and philosophy.* Garden City, NY: Anchor Doubleday Books.

McGrath, J., & Kelly, J. (1986). *Time and human interaction: Toward a social psychology of time.* New York: Guilford Press.

Morgan, P. D. (1998). *Slave counterpoint: Black culture in the eighteenth-century Chesapeake & lowcountry.* Chapel Hill, NC: University of North Carolina Press.

Osborne, J. W. (1995). Academics, self-esteem, and race: A look at the underlying assumptions of the disidentification hypothesis. *Personality and Social Psychology Bulletin, 21,* 449–455.

Oyserman, D., Coon, H. M., & Kimmelmeier, M. (2002). Rethinking individualism and collectivism: Evaluation of theoretical assumptions and meta-analyses. *Psychological Bulletin, 128*(1), 3–72.

Schwartz, S. H. (1992). Universals in the content and structure of values: Theoretical advances and empirical tests in 20 countries. In M. P. Zanna (Ed.), *Advances in experimental social psychology* (Vol. 24, pp. 1–65). San Diego, CA: Academic Press.

Sellers, R. M., Rowley, S. A. J., Chavous, T. M., Shelton, J. N., & Smith, M. A. (1997). Multidimensional inventory of Black identity: A preliminary investigation of reliability and construct validity. *Journal of Personality and Social Psychology, 73*(4), 805–815.

Senghor, L. (1956). L'esprit de la civilisation ou les lois de la culture Negro-africaine. *Presence Africaine.* Paris, France.

Shweder, R., & Sullivan, M. A. (1992). Cultural psychology: Who needs it? *Annual Review of Psychology, 44,* 497–523.

Sidanius, J., & Pratto, F. (1999). *Social dominance: An intergroup theory of social hierarchy and oppression.* New York: Cambridge Press.

Singelis, T. M. (1994). The measurement of independent and interdependent self-construals. *Personality and Social Psychology Bulletin, 20,* 580–591.

Smitherman, G. (1977). *Talkin' and testifyin': The language of Black America.* Detroit, MI: Wayne State University Press.

Sobel, M. (1987). *The world they made together: Black and White values in eighteenth-century Virginia.* Princeton, NJ: Princeton University Press.

Steele, C. M. (1997). A burden of suspicion: How stereotypes shape the intellectual identities and performance of women and African-Americans. *American Psychologist, 52*(6), 613–629.

Tatum, B. D. (1999). *Why are all the Black kids sitting together in the cafeteria? And other conversations about race.* New York: Basic Books.

Thurstone, L. L. (1928). Attitudes can be measured. *American Journal of Sociology, 33,* 529–554.

Triandis, H. C. (1994). *Culture and behavior.* New York: McGraw-Hill.

Woodward, C. V. (1951). *Origins of the new South, 1877–1913.* Baton Rouge, LA: Louisiana State University Press.

Worthy, M., & Markle, A. (1970). Racial differences in reactive versus self-paced sports activities. *Journal of Personality and Social Psychology, 16,* 439–443.

Zaleski, Z. (1994). *Psychology of future time orientation.* Lublin, Poland: Towarzystwo Naukowe KUL.

Zimbardo, P. G., & Boyd, J. N. (1999). Putting time in prespective: A valid, reliable individual-differences metric. *Journal of Personality and Social Psychology, 77*(6), 1271–1288.